Common Law:
1. Unlawful (under the traditional rule husbands are exempted, not under modern statutes);
2. Sexual intercourse (slightest penetration is sufficient);
3. With a woman (gender specific);
4. Without consent (being incapable of giving consent due to unconsciousness, intoxication, or mental condition is sufficient);
5. By force;
6. Against her will.

EXCUSE DEFENSES

INSANITY DEFENSES

State v. Johnson, 399 A.2d 469 (R.I. 1979).
1. M'Naghten Test: The defendant may be found insane if at the time of the act, she was under a defect of reason, as:
   a. She did not know the nature and quality of the act she was doing; OR
   b. If she did know, then she did not know that what she was doing was wrong.
2. Irresistible Impulse Test: A defendant is insane if, as the result of a mental disease or defect, she "acted with an irresistible and uncontrollable impulse."
3. The "Product" Test: A person is excused if her unlawful act was the product of a mental disease or defect.
4. Model Penal Code Test: A person is not responsible for criminal conduct if at the time of the act as a result of mental disease or defect she lacked the substantial capacity to:
   a. Appreciate the criminality of her actions; OR
   b. Conform her conduct to the requirements of the law
   MPC § 4.01(1).
5. Federal Insanity Test: A person is excused if she proves by clear and convincing evidence that at the time of the crime, as the result of a "severe mental disease or defect," she was unable to appreciate the nature and quality or wrongfulness of her conduct.
Note: Since insanity is an affirmative defense, a majority of states and Congress place the burden of proving insanity on the defendant.

MISTAKE OF LAW

1. Generally, it is not a defense (ignorance of the law is NO excuse). *People v. Marrero*, 507 N.E.2d 1068 (N.Y. 1987).
2. Exemptions: (Authorized-Reliance Doctrine):
   a. Law not published. Reasonably relied on statute that was later invalidated.
   b. Reasonably relied on court decision.
   c. Reasonably relied on official in position to interpret statute (i.e., must be someone like the U.S. Attorney General, NOT one's personal attorney).
   d. Statute specifically requires defendant to know that the activity is illegal. MPC § 2.04.

INFANCY

1. If the accused is younger than the age of seven, she has an absolute defense to all crimes.
2. If older than the age of seven but younger than fourteen, then the accused's age is a rebuttable defense.
3. If older than fourteen, a rebuttable presumption that the accused will be treated as an adult.
Note: Modern statutes may modify the above.
4. Model Penal Code: Being under the age of 16 constitutes a defense. MPC § 4.10(1)(a).

VOLUNTARY INTOXICATION

1. Self-induced intoxication is not a tr defense to a crime.
   a. Yet, voluntary intoxication may k as a defense to specific intent c MPC § 2.08(1).
   b. Voluntary intoxication may NOT be used as a "temporary insanity" defense.
   Example: Sarah, the defendant, gets so inebriated that she starts to shoot aimlessly at blurry blobs, not knowing that they are humans. She kills Chenin, an innocent bystander, with a bullet. Voluntary intoxication may be used as a defense against the specific intent crime of first degree murder, but it will not be a defense against lesser degrees of murder that do not require specific intent (i.e., second degree "heat of passion," or common law murder).
2. Intoxication does not of itself constitute mental disease. MPC § 2.08(3).

MISTAKE OF FACT

1. Is only a defense if it negates the mens rea required by the crime.
2. Common Law (majority):
   a. General intent crimes need reasonable mistake of fact.
   b. For specific intent crimes, mistake of fact can be unreasonable (but must be sincere).
   Example: Jacquie, the defendant, sees Bill's bicycle that is EXACTLY like hers in every way. Jacquie sincerely believes that this is her own and she pedals off on it. She is NOT guilty of the specific intent crime of larceny because she had a sincere mistake of fact as to its ownership.
3. Model Penal Code: Under MPC § 2.04(1), ignorance or mistake as to a fact is a defense if it negates the knowledge, recklessness, or negligence required to establish the offense.
4. Mistake of fact cannot be used as a defense in strict liability crimes.

INVOLUNTARY INTOXICATION

Involuntary intoxication occurs when the defendant unknowingly ingests an intoxicant or is coerced through the use of force to ingest alcohol or a narcotic.

1. Involuntary intoxication may be used as a defense equivalent to that of insanity.
2. Thus, involuntary intoxication may be a defense to all crimes.
MPC §2.08(4).

DIMINISHED CAPACITY (MINORITY)

1. As a result of a mental defect (which does not reach insanity), the defendant could not form the requisite mens rea to commit the crime.
2. This only applies to specific intent crimes.
3. Modernly, "partial responsibility" is recognized, if at all, in states adopting the MPC "extreme mental or emotional disturbance" manslaughter provision. MPC § 210.3(1).

   a. Intent to kill.
   b. Intent to inflict grievous bodily injury.
   c. Reckless indifference to human life ("depraved or malignant heart").
   d. Intent to commit a felony (felony murder).
2. **Voluntary Manslaughter** ("Heat of Passion") A killing that would be murder if not for adequate provocation. Provocation is adequate only if:
   a. The provocation would arouse sudden and intense passion in a reasonable person.
   b. There were not enough time for a reasonable person to "cool off" between the provocation and the killing.
   Note: Always carefully examine the adequacy of provocation.
   Important: "Heat of passion" manslaughter is NOT a defense, it merely reduces the crime from common law murder to voluntary manslaughter.
   Example: Eugene, the defendant, walks into his bedroom. He sees his wife in bed with the Marc, the neighbor. Eugene becomes enraged and immediately leaves the room. Eugene plots to kill Marc. Three weeks later he kills Marc. This is NOT voluntary manslaughter. There was too much time for premeditation and deliberation. If Eugene had killed Mark when he caught his wife in bed with him, it might have been voluntary manslaughter.
3. **Involuntary Manslaughter** (Unlawful Act Doctrine):
   a. If a killing occurred through the gross negligence of the defendant, OR
   b. During the commission of an unlawful act (misdemeanor or felony not included in the felony murder rule).
   c. Lack of causation is a defense.
4. **Felony Murder**:
   a. Any death caused in the commission of or in an attempt to commit a felony is murder.
   b. Malice is implied from the intent to commit the underlying felony.
   c. The felony being committed must be inherently dangerous (e.g., burglary, arson, rape, etc.)
   d. The defendant must be guilty of the underlying felony.
   e. The death must have been a foreseeable result of the felony.
   Additional Considerations: The death of the victim must occur a "year and a day" from the day on which the felony occurred.
   Note: Some jurisdictions classify homicides differently according to statute. Most murders would be classified as second degree murder unless the defendant killed in a manner that was deliberate and premeditated in which case, it would be first degree murder.

Criminal Homicide
continues on page

DEFENSE OF PROPERTY

1. Non-deadly force may be applied if reasonably necessary to protect property.
2. Deadly force may NEVER be used to protect property.
3. Model Penal Code: One may use non-deadly force to recapture property, even if the owner is not in pursuit or if the property is no longer in her possession.

Note: In certain conditions, a property owner may use deadly force to prevent a property related felony to her property, even if there is no present risk of bodily injury to the property owner. MPC § 3.06(3)(d)(ii).

ARREST BY CITIZEN

1. Non-deadly force may be used in an arrest by a citizen if the crime has been committed and there is a reasonable belief that the suspect committed it. MPC § 3.07.
2. Deadly force may be used by a private citizen only to prevent escape of a felon who actually committed the crime and is a threat to human life. MPC § 3.07(3).
3. A private person must give notice of her intention to make an arrest.
4. The felony committed must be an atrocious felony in order to use deadly force. Mistake of fact is NOT available as a defense.

ARREST BY POLICE

1. Non-deadly force may be used if reasonably necessary to arrest.
2. Deadly force may be applied only to prevent the escape of a felony suspect who poses a significant threat to human life or safety. *Tennessee v. Garner*, 471 U.S. 1 (1985).
3. Deadly force is necessary to prevent flight. When practical, officer must warn suspect of her intent to use deadly force.
4. Officer must have probable cause as to the threat of the suspect.

NECESSITY

1. One may use the defense of necessity if one reasonably believed that the commission of the crime was necessary to avoid a greater injury (than the crime itself). MPC § 3.02. *Nelson v. State*, 597 P.2d 977 (Alaska 1979).
2. One must use the objective standard. Sincerity is not enough. Deadly force is NOT allowed.
3. If defendant is the one that created the situation requiring necessity, then necessity is not available.
4. Necessity usually involves threats from nature: if there are threats from a human, then use duress.
5. Mode Penal Code: The defense of necessity is similar to common law. MPC § 3.02.
6. Defense not apt to succeed in civil disobedience cases. *U.S. v. Schoon*, 971 F.2d 193 (9th Cir. 1991).

DEFENSE OF HABITATION

1. Non-deadly force may be applied if reasonably necessary to prevent unlawful entry. MPC §§ 3.06, 3.09.
2. Deadly force may be used to prevent a felony being committed or if there is the threat of bodily injury. MPC § 3.06(3)(d).
3. Mode Penal Code: With certain limitations, a person may use deadly force against an intruder who is seeking to dispossess the owner. MPC § 3.06(3)(d)(i).

DEFENSE OF ANOTHER

1. Non-deadly force may be applied if reasonably necessary to protect another.
2. Deadly force may be used if there is a threat of death or great bodily harm. MPC § 3.05. *People v. Kurr*, 654 N.W.2d 651 (Mich. App. 2002).
3. Model Penal Code: In order to be justified in the use of deadly force in defense of another under the MPC, four conditions must be met:
   a. The actor using the deadly force must subjectively believe that she is justified in using deadly force in defense of herself.
   b. The "victim" would also have to be justified in using deadly force in defense of herself.
   c. The use of deadly force must be necessary.
   d. There are no means of retreat. MPC § 3.05(1)-(2).

PROPERTY CRIMES—THEFT

LARCENY

U.S. v. Mafnas, 701 F.2d 83 (9th Cir. 1983).

1. A trespassory;
2. Taking;
3. And carrying away (asportation);
4. Of the personal property (does not include realty, services, and intangibles);
5. Of another;
6. With the intent to permanently deprive.

Notes:

1. The intent to deprive permanently must be formed at the time of the taking (yet, if the intent is formed later, the defendant may be guilty of larceny if the initial taking was wrong).
2. Some jurisdictions combine larceny or similar property crimes into a single consolidated theft statute, modeled after MPC § 223.1.

Defense: Claim of Right.

ROBBERY

All the elements of larceny plus:

1. By force or fear of immediate force; AND
2. From person or in immediate presence and control of victim. MPC § 222.1.

LOST AND MISLAID PROPERTY

1. If there is a reasonable clue to ownership of the property when discovered, the original owner of property has constructive possession of her lost property. (Thus, keeping the property is theft or larceny.) MPC § 223.5.
2. If the finder intends to keep the lost item, despite reasonable clues to the ownership of the item, then the finder is guilty of larceny.

Defense: Claim of Right.

FALSE PRETENSES

People v. Ingram, 76 Cal. Rptr. 2d 553 (Cal. App. 1998).

1. Title is obtained;
2. To personal property of another;
3. Through false representation of existing facts;
4. With intent to defraud.

Note: False pretenses requires that title be surrendered by victim. If the victim is tricked into only giving up possession (by a misrepresentation of fact), then it is larceny by trick.

Defense: Claim of Right.

EMBEZZLEMENT

1. A non-trespassory;
2. Conversion;
3. Of the personal property;
4. Of another;
5. By a person who has been entrusted with that property.

Defense: Claim of Right.

BURGLARY

1. Common Law:
   a. Breaking (creating an entrance with at least minimal force);
   b. And entereing (any part of the defendant's body or instrument used by defendant);
   c. Of a dwelling house;
   d. Of another;
   e. At night;
   f. With intent to commit a felony (felony need not be actually carried out, intent is important).

Note: Many modern statutes modify several of the common law elements described, especially the nocturnal requirement (e). Since burglary is a specific intent crime, that actor must have formed intent necessary to commit the crime. Hence, at the time of breaking and entering, the actor must intend to commit a felony inside the dwelling.

Example: Robin, the defendant, walks by a house at night and sees an open window. She is curious and decides to see if anyone is home. She has no intention of committing any crime, much less a felony. Robin climbs through the window and looks around the house. She is about to leave when at the last minute she sees a very valuable antique. She grabs it and leaves. Robin has committed larceny. She has not committed burglary because she did not have the requisite intent at the time of breaking and entering. Conversely, if she entered the dwelling with an intent to commit a felony, but did not go through with it, Robin would be guilty of burglary. Intent is the focus here.

2. Model Penal Code:
   a. Unauthorized entry;
   b. Structure;
   c. Of another;
   d. With intent to commit any crime. MPC: § 221.1.

RAPE

STATUTORY RAPE

Strict liability crime, thus lack of knowledge or mistake of the victim's age and/or consent by the victim is not a defense. *Garnett v. State*, 632 A.2d 797 (Md. App. 1993).

DEFINITION

Model Penal Code:

1. A male who has sexual intercourse with a female not his wife.
2. Compelled through the use of force or by threat.
3. Of imminent death, serious body injury, extreme pain or kidnapping. MPC § 213.1(1).

Rape
continues on page 3 ►

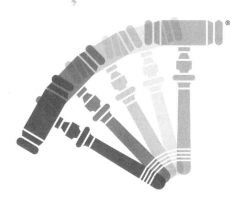

Casenote® *Legal Briefs*

CRIMINAL LAW

Keyed to Courses Using

Kaplan, Weisberg, and Binder's
Criminal Law: Cases and Materials
Seventh Edition

Wolters Kluwer
Law & Business

Copyright © 2012 CCH Incorporated. All Rights Reserved.

Published by Wolters Kluwer Law & Business in New York.

Wolters Kluwer Law & Business serves customers worldwide with CCH, Aspen Publishers, and Kluwer Law International products. (www.wolterskluwerlb.com)

No part of this publication may be reproduced or transmitted in any form or by any means, electronic or mechanical, including photocopy, recording, or utilized by any information storage and retrieval system, without written permission from the publisher. For information about permissions or to request permission online, visit us at wolterskluwerlb.com or a written request may be faxed to our permissions department at 212-771-0803.

To contact Customer Service, e-mail customer.service@wolterskluwer.com, call 1-800-234-1660, fax 1-800-901-9075, or mail correspondence to:

Wolters Kluwer Law & Business
Attn: Order Department
P.O. Box 990
Frederick, MD 21705

Printed in the United States of America.

1 2 3 4 5 6 7 8 9 0

ISBN 978-1-4548-0932-6

About Wolters Kluwer Law & Business

Wolters Kluwer Law & Business is a leading global provider of intelligent information and digital solutions for legal and business professionals in key specialty areas, and respected educational resources for professors and law students. Wolters Kluwer Law & Business connects legal and business professionals as well as those in the education market with timely, specialized authoritative content and information-enabled solutions to support success through productivity, accuracy and mobility.

Serving customers worldwide, Wolters Kluwer Law & Business products include those under the Aspen Publishers, CCH, Kluwer Law International, Loislaw, Best Case, ftwilliam.com and MediRegs family of products.

CCH products have been a trusted resource since 1913, and are highly regarded resources for legal, securities, antitrust and trade regulation, government contracting, banking, pension, payroll, employment and labor, and healthcare reimbursement and compliance professionals.

Aspen Publishers products provide essential information to attorneys, business professionals and law students. Written by preeminent authorities, the product line offers analytical and practical information in a range of specialty practice areas from securities law and intellectual property to mergers and acquisitions and pension/benefits. Aspen's trusted legal education resources provide professors and students with high-quality, up-to-date and effective resources for successful instruction and study in all areas of the law.

Kluwer Law International products provide the global business community with reliable international legal information in English. Legal practitioners, corporate counsel and business executives around the world rely on Kluwer Law journals, looseleafs, books, and electronic products for comprehensive information in many areas of international legal practice.

Loislaw is a comprehensive online legal research product providing legal content to law firm practitioners of various specializations. Loislaw provides attorneys with the ability to quickly and efficiently find the necessary legal information they need, when and where they need it, by facilitating access to primary law as well as state-specific law, records, forms and treatises.

Best Case Solutions is the leading bankruptcy software product to the bankruptcy industry. It provides software and workflow tools to flawlessly streamline petition preparation and the electronic filing process, while timely incorporating ever-changing court requirements.

ftwilliam.com offers employee benefits professionals the highest quality plan documents (retirement, welfare and non-qualified) and government forms (5500/PBGC, 1099 and IRS) software at highly competitive prices.

MediRegs products provide integrated health care compliance content and software solutions for professionals in healthcare, higher education and life sciences, including professionals in accounting, law and consulting.

Wolters Kluwer Law & Business, a division of Wolters Kluwer, is head-quartered in New York. Wolters Kluwer is a market-leading global information services company focused on professionals.

Format for the Casenote® Legal Brief

Nature of Case: This section identifies the form of action (e.g., breach of contract, negligence, battery), the type of proceeding (e.g., demurrer, appeal from trial court's jury instructions), or the relief sought (e.g., damages, injunction, criminal sanctions).

Fact Summary: This is included to refresh your memory and can be used as a quick reminder of the facts.

Rule of Law: Summarizes the general principle of law that the case illustrates. It may be used for instant recall of the court's holding and for classroom discussion or home review.

Facts: This section contains all relevant facts of the case, including the contentions of the parties and the lower court holdings. It is written in a logical order to give the student a clear understanding of the case. The plaintiff and defendant are identified by their proper names throughout and are always labeled with a (P) or (D).

Palsgraf v. Long Island R.R. Co.

Injured bystander (P) v. Railroad company (D)

N.Y. Ct. App., 248 N.Y. 339, 162 N.E. 99 (1928).

Party ID: Quick identification of the relationship between the parties.

NATURE OF CASE: Appeal from judgment affirming verdict for plaintiff seeking damages for personal injury.

FACT SUMMARY: Helen Palsgraf (P) was injured on R.R.'s (D) train platform when R.R.'s (D) guard helped a passenger aboard a moving train, causing his package to fall on the tracks. The package contained fireworks which exploded, creating a shock that tipped a scale onto Palsgraf (P).

🏛 RULE OF LAW
The risk reasonably to be perceived defines the duty to be obeyed.

FACTS: Helen Palsgraf (P) purchased a ticket to Rockaway Beach from R.R. (D) and was waiting on the train platform. As she waited, two men ran to catch a train that was pulling out from the platform. The first man jumped aboard, but the second man, who appeared as if he might fall, was helped aboard by the guard on the train who had kept the door open so they could jump aboard. A guard on the platform also helped by pushing him onto the train. The man was carrying a package wrapped in newspaper. In the process, the man dropped his package, which fell on the tracks. The package contained fireworks and exploded. The shock of the explosion was apparently of great enough strength to tip over some scales at the other end of the platform, which fell on Palsgraf (P) and injured her. A jury awarded her damages, and R.R. (D) appealed.

ISSUE: Does the risk reasonably to be perceived define the duty to be obeyed?

HOLDING AND DECISION: (Cardozo, C.J.) Yes. The risk reasonably to be perceived defines the duty to be obeyed. If there is no foreseeable hazard to the injured party as the result of a seemingly innocent act, the act does not become a tort because it happened to be a wrong as to another. If the wrong was not willful, the plaintiff must show that the act as to her had such great and apparent possibilities of danger as to entitle her to protection. Negligence in the abstract is not enough upon which to base liability. Negligence is a relative concept, evolving out of the common law doctrine of trespass on the case. To establish liability, the defendant must owe a legal duty of reasonable care to the injured party. A cause of action in tort will lie where harm,

though unintended, could have been averted or avoided by observance of such a duty. The scope of the duty is limited by the range of danger that a reasonable person could foresee. In this case, there was nothing to suggest from the appearance of the parcel or otherwise that the parcel contained fireworks. The guard could not reasonably have had any warning of a threat to Palsgraf (P), and R.R. (D) therefore cannot be held liable. Judgment is reversed in favor of R.R. (D).

DISSENT: (Andrews, J.) The concept that there is no negligence unless R.R. (D) owes a legal duty to take care as to Palsgraf (P) herself is too narrow. Everyone owes to the world at large the duty of refraining from those acts that may unreasonably threaten the safety of others. If the guard's action was negligent as to those nearby, it was also negligent as to those outside what might be termed the "danger zone." For Palsgraf (P) to recover, R.R.'s (D) negligence must have been the proximate cause of her injury, a question of fact for the jury.

Concurrence/Dissent: All concurrences and dissents are briefed whenever they are included by the casebook editor.

▶ ANALYSIS

The majority defined the limit of the defendant's liability in terms of the danger that a reasonable person in defendant's situation would have perceived. The dissent argued that the limitation should not be placed on liability, but rather on damages. Judge Andrews suggested that only injuries that would not have happened but for R.R.'s (D) negligence should be compensable. Both the majority and dissent recognized the policy-driven need to limit liability for negligent acts, seeking, in the words of Judge Andrews, to define a framework "that will be practical and in keeping with the general understanding of mankind." The Restatement (Second) of Torts has accepted Judge Cardozo's view.

Analysis: This last paragraph gives you a broad understanding of where the case "fits in" with other cases in the section of the book and with the entire course. It is a hornbook-style discussion indicating whether the case is a majority or minority opinion and comparing the principal case with other cases in the casebook. It may also provide analysis from restatements, uniform codes, and law review articles. The analysis will prove to be invaluable to classroom discussion.

— ▬ —

Quicknotes

FORESEEABILITY A reasonable expectation that change is the probable result of certain acts or omissions.

NEGLIGENCE Conduct falling below the standard of care that a reasonable person would demonstrate under similar conditions.

PROXIMATE CAUSE The natural sequence of events without which an injury would not have been sustained.

— ▬ —

Issue: The issue is a concise question that brings out the essence of the opinion as it relates to the section of the casebook in which the case appears. Both substantive and procedural issues are included if relevant to the decision.

Holding and Decision: This section offers a clear and in-depth discussion of the rule of the case and the court's rationale. It is written in easy-to-understand language and answers the issue presented by applying the law to the facts of the case. When relevant, it includes a thorough discussion of the exceptions to the case as listed by the court, any major cites to the other cases on point, and the names of the judges who wrote the decisions.

Quicknotes: Conveniently defines legal terms found in the case and summarizes the nature of any statutes, codes, or rules referred to in the text.

Wolters Kluwer Law & Business is proud to offer *Casenote® Legal Briefs*—continuing thirty years of publishing America's best-selling legal briefs.

Casenote® Legal Briefs are designed to help you save time when briefing assigned cases. Organized under convenient headings, they show you how to abstract the basic facts and holdings from the text of the actual opinions handed down by the courts. Used as part of a rigorous study regimen, they can help you spend more time analyzing and critiquing points of law than on copying bits and pieces of judicial opinions into your notebook or outline.

Casenote® Legal Briefs should never be used as a substitute for assigned casebook readings. They work best when read as a follow-up to reviewing the underlying opinions themselves. Students who try to avoid reading and digesting the judicial opinions in their casebooks or online sources will end up shortchanging themselves in the long run. The ability to absorb, critique, and restate the dynamic and complex elements of case law decisions is crucial to your success in law school and beyond. It cannot be developed vicariously.

Casenote® Legal Briefs represents but one of the many offerings in Legal Education's Study Aid Timeline, which includes:

- *Casenote® Legal Briefs*
- *Emanuel® Law Outlines*
- Emanuel® *Law in a Flash* Flash Cards
- Emanuel® *CrunchTime®* Series
- *Siegel's Essay and Multiple-Choice Questions and Answers Series*

Each of these series is designed to provide you with easy-to-understand explanations of complex points of law. Each volume offers guidance on the principles of legal analysis and, consulted regularly, will hone your ability to spot relevant issues. We have titles that will help you prepare for class, prepare for your exams, and enhance your general comprehension of the law along the way.

To find out more about Wolters Kluwer Law & Business' study aid publications, visit us online at *www.wolterskluwerlb.com* or email us at *legaledu@wolterskluwer.com*. We'll be happy to assist you.

How to Brief a Case

A. Decide on a Format and Stick to It

Structure is essential to a good brief. It enables you to arrange systematically the related parts that are scattered throughout most cases, thus making manageable and understandable what might otherwise seem to be an endless and unfathomable sea of information. There are, of course, an unlimited number of formats that can be utilized. However, it is best to find one that suits your needs and stick to it. Consistency breeds both efficiency and the security that when called upon you will know where to look in your brief for the information you are asked to give.

Any format, as long as it presents the essential elements of a case in an organized fashion, can be used. Experience, however, has led *Casenote® Legal Briefs* to develop and utilize the following format because of its logical flow and universal applicability.

NATURE OF CASE: This is a brief statement of the legal character and procedural status of the case (e.g., "Appeal of a burglary conviction").

There are many different alternatives open to a litigant dissatisfied with a court ruling. The key to determining which one has been used is to discover *who is asking this court for what.*

This first entry in the brief should be kept as *short as possible.* Use the court's terminology if you understand it. But since jurisdictions vary as to the titles of pleadings, the best entry is the one that addresses who wants what in this proceeding, not the one that sounds most like the court's language.

RULE OF LAW: A statement of the general principle of law that the case illustrates (e.g., "An acceptance that varies any term of the offer is considered a rejection and counteroffer").

Determining the rule of law of a case is a procedure similar to determining the issue of the case. Avoid being fooled by red herrings; there may be a few rules of law mentioned in the case excerpt, but usually only one is *the* rule with which the casebook editor is concerned. The techniques used to locate the issue, described below, may also be utilized to find the rule of law. Generally, your best guide is simply the chapter heading. It is a clue to the point the casebook editor seeks to make and should be kept in mind when reading every case in the respective section.

FACTS: A synopsis of only the essential facts of the case, i.e., those bearing upon or leading up to the issue.

The facts entry should be a short statement of the events and transactions that led one party to initiate legal proceedings against another in the first place. While some cases conveniently state the salient facts at the beginning of the decision, in other instances they will have to be culled from hiding places throughout the text, even from concurring and dissenting opinions. Some of the "facts" will often be in dispute and should be so noted. Conflicting evidence may be briefly pointed up. "Hard" facts must be included. Both must be *relevant* in order to be listed in the facts entry. It is impossible to tell what is relevant until the entire case is read, as the ultimate determination of the rights and liabilities of the parties may turn on something buried deep in the opinion.

Generally, the facts entry should not be longer than three to five *short* sentences.

It is often helpful to identify the role played by a party in a given context. For example, in a construction contract case the identification of a party as the "contractor" or "builder" alleviates the need to tell that that party was the one who was supposed to have built the house.

It is always helpful, and a good general practice, to identify the "plaintiff" and the "defendant." This may seem elementary and uncomplicated, but, especially in view of the creative editing practiced by some casebook editors, it is sometimes a difficult or even impossible task. Bear in mind that the *party presently* seeking something from this court may not be the plaintiff, and that sometimes only the cross-claim of a defendant is treated in the excerpt. Confusing or misaligning the parties can ruin your analysis and understanding of the case.

ISSUE: A statement of the general legal question answered by or illustrated in the case. For clarity, the issue is best put in the form of a question capable of a "yes" or "no" answer. In reality, the issue is simply the Rule of Law put in the form of a question (e.g., "May an offer be accepted by performance?").

The major problem presented in discerning what is *the* issue in the case is that an opinion usually purports to raise and answer several questions. However, except for rare cases, only one such question is really the issue in the case. Collateral issues not necessary to the resolution of the matter in controversy are handled by the court by language known as *"obiter dictum"* or merely *"dictum."* While dicta may be included later in the brief, they have no place under the issue heading.

To find the issue, ask *who wants what* and then go on to ask *why did that party succeed or fail in getting it.* Once this is determined, the "why" should be turned into a question.

The complexity of the issues in the cases will vary, but in all cases a single-sentence question should sum up the issue. *In a few cases,* there will be two, or even more rarely, three issues of equal importance to the resolution of the case. Each should be expressed in a single-sentence question.

Since many issues are resolved by a court in coming to a final disposition of a case, the casebook editor will reproduce the portion of the opinion containing the issue or issues most relevant to the area of law under scrutiny. A noted law professor gave this advice: "Close the book; look at the title on the cover." Chances are, if it is Property, you need not concern yourself with whether, for example, the federal government's treatment of the plaintiff's land really raises a federal question sufficient to support jurisdiction on this ground in federal court.

The same rule applies to chapter headings designating sub-areas within the subjects. They tip you off as to what the text is designed to teach. The cases are arranged in a casebook to show a progression or development of the law, so that the preceding cases may also help.

It is also most important to remember to *read the notes and questions* at the end of a case to determine what the editors wanted you to have gleaned from it.

HOLDING AND DECISION: This section should succinctly explain the rationale of the court in arriving at its decision. In capsulizing the "reasoning" of the court, it should always include an application of the general rule or rules of law to the specific facts of the case. Hidden justifications come to light in this entry: the reasons for the state of the law, the public policies, the biases and prejudices, those considerations that influence the justices' thinking and, ultimately, the outcome of the case. At the end, there should be a short indication of the disposition or procedural resolution of the case (e.g., "Decision of the trial court for Mr. Smith (P) reversed").

The foregoing format is designed to help you "digest" the reams of case material with which you will be faced in your law school career. Once mastered by practice, it will place at your fingertips the information the authors of your casebooks have sought to impart to you in case-by-case illustration and analysis.

B. Be as Economical as Possible in Briefing Cases

Once armed with a format that encourages succinctness, it is as important to be economical with regard to the time spent on the actual reading of the case as it is to be economical in the writing of the brief itself. This does not mean "skimming" a case. Rather, it means reading the case with an "eye" trained to recognize into which "section" of your brief a particular passage or line fits and having a system for quickly and precisely marking the case so that the passages fitting any one particular part of

the brief can be easily identified and brought together in a concise and accurate manner when the brief is actually written.

It is of no use to simply repeat everything in the opinion of the court; record only enough information to trigger your recollection of what the court said. Nevertheless, an accurate statement of the "law of the case," i.e., the legal principle applied to the facts, is absolutely essential to class preparation and to learning the law under the case method.

To that end, it is important to develop a "shorthand" that you can use to make marginal notations. These notations will tell you at a glance in which section of the brief you will be placing that particular passage or portion of the opinion.

Some students prefer to underline all the salient portions of the opinion (with a pencil or colored underliner marker), making marginal notations as they go along. Others prefer the color-coded method of underlining, utilizing different colors of markers to underline the salient portions of the case, each separate color being used to represent a different section of the brief. For example, blue underlining could be used for passages relating to the rule of law, yellow for those relating to the issue, and green for those relating to the holding and decision, etc. While it has its advocates, the color-coded method can be confusing and time-consuming (all that time spent on changing colored markers). Furthermore, it can interfere with the continuity and concentration many students deem essential to the reading of a case for maximum comprehension. In the end, however, it is a matter of personal preference and style. Just remember, whatever method you use, underlining must be used sparingly or its value is lost.

If you take the marginal notation route, an efficient and easy method is to go along underlining the key portions of the case and placing in the margin alongside them the following "markers" to indicate where a particular passage or line "belongs" in the brief you will write:

N (NATURE OF CASE)
RL (RULE OF LAW)
I (ISSUE)
HL (HOLDING AND DECISION, relates to the RULE OF LAW behind the decision)
HR (HOLDING AND DECISION, gives the RATIONALE or reasoning behind the decision)
HA (HOLDING AND DECISION, APPLIES the general principle(s) of law to the facts of the case to arrive at the decision)

Remember that a particular passage may well contain information necessary to more than one part of your brief, in which case you simply note that in the margin. If you are using the color-coded underlining method instead of marginal notation, simply make asterisks or checks in the margin next to the passage in question in the colors that indicate the additional sections of the brief where it might be utilized.

The economy of utilizing "shorthand" in marking cases for briefing can be maintained in the actual brief writing process itself by utilizing "law student shorthand" within the brief. There are many commonly used words and phrases for which abbreviations can be substituted in your briefs (and in your class notes also). You can develop abbreviations that are personal to you and which will save you a lot of time. A reference list of briefing abbreviations can be found on page xii of this book.

C. Use Both the Briefing Process and the Brief as a Learning Tool

Now that you have a format and the tools for briefing cases efficiently, the most important thing is to make the time spent in briefing profitable to you and to make the most advantageous use of the briefs you create. Of course, the briefs are invaluable for classroom reference when you are called upon to explain or analyze a particular case. However, they are also useful in reviewing for exams. A quick glance at the fact summary should bring the case to mind, and a rereading of the rule of law should enable you to go over the underlying legal concept in your mind, how it was applied in that particular case, and how it might apply in other factual settings.

As to the value to be derived from engaging in the briefing process itself, there is an immediate benefit that arises from being forced to sift through the essential facts and reasoning from the court's opinion and to succinctly express them in your own words in your brief. The process ensures that you understand the case and the point that it illustrates, and that means you will be ready to absorb further analysis and information brought forth in class. It also ensures you will have something to say when called upon in class. The briefing process helps develop a mental agility for getting to the *gist* of a case and for identifying, expounding on, and applying the legal concepts and issues found there. The briefing process is the mental process on which you must rely in taking law school examinations; it is also the mental process upon which a lawyer relies in serving his clients and in making his living.

Abbreviations for Briefs

Table of Cases

The Purposes and Limits of Punishment

Quick Reference Rules of Law

Kansas v. Hendricks

State (P) v. Child molester (D)

521 U.S. 346 (1997).

NATURE OF CASE: Certiorari review of a Kansas Supreme Court decision.

FACT SUMMARY: Kansas enacted a Sexually Violent Predator Act, which it invoked for the first time in committing Hendricks (D) to a mental hospital when he was scheduled for release from prison. The Kansas Supreme Court invalidated the Act. The Supreme Court of the United States granted certiorari review.

🏛 **RULE OF LAW**
A statute is constitutional if it provides for civil commitment and long-term treatment of persons who have been convicted of sexually violent offenses who suffer from mental abnormalities or personality disorders making them likely to engage in predatory behavior.

FACTS: Hendricks (D) had a long history of molesting children. He had been incarcerated on several occasions and, upon release, had molested more children. In 1984, he was convicted of "taking indecent liberties" with two teenaged boys. Hendricks (D) was scheduled for release after serving about ten years of his sentence, which was about the same time the Kansas Legislature passed the Sexually Violent Predator Act to address repeat sexual offenders. His scheduled release prompted the state to file a petition seeking his civil commitment under the Act. Hendricks (D) agreed with his diagnosis of pedophilia and did not believe he could be treated. A jury found beyond a reasonable doubt that Hendricks (D) was a sexually violent predator and Hendricks (D) appealed. The Kansas Supreme Court found that the Act was unconstitutional. The United States Supreme Court granted certiorari review.

ISSUE: Is a statute providing for the long-term civil commitment and treatment of persons who have been convicted of sex offenses, who have been determined to have mental defects or personality disorders that make them likely to engage in predatory acts, constitutional?

HOLDING AND DECISION: (Thomas, J.) Yes. A statute is constitutional if it provides for civil commitment and long-term treatment of persons who have been convicted of sexually violent offenses, who suffer from mental abnormalities or personality disorders making them likely to engage in predatory behavior. Hendricks (D) first asserts the Act violates substantive due process, but states can forcibly restrain persons who are a danger to society because of an inability to control behavior. Hendricks (D) next argues that the Act violates principles of double jeopardy. Specifically, he asserts that the Act provides for punishment of a prior crime for which he has previously served a prison sentence. The statute provides for civil commitment, and the legislative intent was not punitive but, rather, therapeutic in nature, so the Act is civil. Criminal punishment has retribution or deterrence as its primary objectives and the Act does not implicate either. Intent does not play a role in the Act, unlike a criminal statute, because the focus is on the "mental abnormality" instead of scienter. The threat of confinement would not deter a predator suffering from a "mental abnormality", so the Act is not a deterrent. Accordingly, principles of double jeopardy are not applicable. The Kansas Sexually Violent Predator Act does not violate principles of double jeopardy. Reversed.

▶ **ANALYSIS**

The Kansas Sexually Violent Predator Act, in effect, supplements criminal penalties of sex offenders. It is imposed only after the criminal sentence is served. In cases where a person is convicted of a sexually violent crime and sentenced to life in prison, the statute is unnecessary. Therefore, it is debatable whether or not, as the dissent argues, Kansas's statute is actually a further criminal penalty in the guise of a civil commitment.

■■■

Quicknotes

CERTIORARI A discretionary writ issued by a superior court to an inferior court in order to review the lower court's decisions; the Supreme Court's writ ordering such review.

DOUBLE JEOPARDY A prohibition against a second prosecution for the same offense after an acquittal or conviction for that offense in a prior proceeding or against multiple punishments for the same offense.

SUBSTANTIVE DUE PROCESS A constitutional safeguard limiting the power of the state, irrespective of how fair its procedures may be; substantive limits placed on the power of the state.

■■■

Graham v. Florida

Juvenile convicted of armed burglary (D) v. State (P)

130 S. Ct. 2011 (2010).

NATURE OF CASE: Appeal by a juvenile from the affirmance of the denial of his motion challenging a sentence of life without parole for armed burglary.

FACT SUMMARY: Graham (D), a juvenile, was convicted as an adult of various offenses, including armed burglary. After violating probation and committing new offenses, the trial court imposed a sentence of life without parole.

RULE OF LAW
The Constitution does not permit a juvenile offender to be sentenced to life in prison without parole for a nonhomicide crime.

FACTS: Graham (D), a juvenile, was charged as an adult for various offenses, including armed burglary, which carried a maximum sentence of life imprisonment without parole, and attempted armed robbery, which carried a 15-year term. Graham (D) pleaded guilty and the trial court withheld the adjudication of guilt. The court sentenced Graham (D) to concurrent three-year terms of probation. After spending the first 12 months in jail, he was released and subsequently violated probation within six months by committing new offenses. Graham (D) was then re-arrested and the trial court that adjudicated guilt for his prior crimes sentenced him to life imprisonment without parole for the armed burglary and 15 years for the attempted armed robbery. Graham (D) filed a motion challenging the sentence of life imprisonment without parole, on the grounds that it violated the "proportionality test" under the Eighth Amendment. The motion was denied. The state's intermediate appellate court affirmed and its highest court denied review. The United States Supreme Court granted certiorari.

ISSUE: Does the Constitution permit a juvenile offender to be sentenced to life in prison without parole for a nonhomicide crime?

HOLDING AND DECISION: (Kennedy, J.) No. The Constitution does not permit a juvenile offender to be sentenced to life in prison without parole for a nonhomicide crime. The Eighth Amendment's prohibition against cruel or unusual punishment is measured by "evolving standards of decency that mark the progress of a maturing society." The concept of "proportionality" is central to the Eighth Amendment so that the punishment for a crime is graduated and proportioned to the offense. Addressing the proportionality of sentences falls within two general classifications. The first involves challenges to the length of term-of years for sentences given consideration to the

circumstances in a particular case. The second generally comprises the proportionality standard by certain categorical restrictions on the death penalty. In the first classification, a review of all of the circumstances of the case is necessary to determine whether the sentence is unconstitutionally excessive. Under this approach, if a comparison of a defendant's sentence with the sentences received by other offenders in the same jurisdiction and those imposed for the same crime in other jurisdictions is "grossly disproportionate," then the defendant's sentence is cruel and unusual. For example, a term of life without parole for a defendant's seventh nonviolent felony of passing a worthless check, was found to be unconstitutional. Similarly, a sentence of 25 years to life for the theft of a few golf clubs was grossly disproportionate. The second classification uses categorical rules to define Eighth Amendment standards. In previous cases involving the death penalty, two subsets were considered. One subset measured the nature of the offense, and the other subset considered the characteristics of the offender. Capital punishment is impermissible for some nonhomicide crimes against individuals. Where the characteristics of the offender are below the age of 18 or who whose intellectual functioning is in a low range, a life without parole sentence is not allowed. Two considerations are made: first, whether the "objective indicia of society's standards, as expressed in legislative enactments and state practice" determines whether or not there is a national consensus and, second, if the Court's own independent judgment concludes that such a punishment violates the Constitution.

With regard to Graham (D), sentences of life without parole for a juvenile nonhomicide offender are permitted in some jurisdictions and there is no national consensus against it. However, a comparison of actual sentencing practices suggests that in proportion to the opportunities to impose life without parole, such sentences for juveniles convicted of nonhomicide crimes are rare.

In the judicial exercise of independent judgment, the inquiry focuses on the consideration of the culpability of the offenders in light of the crime and characteristics, along with the severity of the punishment in question and whether the punishment serves legitimate penological goals. Legitimate goals, such as retribution, deterrence, incapacitation, and rehabilitation are justifiable. However, a sentence of life without parole does not serve the desired deterrence for juveniles like Graham (D) who lack maturity and are impulsive. Incapacitation does not apply because a determination that a juvenile is forever incorrigible is

Continued on next page.

questionable. Likewise, a sentence of life imprisonment without parole is inconsistent with the goal of rehabilitation. For someone like Graham (D) the State (P) must give some meaningful opportunity to obtain release based on demonstrated maturity and rehabilitation. A sentence of life without parole for juvenile convicted of a nonhomicide offense is, therefore, grossly disproportionate, cruel and unusual, and unconstitutional. Reversed and remanded.

▶ *ANALYSIS*

In *Graham*, the Court continued the trend in treating minors and mentally challenged individuals differently, disavowing life imprisonment for nonhomicide offenses. In reviewing the proportionality test, the Court took note of actual sentencing trends and the goals of sentencing to determine that convicted juvenile offenders should be given an opportunity to gain release at some point in the future.

■═■

Kennedy v. Louisiana

Convicted child rapist (P) v. State (D)

554 U.S. 407 (2008).

NATURE OF CASE: Appeal of a sentence of death that resulted from a conviction for rape of a child.

FACT SUMMARY: Kennedy (P) was convicted of the aggravated rape of his then eight-year-old step-daughter, which did not result in her death. Kennedy (P) was sentenced to death under the applicable state law, which was challenged as unconstitutional.

🏛 RULE OF LAW
The Constitution bars a convicted offender from being sentenced to death for the rape of a child where the crime did not result, and was not intended to result, in death of the victim.

FACTS: Petitioner Kennedy was charged with the aggravated rape of his then eight-year-old stepdaughter. The victim's injuries required emergency surgery, but did not result in her death. After a jury trial, Kennedy (P) was convicted and sentenced to death under a state statute authorizing capital punishment for the rape of a child under 12 years of age. The conviction was affirmed by the state's highest court, and the United States Supreme Court granted certiorari.

ISSUE: Does the Constitution bar a convicted offender from being sentenced to death for the rape of a child where the crime did not result, and was not intended to result, in death of the victim?

HOLDING AND DECISION: (Kennedy, J.) Yes. The Constitution bars a convicted offender from being sentenced to death for the rape of a child where the crime did not result, and was not intended to result, in death of the victim. A capital punishment must be limited to those offenders who commit a narrow category of the most serious crimes and whose extreme culpability makes them the most deserving of execution. Guidance is taken by "objective indicia of society's standards, as expressed in legislative enactments and state practice with respect to executions." Whether the death penalty is disproportionate to the crime committed depends as well upon the standards elaborated the Court's own understanding and interpretation of the Eighth Amendment. The Eighth Amendment prohibits cruel and unusual punishment. One such standard is whether there is evidence of a national consensus with respect to the death penalty for child rapists. A review shows that there have been no executions for the rape of an adult or child since 1964, and no execution for any other nonhomicide offense has been conducted since 1963. While one state (Louisiana) has sentenced one individual to death for the crime of child rape, there is no national consensus to justify a sentence of death for such a nonhomicide offense.

While there are moral grounds to permit the imposition of a death sentence for nonhomicide offenses that result in the victim's fright, the sense of betrayal, and the nature of their injuries that cause prolonged physical and mental suffering, consistent with evolving standards of decency, there is a distinction between intentional first-degree murder on the one hand and nonhomicide crimes against individual persons, even including child rape. Permitting executions for child rape is grossly out of proportion to the crime and does not fulfill the two distinct social purposes, the goals of retribution and deterrence. Forcing such a long-term commitment on child victims to testify in multiple proceedings creates an unfair moral choice and is burdensome. The consequence of a death sentence would increase the risk of the nonreporting of child rape, particularly those committed by family members, and therefore does not serve the goals of deterrence or more effective enforcement. Reversed.

▶ ANALYSIS

The Court found that capital punishment is excessive and focused on the penological goals of retribution and deterrence. While concerned that a sentence of death for a nonhomicide crime was permitted in some instances, it may not serve a child victim's interests particularly given the prospect of a disincentive to report child abuse against a family if the punishment is so severe.

■==■

Quicknotes

CAPITAL PUNISHMENT Punishment by death.

FIRST-DEGREE MURDER The willful killing of another person with deliberation and premeditation; first-degree murder also encompasses those situations in which a person is killed within the perpetration of, or attempt to perpetrate, specified felonies.

■==■

Ewing v. California

Convicted felon (D) v. State (P)

538 U.S. 11 (2003).

NATURE OF CASE: Appeal from conviction under a "three strikes" law.

FACT SUMMARY: When Ewing (D) was sentenced to 25 years to life for stealing three golf clubs, under California's "three strikes" law, he argued that such sentence violated the Eighth Amendment's prohibition against cruel and unusual punishment.

🏛 RULE OF LAW
The Eighth Amendment does not prohibit a state from sentencing a repeat felon to a prison term of 25 years to life under the state's "Three Strikes and You're Out" law.

FACTS: On parole from a 9-year prison term, Gary Ewing (D) walked into the pro shop of a golf shop and walked out with three golf clubs, priced at $399 apiece, concealed in his pants leg. He was convicted of one count of felony grand theft of personal property in excess of $400. Ewing (D) had been convicted previously of four serious or violent felonies for three prior burglaries and a robbery in an apartment complex. As a newly convicted felon with two or more serious or violent felony convictions in his past, Ewing (D) was convicted under California's newly enacted "three strikes law" to 25 years to life. He appealed, arguing that the sentence violated the Eighth Amendment prohibition against cruel and unusual punishment in that the sentence was grossly disproportionate to his crime.

ISSUE: Does the Eighth Amendment prohibit a state from sentencing a repeat felon to a prison term of 25 years to life under the state's "Three Strikes and You're Out" law?

HOLDING AND DECISION: (O'Connor, J.) No. The Eighth Amendment does not prohibit a state from sentencing a repeat felon to a prison term of 25 years to life under the state's "Three Strikes and You're Out" law. Ewing's (D) sentence is justified by the state's public safety interest in incapacitating and deterring recidivist felons, and amply supported by his own long, serious criminal record. To be sure, his sentence is a long one. However, it reflects a rational legislative judgment, entitled to deference, that offenders who have committed serious or violent felonies and who continue to commit felonies must be incapacitated. This is not the rare case in which the threshold comparison of the crime committed and the sentence imposed leads to an inference of gross disproportionality. In weighing the gravity of Ewing's (D) offense, the Court must place on the scales not only his current felony, but also his long history of felony recidivism. Any other approach would fail to accord proper deference to the policy judgments that find expression in the legislature's choice of sanctions. The Eighth Amendment does not require strict proportionality between crime and sentence. Rather, it forbids only extreme sentences that are grossly disproportionate to the crime. Conviction affirmed.

CONCURRENCE: (Scalia, J.) The concept of proportionality is inherently a concept tied to the penological goal of retribution. It becomes difficult even to speak intelligently of proportionality once deterrence and rehabilitation are given significant weight. All punishment should reasonably pursue the multiple purposes of the criminal law.

▶ ANALYSIS

In *Ewing*, the Supreme Court pointed out that although three strikes laws are relatively new, the Court's tradition of deferring to state legislatures in making and implementing such important policy decisions is long-standing. This traditional deference to legislative policy choices finds a corollary in the principle that the Constitution does not mandate adoption of any one penological theory.

■■■

Quicknotes

CRUEL AND UNUSUAL PUNISHMENT Punishment that is excessive or disproportionate to the offense committed and which is prohibited by the Eighth Amendment to the United States Constitution.

■■■

Apprendi v. New Jersey

Violator of Hate Crime Statute (P) v. State (D)

530 U.S. 466 (2000).

NATURE OF CASE: Certiorari review.

FACT SUMMARY: Apprendi (P) shot a gun into the home of a black family. The judge found by a preponderance of the evidence that his crime was bias motivated and he was sentenced to a term equal to double the maximum sentence provided for by the statute under which he was originally charged. Apprendi (P) appealed his sentence and the Supreme Court of the United States granted certiorari review.

🏛 RULE OF LAW
A fact, other than a prior conviction, that increases the sentence for a crime beyond the statutory maximum must be submitted to a jury and proven beyond a reasonable doubt.

FACTS: Apprendi (P) fired shots into the home of a black family who had recently moved into an all-white neighborhood. After being apprehended by police, Apprendi (P) admitted that the motivation for his crime was racial bias. Apprendi (P) reached a plea agreement with prosecutors. After a judge found by a preponderance of the evidence that Apprendi's (P) crime was bias motivated, he imposed a sentence beyond the statutory maximum. Apprendi (P) filed an appeal arguing that the Due Process Clause requires that a finding of bias must be proved to a jury beyond a reasonable doubt. The United States Supreme Court granted certiorari review.

ISSUE: Must a fact that increases the sentence for a crime beyond the statutory maximum be submitted to a jury and proven beyond a reasonable doubt?

HOLDING AND DECISION: (Stevens, J.) Yes. A fact, other than a prior conviction, that increases the sentence for a crime beyond the statutory maximum must be submitted to a jury and proven beyond a reasonable doubt. The statute at issue allows a jury to convict a defendant of a second-degree offense if it finds beyond a reasonable doubt that the defendant unlawfully possessed a firearm. Additionally, the statute allows for a separate sentencing proceeding during which a judge may decide to impose a sentence reserved for first-degree felonies in the event that he or she finds by a preponderance of the evidence that the crime was racially motivated. In the present case, a judge so found, and the defendant was sentenced accordingly. It has long been held that all elements of a crime must be proven beyond a reasonable doubt. We have noted, in prior cases, that it is unconstitutional for a legislature to prevent the jury from assessing facts that increase the defendant's range of penalties for the crime charged. Today, we find that any fact, other than a prior conviction, that increases the defendant's possible sentence beyond the statutory maximum must be submitted to the jury and proven beyond a reasonable doubt. Reversed and remanded.

▶ ANALYSIS

Judges have discretion to impose sentences after considering aggravating and mitigating circumstances. However, in general, the judge is deciding on a sentence within the guidelines provided in a statute. For example, a judge might decide to impose a sentence of three years, based on mitigating factors, when a statute provides for a penalty of between 3 and 5 years. In *Apprendi*, the difference is that the judge has decided to impose a sentence that goes beyond the maximum penalty provided for in the statute. Essentially, the Court decided that any factor that could increase the defendant's sentence beyond the maximum sentence provided by statute rises to the level of being an element of the crime which must be submitted to a jury and proven beyond a reasonable doubt.

■■■

Quicknotes

PREPONDERANCE OF THE EVIDENCE Standard of proof requiring the trier of fact to determine whether the fact sought to be established is more probable than not.

REASONABLE DOUBT Standard of proof necessary to convict a defendant, requiring the absence of evidence that would cause a reasonable person to hesitate in making an important decision in his personal affairs.

■■■

The Criminal Act

Quick Reference Rules of Law

Proctor v. State

Property owner (D) v. State (P)

Okla. Crim. App. Ct., 176 P. 771 (1918).

NATURE OF CASE: Appeal from conviction of violating alcoholic beverage control laws.

FACT SUMMARY: Proctor (D) was convicted of keeping a dwelling with the intent of selling alcoholic beverages there.

 RULE OF LAW
A criminal conviction requires an overt illegal act.

FACTS: Proctor (D) was charged with keeping a place with the intent of selling alcoholic beverages there, in contravention of state laws. Neither Proctor (D) nor the state alleged that he actually sold liquor there. Proctor (D) was convicted, and he appealed.

ISSUE: Does a criminal conviction require an overt illegal act?

HOLDING AND DECISION: (Galbraith, Spec. J.) Yes. A criminal conviction requires an overt illegal act. It is basic to the criminal justice system that criminal intent alone is insufficient to convict a person. Some sort of illegal act must be performed in furtherance of the intent. Here, all that Proctor (D) did was "keep a place." He did not actually perform any illegal activity there. Keeping a place is not illegal. Since no illegal act was performed by Proctor (D), the statute under which he was convicted is invalid, and the conviction must be vacated.

▶ *ANALYSIS*

It is a universal requirement in criminal law that an act is required for a crime to be committed. The reasons for this seem obvious: the difficulty of proving intent without an act, and the fact that criminal law is meant to shape conduct. The problem, of course, is defining exactly what constitutes an act.

■═■

Quicknotes

OVERT ACT An open act evidencing an intention to commit a crime.

■═■

Jones v. United States

Convicted murderer (D) v. Federal government (P)

308 F.2d 307 (D.C. Cir. 1962).

NATURE OF CASE: Appeal from conviction for involuntary manslaughter.

FACT SUMMARY: Jones was found guilty of the involuntary manslaughter of Green, a 10-month-old baby belonging to Shirley Green, who placed her baby in Jones's (D) care.

🏛 RULE OF LAW
Under some circumstances, the omission of a legal duty owed by one individual to another, where such omission results in the death of the one to whom the duty is owed, will make the other chargeable with manslaughter.

FACTS: Anthony Green, the 10-month-old illegitimate child of Shirley Green, was placed in the care of Jones (D), a family friend. The baby died of neglect and malnutrition. Jones (D) was convicted of involuntary manslaughter. There was a conflict in the evidence over whether Jones (D) was paid to take care of the baby. Medical evidence clearly showed the baby to have been shockingly neglected. Jones (D) had ample means to provide food and medical care. Jones (D) took exception to the trial court's failure to instruct the jury that it must find beyond a reasonable doubt that, as an element of the case, she was under a legal duty to provide for the baby.

ISSUE: Will omission of a legal duty owed by one individual to another, where such omission results in the death of the one to whom the duty is owed, make the other chargeable with manslaughter?

HOLDING AND DECISION: (Wright, J.) Yes. The omission of a legal duty owed by one individual to another, where such omission results in the death of the one to whom the duty is owed, will make the other chargeable with manslaughter. The duty must be imposed by law or contract. The omission must be the immediate cause of death. Breach of a legal duty can arise in four situations: (1) where a statute imposes the duty; (2) where one is in a certain status relationship to another; (3) where one has assumed a contractual duty to care for another; and (4) where one has voluntarily assumed the care of another. Whether Jones (D) fits any of those four situations is a question for the jury. Evidence was in conflict particularly on the third and fourth situations. Failure to instruct the jury on a critical element of the crime requires a reversal of the conviction with the matter to be remanded for a new trial.

▶ ANALYSIS

A tentative draft of the Model Penal Code dealing with the issue confronted in the instant case states, "Liability for the commission of an offense may not be based on an omission unaccompanied by action unless: (a) the omission is expressly made sufficient by the law defining the offense; or (b) a duty to perform the omitted act is otherwise imposed by law." M.P.C., Tent. Draft No. 4 (1955), § 2.01(3). Here, whether there was a duty was an element of the crime. Failure to find beyond a reasonable doubt on any element of a crime prohibits a conviction. Note that the duty must be legal, not merely moral.

■══■

Quicknotes

INVOLUNTARY MANSLAUGHTER The killing of another person without premeditation or deliberation or with the intent to kill or to commit a felony, which may be reasonably expected to result in death or serious bodily injury; involuntary manslaughter is characterized by reckless conduct in the commission of a lawful act, or by the commission of an unlawful act that is not a felony, but which leads to the killing of another.

LEGAL DUTY TO ACT The duty to take some action to assist another in danger; such a duty is only imposed under certain circumstances, such as in accordance with a statute, contract, or relationship between the parties; when the defendant voluntarily assumes responsibility for care of the victim; or if the defendant creates the circumstances placing the victim in danger.

OMISSION The failure to perform an act or obligation that one is required to perform by law.

REASONABLE DOUBT Standard of proof necessary to convict a defendant, requiring the absence of evidence that would cause a reasonable person to hesitate in making an important decision in his personal affairs.

■══■

United States v. Maldonado

Federal government (P) v. Cocaine distributor (D)

23 F.3d 4 (lst Cir. 1994).

NATURE OF CASE: Appeal from conviction for cocaine possession.

FACT SUMMARY: When cocaine was found in Maldonado's (Zavala) (D) hotel room, he argued there was insufficient evidence that he "possessed" the cocaine within the meaning of federal drug legislation.

🏛 RULE OF LAW
A person with cocaine in his room constructively "possesses" the cocaine where the person's knowledge of its existence can reasonably be inferred.

FACTS: Santos, a seaman acting on behalf of federal customs agents, went to a hotel in Puerto Rico with drugs (being tracked by the agents) and asked at the desk for Palestino, the suspected dealer. The desk clerk called the room, and Rafael Angel Zavala Maldonado (Zavala) (D) came to the lobby and took Santos to the hotel room. There, Santos (who had the drugs in a bag with him), told Zavala (D) he had the drugs for Palestino. Zavala (D) told Santos he was a friend of Palestino and would have Palestino come to the hotel. While waiting for Palestino's arrival, Santos placed the bag in the closet of the room, and both Santos and Zavala (D) intended to leave the hotel for a while. However, when they reached the corridor, they were detained by the supervising customs agent and ultimately arrested. Zavala (D) was tried and convicted for possession of cocaine with intent to distribute. He appealed, arguing there was insufficient evidence he was in "possession" of cocaine, within the meaning of the drug statute.

ISSUE: Does a person with cocaine in his room constructively "possess" the cocaine where the person's knowledge of its existence can reasonably be inferred?

HOLDING AND DECISION: (Boudin, J.) Yes. A person with cocaine in his room constructively "possesses" the cocaine where the person's knowledge of its existence can reasonably be inferred. Constructive possession is the power and intention to exercise control, or dominion and control, over an object not in one's actual possession. One can constructively possess an object while it is hidden at home in a bureau drawer, or while held by an agent, or even while it is secured in a safe deposit box at the bank. Here, although Zavala (D) arguably did not even constructively possess the cocaine while he and Santos were in the hotel room together, once both parties departed from the room leaving the drugs inside, the situation altered. First, Santos surrendered his actual possession of the drugs. Second, with the acquiescence of both parties, the drugs were secured in Zavala's (D) room. In the context of this factual setting, a jury could reasonably have found both requisites of constructive possession: Zavala (D) had sufficient power to control the drugs and an intention to exercise that power. Clearly, the drugs were left in his room with his knowledge and consent while he was awaiting the arrival of an accomplice to pay for them. Zavala's (D) intention to have the drugs stored in his room, incident to their intended transfer to a confederate, is an intention intimately related to his power to control the drugs. Conviction affirmed.

▶ ANALYSIS

The location of drugs or firearms in a defendant's home or car is a common basis for attributing possession to the defendant. As the *Maldonado* case illustrates, this is so even if the residence or room is shared by others. The cases do not, however, say that possession is automatic, but rather that the location of the object in a domain especially accessible to the defendant can (at least where knowledge is admitted or inferred) be enough to permit the jury to find possession.

◼◼◼

State v. Barger

State (P) v. Child pornographer (D)

Ore. Sup. Ct., 247 P.3d 309 (2011).

NATURE OF CASE: Appeal from conviction for possession of child pornography, based on the trial court's failure to grant the defendant's motion for judgment of acquittal.

FACT SUMMARY: Barger (D) was convicted of possessing child pornography after a search of his computer found images in the temporary internet cache. These images, which were not saved to his computer, were nevertheless accessible to Barger (D).

🏛 RULE OF LAW

A person may not be found guilty of possessing or controlling digital images of sexually explicit conduct involving a child based on evidence showing only that the person searched for and found such images through the Internet on his computer.

FACTS: In the course of investigating a report that Barger (D) had sexually abused a child, the police conducted a search of his computer. Pornographic images of children were discovered on Barger's (D) computer in the temporary internet cache which stores web pages from sites visited by the user. These images were not found saved to the computer's hard drive. Barger's (D) motion for judgment of acquittal at the end of State's (P) case was denied, and a jury convicted him. The conviction was affirmed by the Oregon Court of Appeals, but reversed by the Supreme Court of Oregon.

ISSUE: May a person be found guilty of possessing or controlling digital images of sexually explicit conduct involving a child based on evidence showing only that the person searched for and found such images through the Internet on his computer?

HOLDING AND DECISION: (Dyke, J.) No. A person may not be found guilty of possessing or controlling digital images of sexually explicit conduct involving a child based on evidence showing only that the person searched for and found such images through the Internet on his or her computer. The statute in question requires something more than simply accessing and looking at incorporeal material of the kind involved here to "possess" or "control" that material. While Barger's (D) computer demonstrated that someone had accessed three web sites and that all appeared to contain prohibited child pornography, there was no evidence than any such images had been purposefully copied and saved in any user's personal files. Computer users with ordinary skills would not necessarily be aware of the function to recall images or know how to go about accessing information stored in the temporary

Internet file cache. The intangible nature of a web image is analogous to seeing something that a visitor has temporarily placed in one's own home. One may be aware of it, may even have asked the visitor to bring it for viewing, but one does not thereby possess the item. There is no support for the idea that a mere unexercised ability to manipulate a thing, such as to direct or influence an image, constitutes constructive possession. The argument that the mere ability to cause an item to appear on a computer screen is sufficient to constitute "control" or constructive "possession" of the item would improperly imply that any person who uses the Internet (and, indeed, any person who is within physical reach of some tangible item of child pornography) can be deemed to be guilty of violating that statute, at least insofar as the element of possession or control is involved. The statute embodies a considered legislative choice not to criminalize the mere "obtaining" or "viewing" of child pornography without consideration. Thus, the acts at issue here (navigating to a website and bringing the images that the site contains to a computer screen) are not acts that the legislature intended to criminalize. The Defendant's motion for a judgment of acquittal should have been granted. Reversed.

▶ ANALYSIS

The court found that a computer user's act of accessing an Internet web page and intentionally calling digital images of child sexual abuse onto a computer screen did not constitute possession or control of those images within the meaning of that statute. The mere ability to access prohibited child pornography does not equal constructive possession.

■=■

Lawrence v. Texas

Homosexual convicted of deviate sexual intercourse (D) v. State (P)

539 U.S. 558 (2003).

NATURE OF CASE: Appeal from conviction of deviate sexual intercourse.

FACT SUMMARY: Lawrence (D) and Garner (D), men who were convicted of engaging in deviate sexual intercourse, argued that the state statute that criminalized sexual intimacy between adult members of the same sex violated their rights to equal protection and due process under the Constitution.

🏛 **RULE OF LAW**

A statute making it a crime for two adult persons of the same sex to engage in certain consensual intimate sexual conduct violates the Due Process Clause.

FACTS: Responding to a reported weapons disturbance in a private residence, police entered Lawrence's (D) apartment and saw him and another adult man, Garner (D), engaging in a private, consensual sexual act (anal sex). They were arrested and convicted of deviate sexual intercourse in violation of a Texas statute forbidding two persons of the same sex to engage in certain intimate sexual conduct involving any contact between any part of the genitals of one person and the mouth or anus of another person, or the penetration of the genitals or the anus of another person with an object. In affirming, the state court of appeals held, inter alia, that the statute was not unconstitutional under the Due Process Clause of the Fourteenth Amendment. The court considered *Bowers v. Hardwick*, 478 U.S. 186 (1986), controlling on that point. The United States Supreme Court granted certiorari.

ISSUE: Does a statute making it a crime for two adult persons of the same sex to engage in certain consensual intimate sexual conduct violate the Due Process Clause?

HOLDING AND DECISION: (Kennedy, J.) Yes. A statute making it a crime for two adult persons of the same sex to engage in certain consensual intimate sexual conduct violates the Due Process Clause. Resolution of this case depends on whether Lawrence (D) and Garner (D) were free as adults to engage in private conduct in the exercise of their liberty under the Due Process Clause. For this inquiry, it is necessary to reconsider the *Bowers* holding. The *Bowers* Court's initial substantive statement— "The issue presented is whether the Federal Constitution confers a fundamental right upon homosexuals to engage in sodomy . . ."—discloses the Court's failure to appreciate the extent of the liberty at stake. To say that the issue in *Bowers* was simply the right to engage in certain sexual conduct demeans the claim the individual put forward, just as it would demean a married couple were it said that marriage is only about the right to have sexual intercourse. Although the laws involved in *Bowers* and here purport to do no more than prohibit a particular sexual act, their penalties and purposes have more far-reaching consequences, touching upon the most private human conduct, sexual behavior, and in the most private of places, the home. They seek to control a personal relationship that, whether or not entitled to formal recognition in the law, is within the liberty of persons to choose without being punished as criminals. The liberty protected by the Constitution allows homosexual persons the right to choose to enter upon relationships in the confines of their homes and their own private lives and still retain their dignity as free persons.

Having misapprehended the liberty claim presented to it, the *Bowers* Court stated that proscriptions against sodomy have ancient roots. It should be noted, however, that there is no long-standing history in this country of laws directed at homosexual conduct as a distinct matter. Early American sodomy laws were not directed at homosexuals as such, but instead sought to prohibit nonprocreative sexual activity more generally, whether between men and women or men and men. Moreover, early sodomy laws seem not to have been enforced against consenting adults acting in private. Instead, sodomy prosecutions often involved predatory acts against those who could not or did not consent: relations between men and minor girls or boys, between adults involving force, between adults implicating disparity in status, or between men and animals. The long-standing criminal prohibition of homosexual sodomy upon which *Bowers* placed such reliance is as consistent with a general condemnation of nonprocreative sex as it is with an established tradition of prosecuting acts because of their homosexual character. Far from possessing "ancient roots," American laws targeting same-sex couples did not develop until the last third of the 20th century. Even now, only nine states have singled out same-sex relations for criminal prosecution. Thus, the historical grounds relied upon in *Bowers* are more complex than the majority opinion and the concurring opinion by Chief Justice Burger there indicated. They are not without doubt and, at the very least, are overstated. The *Bowers* Court was, of course, making the broader point that for centuries there have been powerful voices to condemn homosexual conduct as immoral, but this Court's obligation is to define the liberty of all, not to mandate its own moral code. The nation's laws and traditions in the past half century are most relevant here. They show an emerging awareness that liberty gives substantial

Continued on next page.

protection to adult persons in deciding how to conduct their private lives in matters pertaining to sex.

Bowers's deficiencies became even more apparent in the years following its announcement. The 25 states with laws prohibiting the conduct referenced in *Bowers* are reduced now to 13, of which four enforce their laws only against homosexual conduct. In those states, including Texas, that still proscribe sodomy (whether for same-sex or heterosexual conduct), there is a pattern of nonenforcement with respect to consenting adults acting in private. One of the cases decided after *Bowers*, *Planned Parenthood of Southeastern Pa. v. Casey*, 505 U.S. 833, confirmed that the Due Process Clause protects personal decisions relating to marriage, procreation, contraception, family relationships, child rearing, and education. The heart of liberty involves a person's autonomy in making those intimate and personal decisions. Here, the petitioners seek a right integral to human freedom in other countries and this country fails to show a legitimate governmental interest in denying them that right. The private sexual conduct here is not a crime. Reversed and remanded.

▶ ANALYSIS

Only 17 years elapsed between the time *Bowers* was decided and this case. As Justice Scalia pointed out in his dissent, social perceptions of sexual and other morality change over time. With regard to homosexual intimacy, the change occurred rapidly, rendering the dissenting views in *Bowers* the prevailing view in this case. The dissent in *Bowers* argued for the recognition of an expansive fundamental right that "all individuals have in controlling the nature of their intimate associations with others," and Justice Blackmun in his dissent, argued that there is a fundamental right of an individual to conduct intimate relationships in the intimacy of his or her own home. It seems that it is these rights that the Court implicitly found were "fundamental," not, as Scalia emphasizes, that homosexual sodomy is per se a fundamental right.

■=■

Quicknotes

DUE PROCESS CLAUSE Clauses found in the Fifth and Fourteenth Amendments to the United States Constitution providing that no person shall be deprived of "life, liberty, or property, without due process of law."

EQUAL PROTECTION CLAUSE A constitutional guarantee that no person should be denied the same protection of the laws enjoyed by other persons in like circumstances.

FOURTEENTH AMENDMENT Declares that no state shall make or enforce any law which shall abridge the privileges and immunities of citizens of the United States.

RATIONAL BASIS REVIEW A test employed by the court to determine the validity of a statute in equal protection actions, whereby the court determines whether the challenged statute is rationally related to the achievement of a legitimate state interest.

STARE DECISIS Doctrine whereby courts follow legal precedent unless there is good cause for departure.

■=■

People v. Newton

State (P) v. Firearm carrier (D)

N.Y. Sup. Ct., App. Div., 72 Misc. 2d 646, 340 N.Y.S.2d 77 (1973).

NATURE OF CASE: Appeal of conviction for carrying a firearm on an airplane.

FACT SUMMARY: Newton (D), carrying a firearm on an airplane, was arrested when the plane made an unscheduled stop in New York.

🏛 RULE OF LAW
The criminal act of which a defendant is accused must have been voluntary for a conviction to be legitimate.

FACTS: Newton (D) carried a firearm onto an airplane. The flight was not scheduled to enter U.S. airspace. During the course of the flight, the pilot elected to make an emergency stop in New York. The firearm was found by authorities. Newton (D) was convicted under New York law of carrying a firearm on an airplane. Newton (D) appealed.

ISSUE: For a conviction to be legitimate, must the criminal act of which a defendant is accused have been voluntary?

HOLDING AND DECISION: (Weinstein, J.) Yes. The criminal act of which a defendant is accused must have been voluntary for a conviction to be legitimate. Newton (D) had no intention of availing himself of New York jurisdiction. His being in New York was entirely due to the actions of another. For this reason the violation of the New York statute was not voluntary on his part and consequently he committed no penal violation. Reversed.

⟩ ANALYSIS

This case raises interesting questions about the nature of volition. An argument can be made that the act of carrying a firearm was the act in question, and that the actor must take the laws as he finds them. Also, there is some indication in the opinion that the pilot made the stop because he became aware of the firearm. This adds a dimension that the court did not address.

∎═∎

Martin v. State

Public drunk (D) v. State (P)

Ala. Ct. App., 17 So. 2d 427 (1944).

NATURE OF CASE: Appeal from conviction for public drunkenness.

FACT SUMMARY: When Martin (D) was taken from his home by the police and placed onto a public highway, then charged with being drunk in public, he argued he could not be found guilty of the crime since he was involuntarily taken to the public highway.

🏛 RULE OF LAW
Under a public drunkenness statute, a voluntary appearance by the accused is presupposed.

FACTS: Police officers arrested Martin (D) at his home and took him onto a public highway where he manifested a drunken condition by using loud and profane language. Martin (D) was convicted for public intoxication and appealed, arguing that the police had involuntarily taken him to the public place.

ISSUE: Under a public drunkenness statute, is a voluntary appearance by the accused presupposed?

HOLDING AND DECISION: (Simpson, J.) Yes. Under a public drunkenness statute, a voluntary appearance by the accused is presupposed. The pertinent provisions of the statute here at issue are that any person who, while intoxicated or drunk, appears in any public place where one or more persons are present and manifests a drunken condition by boisterous or indecent conduct, or loud and profane discourse, shall, on conviction, be fined. Under the plain terms of this statute, a voluntary appearance is presupposed. The sound rule is that an accusation of drunkenness in a designated public place cannot be established by proof that the accused, while in an intoxicated condition, was, as here, involuntarily and forcibly carried to that place by the arresting officer. Conviction reversed.

▶ ANALYSIS

The Model Penal Code § 2.01(1) provides that a person is not guilty of an offense unless his or her liability is based on conduct that includes a voluntary act. The point is that the criminal law cannot hope to deter involuntary behavior thus cannot deter any crime by making an individual liable for actions he or she cannot control.

▪═▪

People v. Grant

State (P) v. Epileptic (D)

Ill. Ct. App., 360 N.E.2d 809 (1977).

NATURE OF CASE: Appeal of conviction of aggravated battery.

FACT SUMMARY: Grant (D), an epileptic prone to violent episodes, attempted to assault an officer making an arrest.

⛫ RULE OF LAW
A person is not criminally responsible for his acts if he has no conscious control over them.

FACTS: Grant (D) suffered from psychomotor epilepsy, which inclined him toward seizures and violent outbursts. While watching an arrest outside a tavern, Grant (D) suddenly threw himself on the officer, attempting to foil the arrest. Grant (D) was himself arrested. He later had a serious seizure and was hospitalized. Grant (D) argued that the whole episode was the result of his illness. The court gave no instruction regarding automatic behavior, although it did instruct the jury regarding insanity. Grant (D) was convicted, and he appealed.

ISSUE: Is a person criminally responsible for his acts if he has no conscious control over them?

HOLDING AND DECISION: (Reardon, J.) No. A person is not criminally responsible for his acts if he has no conscious control over them. Automatic acts must be distinguished from insanity. An insane person may not be able to comprehend the criminal nature of his behavior. One committing automatic acts does, but has no control over his behavior. An instruction on insanity was given, but not on automatism. However, an automatic act is not voluntary and will exculpate a defendant. The jury should have been allowed to consider this issue. Reversed.

▶ ANALYSIS

Insanity relates to the mental aspect of criminal law. Automatism goes to the volitional aspect. The linchpin of this issue concerns conscious control over one's acts. If the conscious mind loses control over the body's acts, then the act in question was not voluntary.

■═■

Quicknotes

BATTERY Unlawful contact with the body of another person.

■═■

Robinson v. California

Narcotics addict (D) v. State (P)

370 U.S. 660 (1962).

NATURE OF CASE: Appeal from conviction for narcotics addiction.

FACT SUMMARY: Robinson (D) was convicted of being a narcotics addict.

 RULE OF LAW
States may not outlaw the condition of narcotics addiction.

FACTS: The police observed track marks on Robinson (D), who also admitted to occasional drug use. Robinson (D) appealed. Robinson (D) was convicted under a California statute that made it a criminal offense for a person to "be addicted to the use of narcotics."

ISSUE: May states outlaw the condition of narcotics addiction?

HOLDING AND DECISION: (Stewart, J.) No. States may not outlaw the condition of narcotics addiction. States may punish a person for use, purchase, or sale of narcotics, or for antisocial behavior resulting from their use. However, the statute under which Robinson (D) was convicted punishes the status of addiction rather than any actual use. Narcotics addiction is an illness, which may be contracted involuntarily. Therefore, the California statute inflicts a cruel and unusual punishment in violation of the Eighth and Fourteenth Amendments by imprisoning a person for their addicted status. Reversed.

CONCURRENCE: (Harlan, J.) Addiction alone does not amount to more than a propensity to use narcotics. Thus, the law authorized criminal punishment for the mere desire to commit a criminal act.

DISSENT: (White, J.) The law should be read as prohibiting the regular, repeated, or habitual use of narcotics immediately prior to Robinson's (D) arrest.

▌ ANALYSIS

Justice Stewart noted that usually a punishment of ninety days in prison would not implicate the Eighth Amendment's ban on cruel and unusual punishment. Justice Harlan's concurrence accurately describes one line of reasoning for striking down the law—there was no criminal act because Robinson's (D) conduct was involuntary. However, another rationale has also been advanced: only past conduct is punishable by law, whereas an addict convicted under the California statute risked being punished for a mere future propensity to violate the statute.

Quicknotes

EIGHTH AMENDMENT Prohibits the imposition of excessive bail, fines, and cruel and unusual punishment.

FOURTEENTH AMENDMENT Declares that no state shall make or enforce any law which shall abridge the privileges and immunities of citizens of the United States.

Johnson v. State

Mother (D) v. State (P)

Fla. Sup. Ct., 602 So. 2d 1288 (1992).

NATURE OF CASE: Appeal from conviction for delivering narcotics to a child.

FACT SUMMARY: Johnson (D) was convicted of delivery of a controlled substance to her two children after she transmitted cocaine to her babies during childbirth by ingesting cocaine earlier in the day.

RULE OF LAW
Mothers may not be convicted of delivering narcotics to their newborn children through the umbilical cord during the birth process.

FACTS: Johnson (D) used crack cocaine before and during her labor for the birth of her son and daughter. Florida (P) prosecuted Johnson (D) for delivering a controlled substance to her children via blood flowing through the umbilical cord in the short period after the children were born but prior to the severing of the cord. The prosecution's (P) medical witness testified that cocaine would have remained in Johnson's (D) bloodstream through the birthing. A defense expert testified that it was impossible to tell whether the cocaine found in the children's blood had been transferred before or after their birth. Johnson (D) was convicted and appealed.

ISSUE: May mothers be convicted of transmitting narcotics to their newborn children through the umbilical cord during the birth process?

HOLDING AND DECISION: (Harding, J.) No. Mothers may not be convicted of transmitting narcotics to their newborn children through the umbilical cord during the birth process. The Florida statute at issue in this case was enacted to deal with the problems of child abuse and neglect. During the legislative process, the bill was amended to provide that no parent of a drug-dependent newborn would be subject to criminal investigation solely on the basis of the infant's drug dependency. Thus, it is clear that the Florida legislature considered and rejected a provision authorizing criminal penalties against mothers for delivering drug-affected children. Therefore, it did not intend to sanction prosecutions against mothers who take illegal drugs close enough in time that the drugs could theoretically pass through the umbilical cord after birth. In any event, the medical testimony does not support the trial court's finding. Johnson's (D) conviction is reversed.

▌ ANALYSIS

The court did note that up to 11% of pregnant women have used an illegal drug during their pregnancies. Cocaine-exposed babies have a variety of medical afflictions. The court was swayed in part by the belief that prosecuting women was the least effective response to the crisis and would undermine Florida's policy of keeping families intact.

■═■

Quicknotes

CONTROLLED SUBSTANCE A drug whose medical distribution is regulated by the federal government; certain classifications are unlawful.

■═■

Keeler v. Superior Court of Amador County

Ex-husband (D) v. State (P)

Cal. Sup. Ct., 2 Cal. 3d 619, 470 P.2d 617 (1970).

NATURE OF CASE: Petition for a writ of prohibition in murder prosecution.

FACT SUMMARY: Keeler (D) was charged with murder after causing the death of an unborn viable fetus by kicking the mother in her abdomen.

> **RULE OF LAW**
> Causing the death of a viable fetus is not a homicide.

FACTS: Upon learning that his ex-wife was pregnant with another man's child, Keeler (D) kicked her in the abdomen. The fetus was delivered stillborn via a caesarian section. Medical evidence proved that Keeler's (D) assault had killed the fetus. He was charged with murder. He moved to dismiss, contending that a fetus was not a "human being" within the meaning of the statute defining murder. The motion was denied. A petition for writ of prohibition was granted by the California Supreme Court.

ISSUE: Is causing the death of a viable fetus a homicide?

HOLDING AND DECISION: (Mosk, J.) No. Causing the death of a viable fetus is not a homicide. California's murder statute, Penal Code § 187, defines murder as "the unlawful killing of a human being, with malice aforethought." This law, adopted in 1872, has never been modified. The original codification of California law was meant to be based on common law principles. Under common law existing since at least 1797, an unborn child was not considered a person for purposes of supporting a murder charge. Under rules of statutory construction, it is to be assumed that the legislature was aware of the common law meanings of the terms it incorporated into the law it enacted. This being so, § 187's term "human being" does not include a viable fetus. Writ granted.

DISSENT: (Burke, Acting J.) Penal statutes do not have to be strictly construed. Common law changes with public mores. The holding here defies reason, logic, and common sense.

▶ *ANALYSIS*

The present decision was very unpopular. Within months, the California legislature amended § 187 to include "fetus" within the statute. The law now reads as follows: "(a) Murder is the unlawful killing of a human being, or a fetus, with malice aforethought. (b) This section shall not apply [if] (1) The act complied with Therapeutic Abortion Act. (2) . . . [T]he result of childbirth would be death to the mother . . . (3) The act was . . . consented to by the mother." Note that the amendment to § 187 does not mention viability of the fetus as a criterion.

■═■

Quicknotes

VIABLE FETUS The point at which a child is capable of living outside of its mother's womb.

■═■

United States v. Hudson and Goodwin

Federal government (P) v. Publishers of a libel (D)

11 U.S. (7 Cranch) 32 (1812).

NATURE OF CASE: Appeal from a demurrer to an indictment for a libel on the President and Congress.

FACT SUMMARY: When Hudson (D) and Goodwin (D) were indicted for a newspaper libel against the President and Congress of the United States, they argued that the circuit courts of the United States had no common law jurisdiction in cases of libel.

🏛 RULE OF LAW
United States courts may not exercise common law jurisdiction in criminal cases.

FACTS: Hudson (D) and Goodwin (D) were indicted for a libel against the President and Congress of the United States appearing in a newspaper. They both filed a general demurrer in the federal Circuit Court which was divided as to whether the circuit courts of the United States had a common law jurisdiction in cases of libel. The case was certified to the United States Supreme Court.

ISSUE: May United States courts exercise common law jurisdiction in criminal cases?

HOLDING AND DECISION: (Johnson, J.) No. United States courts may not exercise common law jurisdiction in criminal cases. The powers of the general government are made up of concessions from the several states. Whatever is not expressly given to the former, the latter reserve. The judicial power of the United States is a constituent part of those concessions, namely, that power is to be exercised by courts organized for the purpose and brought into existence by an effect of the legislative power of the Union. Of all the courts which the United States may, under their general powers, constitute, one only, the Supreme Court, possesses jurisdiction derived immediately from the Constitution, and of which the legislative power cannot deprive it. All other courts created by the general government possess no jurisdiction except what is given them by the power that creates them, and can be vested with none but what the power ceded to the general government will authorize them to confer. The legislative authority of the Union must first make an act a crime, affix a punishment to it, and declare the court that shall have jurisdiction of the offense.

▶ ANALYSIS

In *Hudson and Goodwin*, the Supreme Court established that the federal courts could impose liability only for crimes defined by statute.

■=■

Quicknotes

INDICTMENT A formal written accusation made by the prosecution to the grand jury under oath, charging an individual with a criminal offense.

LIBEL A false or malicious publication subjecting a person to scorn, hatred or ridicule, or injuring him or her in relation to his or her occupation or business.

■=■

Rogers v. Tennessee

Murderer (D) v. State (P)

532 U.S. 451 (2001).

NATURE OF CASE: Appeal from a murder conviction.

FACT SUMMARY: When Rogers (D) was convicted of murder after the Tennessee Supreme Court abolished the common law year and a day rule, he argued that his conviction violated *ex post facto* principles.

> ## 🏛 RULE OF LAW
> A judicial alteration of a common law doctrine of criminal law violates ex post facto principles only where it is unexpected and indefensible by reference to the law which had been expressed prior to the conduct in issue.

FACTS: Wilbert Rogers (D) was convicted in a Tennessee state court of second degree murder. Rogers (D) had stabbed the victim in the heart, causing cardiac arrest and a coma. The victim died of a kidney infection, a common complication of comas, after 15 months. At common law, the year and a day rule provided that no defendant could be convicted of murder unless the victim died by the defendant's act within a year and a day of the act. The Tennessee Supreme Court abolished the rule as it had existed at common law in Tennessee and applied its decision to Rogers (D) to uphold the conviction. The state murder statute made no mention of the year and a day rule. Rogers (D) appealed, arguing that, despite its absence from the murder statute, the year and a day rule persisted as part of the common law of Tennessee and, as such, precluded his conviction.

ISSUE: Does a judicial alteration of a common law doctrine of criminal law violate *ex post facto* principles only where it is unexpected and indefensible by reference to the law which had been expressed prior to the conduct in issue?

HOLDING AND DECISION: (O'Connor, J.) Yes. A judicial alteration of a common law doctrine of criminal law violates *ex post facto* principles only where it is unexpected and indefensible by reference to the law which had been expressed prior to the conduct in issue. The Tennessee court's abolition of the year and a day rule was not unexpected and indefensible. The rule is widely viewed as an "outdated relic" of the common law. Since no good reasons exist for retaining the rule, the rule has been legislatively and judicially abolished in the vast majority of jurisdictions recently to have addressed the issue. Common law courts frequently look to the decisions of other jurisdictions in determining whether to alter or modify a common law rule in light of changed circumstances, increased knowledge, and general logic and experience. Due process does not require a person to apprise themselves of the common law of all 50 states in order to guarantee that their actions will not subject them to punishment in light of a developing trend in the law that has not yet made its way to their own state. At the same time, however, the fact that a vast number of jurisdictions have abolished a rule that has so clearly outlived its purpose is surely relevant to whether the abolition of the rule in a particular case can be said to be unexpected and indefensible by reference to the law as it then existed. Affirmed.

DISSENT: (Scalia, J.) The Court has approved the conviction of a man for a murder that was not murder (but only manslaughter) when the offense was committed. It thus violates the principle of no penalty without law, dating from the ancient Greeks and described as one of the most widely held principles in the entire history of human thought.

▶ ANALYSIS

In the *Rogers* case, the Supreme Court noted that, at the time of the crime, the year and a day rule had only "the most tenuous foothold" as part of the criminal law of Tennessee. The rule did not exist as part of the state's statutory criminal code and had never once served as a ground of decision in any prosecution for murder in the state.

Quicknotes

COMMON LAW A body of law developed through the judicial decisions of the courts as opposed to the legislative process.

EX POST FACTO After the fact; a law that makes criminal activity or increases the punishment for a crime that occurred, or eliminates a defense that was available to the defendant, prior to its passage.

MANSLAUGHTER The killing of another person without premeditation, deliberation or with the intent to kill or to commit a felony, which may be reasonably expected to result in death or serious bodily injury; manslaughter is characterized by reckless conduct or by some adequate provocation on the part of the actor, as determined by a subjective standard.

SECOND-DEGREE MURDER The unlawful killing of another person, without premeditation, and characterized by either an intent to kill or by a reckless disregard for human life.

Chicago v. Morales

Municipality (P) v. Accused gang member (D)

527 U.S. 41 (1999).

NATURE OF CASE: United States Supreme Court review of state court ruling on constitutionality of city ordinance.

FACT SUMMARY: Morales (D) challenged an anti-gang ordinance passed by the City of Chicago (P) on the basis that the wording of the statute defining "loitering" was so vague as to make the statute unconstitutional.

🏛 RULE OF LAW
A statute providing penalties for criminal conduct is unconstitutionally vague if it fails to give sufficient notice regarding the type of conduct prohibited.

FACTS: Morales (D) and others were accused as "criminal street gang members" under a new ordinance passed by the City of Chicago (P) prohibiting persons from "loitering" with one another in public places. A City of Chicago (P) commission solicited witness testimony and made a series of findings suggesting that an increase in street activity was a primary cause of the escalation in violent and drug-related crimes, and that a common function of loitering was to enable a street gang to establish control over particular areas. In addition, the commission discovered that loitering by street gang members in public places intimidated law-abiding citizens and limited access to these areas by creating a "justifiable fear for the safety of persons and property" in the areas where loitering took place. In response, the City of Chicago (P) passed the Gang Congregation Ordinance, which created a criminal offense punishable by a fine of up to $500, as well as imprisonment and community service, for "loitering" by suspected street gang members in public places. The statute defined four elements of the crime of "loitering": first, a police officer must reasonably believe that at least two or more persons present in a public place are gang members; second, these persons must be "loitering" by remaining in one place with no apparent purpose; third, the officer must order these persons to disperse; and finally, the order to disperse must be disobeyed by the suspected gang members. Morales (D) challenged the ordinance on the basis that it broadly covered a significant amount of additional activity beyond what should be interpreted as "loitering" and was therefore unconstitutionally vague. The Supreme Court of Illinois concluded the ordinance was unconstitutionally vague because it did not provide specific limits on the discretion of police officers to determine what conduct constituted "loitering," and the City of Chicago (P) filed for review of that determination.

ISSUE: Is a statute which provides penalties for criminal conduct unconstitutionally vague if it fails to give sufficient notice regarding the type of conduct prohibited?

HOLDING AND DECISION: (Stevens, J.) Yes. A statute providing penalties for criminal conduct is unconstitutionally vague if it fails to give sufficient notice regarding the type of conduct prohibited. Clearly, a law directly prohibiting intimidating conduct similar to that described by the City of Chicago (P) commission is constitutional on its face. However, such a law may still be found unconstitutionally vague for two reasons: first, the law fails to provide the type of notice that permits ordinary persons to understand the conduct prohibited; and second, the wording of the law encourages arbitrary and discriminatory enforcement. Citizens should not have to speculate as to the meaning of a law. The requirement of notice is not met here because the order to disperse takes place before an officer knows whether the prohibited conduct has occurred, and is therefore an unjustifiable impairment of liberty if the loiterer is harmless and innocent. In addition, the statute establishes only minimal guidelines for law enforcement to follow. Police officers may exercise absolute discretion when assessing a group of bystanders for dispersal. The City of Chicago (P) asserts that the statute provides limitations on a police officer's discretion, because it does not permit a dispersal order to issue if a person has an apparent purpose, or until the officer reasonably believes that "loitering" is taking place. However, these limitations are insufficient because they do no directly address the degree of discretion an officer may exercise. The ability to assess a "loitering" situation is only subjectively limited by the officer's own evaluation of the circumstances. The Illinois Supreme Court's ruling that the statute in question is unconstitutional was correctly concluded, and is therefore affirmed.

▶ ANALYSIS

Justice Stevens's opinion suggests that the Gang Congregation Ordinance could have been worded optimally to include conduct that was apparent, such as the effort by gang members to publicize the gang's dominance over a certain area. Use of this phrasing explicitly would have satisfied constitutional concerns of specificity; however, the Court ironically noted that the absence of this descriptive language not only expanded the statute's inclusion of harmless behavior, but excluded those exact

Continued on next page.

circumstances where the statute would have played a critical role in addressing the intended problem.

■═■

Quicknotes

FOURTEENTH AMENDMENT Declares that no state shall make or enforce any law which shall abridge the privileges and immunities of citizens of the United States.

VAGUENESS AND OVERBREADTH Characteristics of a statute that make it difficult to identify the limits of the conduct being regulated.

■═■

The Guilty Mind

Quick Reference Rules of Law

People v. Dillard

State (P) v. Firearm offender (D)

Cal. Ct. App., 154 Cal. App. 3d 261, 201 Cal. Rptr. 136 (1984).

NATURE OF CASE: Appeal from conviction for carrying a loaded weapon in a public place.

FACT SUMMARY: When Dillard (D) was convicted of carrying a loaded firearm in a public place, he argued that knowledge that the weapon is loaded should be deemed to be an element of the offense

🏛 RULE OF LAW
Knowledge that a firearm is loaded is not an element of the offense of carrying a loaded firearm in a public place.

FACTS: In the early morning hours, a police officer observed Moses Dillard (D) riding a bicycle and carrying what appeared to be a rifle case. The officer unzipped the case and found a 30.30 Winchester with one round of ammunition inside the chamber and six additional rounds inside the cylinder. Seven more rounds were loose in the case. At his trial for the misdemeanor offense of carrying a loaded firearm on his person in a public place, Dillard (D) testified that he had picked up the rifle from his stepfather's house three hours before he was stopped and never opened the carrying case between the time he picked up the weapon and his stop by the police officer. Dillard (D) was convicted and appealed, arguing that the trial judge had improperly instructed the jury that knowledge that the weapon is loaded is not an element of the offense.

ISSUE: Is knowledge that a firearm is loaded an element of the offense of carrying a loaded firearm in a public place?

HOLDING AND DECISION: (Panelli, J.) No. Knowledge that a firearm is loaded is not an element of the offense of carrying a loaded firearm in a public place. Although criminal sanctions are relied upon, the primary purpose of some statutes, such as the one here under consideration, is regulation rather than punishment. To this extent, "the offenses are not crimes in the orthodox sense," and wrongful intent is not required in the interests of enforcement. When the instant legislation was enacted, the legislature declared it to be an urgency statute necessary for the immediate preservation of the public peace, health, and safety. The legislature pointed to the grave dangers from increased incidence of organized groups of individuals arming themselves and the inadequacy of existing laws to protect the people from either the use of such weapons or from violent incidents arising from the mere presence of such armed individuals in public places. The carrying of a loaded weapon in a public place falls within the class of cases involving "acts that are so destructive of the social order, or where the ability of the state to establish the element of criminal intent would be so extremely difficult if not impossible to prove," that in the interest of justice the legislature has provided that the doing of the act constitutes a crime, regardless of knowledge or criminal intent on the part of the defendant. The instant legislation is a quintessential public welfare statute which embraces a legitimate legislative judgment that, in the interest of the larger good, the burden of acting at hazard is placed upon a person who, albeit innocent of criminal intent, is in a position to avert the public danger. Affirmed.

▶ ANALYSIS

In California, the common law concept of scienter, or mens rea, is codified in a statute which provides that in every crime or public offense there must exist a union, or joint operation of act and intent, or criminal negligence. Nevertheless, as effectively illustrated in the *Dillard* case, notwithstanding this statutory admonition and the common law tradition upon which it is based, the courts, albeit with some reluctance, have recognized that certain kinds of regulatory offenses enacted for the protection of the public health and safety are punishable despite the absence of culpability or criminal intent in the accepted sense.

■══■

Quicknotes

MISDEMEANOR Any offense that does not constitute a felony, which is generally less severe and for which a lesser punishment is imposed.

SCIENTER Knowledge of certain facts; often refers to "guilty knowledge," which implicates liability.

■══■

United States v. Wulff

Federal government (P) v. Alleged violator of federal act (D)

758 F.2d 1121 (6th Cir. 1985).

NATURE OF CASE: Government's appeal from dismissal of an indictment charging violation of the Migratory Bird Treaty Act.

FACT SUMMARY: When Wulff (D) was indicted for selling migratory bird parts in violation of the Migratory Bird Treaty Act, he argued that since the statute does not require guilty knowledge, imposition of a felony conviction would violate his due process.

RULE OF LAW

Absence of a requirement that the government must prove some degree of scienter for a felony conviction violates due process.

FACTS: A federal grand jury returned a one-count indictment charging Robert Wulff (D) with selling migratory bird parts in violation of the Migratory Bird Treaty Act (MBTA) which makes it a felony to sell any migratory bird. The indictment was based on a sale made by Wulff (D) to a government agent of a necklace made of a red-tailed hawk and great-horned owl talons. Both birds are protected species under the MBTA. Wulff (D) moved to dismiss on the grounds that the statute does not require guilty knowledge and that therefore imposition of a felony conviction would be a violation of due process. The federal district court agreed and dismissed the indictment. The Government (P) appealed.

ISSUE: Does absence of a requirement that the government must prove some degree of scienter for a felony conviction violate due process?

HOLDING AND DECISION: (Milburn, J.) Yes. Absence of a requirement that the government must prove some degree of scienter for a felony conviction violates due process. The question here is not whether scienter is an element of the offense or whether Congress made a rational choice in legislating a felony conviction for the commercialization of protected birds. Rather, the issue is whether the absence of a requirement that the government must prove some degree of scienter for a felony conviction violated Wulff's (D) right to due process. Here, it does. The elimination of the element of criminal intent does not violate the due process clause only (1) where the penalty is relatively small and (2) conviction would not irreparably damage one's reputation. The MBTA fails to meet this criteria. The felony penalty carries a maximum sentence of two years' imprisonment or two thousand dollars fine, or both. This is not a relatively small penalty. Furthermore, a felony conviction irreparably damages one's reputation. To wit, a convicted felon loses, among other civil rights, the

right to sit on a jury and the right to possess a gun. Affirmed.

ANALYSIS

As the *Wulff* case illustrates, in order for one to be convicted of a felony under the MBTA, a crime unknown to the common law which carries a substantial penalty, Congress must require the prosecution to prove the defendant acted with some degree of scienter. Otherwise, a person acting with a completely innocent state of mind could be subjected to a severe penalty and experience grave damage to their reputation. This, notes the court in *Wulff,* "the Constitution does not allow."

Quicknotes

DUE PROCESS RIGHTS The constitutional mandate requiring the courts to protect and enforce individuals' rights and liberties consistent with prevailing principles of fairness and justice and prohibiting the federal and state governments from such activities that deprive its citizens of a life, liberty or property interest.

FELONY A criminal offense of greater seriousness than a **misdemeanor;** felonies are generally defined pursuant to statute as any crime that is punishable by death or by a term of imprisonment exceeding one year.

SCIENTER Knowledge of certain facts; often refers to "guilty knowledge," which implicates liability.

Lambert v. California

Convicted forger (D) v. State (P)

355 U.S. 225 (1957).

NATURE OF CASE: Appeal from conviction for failure to register under a California law that requires registration of convicted felons.

FACT SUMMARY: Lambert (D), a convicted forger who was living in Los Angeles, did not register with the authorities as a convicted felon and was charged with failing to do so (in violation of Los Angeles Municipal Code § 52.39).

🏛 RULE OF LAW
One may not be punished for failure to register as a convicted felon (consistent with the requirements of the due process) unless the state can show: (1) circumstances that might move one to inquire as to the necessity of registration or (2) actual knowledge of the duty to register.

FACTS: Lambert (D) was a convicted forger who had been living in Los Angeles for seven years. Los Angeles Municipal Code § 52.39 made it unlawful for any convicted felon to be, or remain, in Los Angeles for a period of more than five days without registering. Lambert (D), who claimed to have no actual knowledge of the duty to register, had not registered, was arrested, and was convicted. The appeal raised the issue of whether or not some mens rea was required in this circumstance by the Due Process Clause of the Fourteenth Amendment.

ISSUE: May one be punished for failure to register as a convicted felon (consistent with the requirements of due process) if the state can show neither circumstances that might move one to inquire as to the necessity of registration nor actual knowledge of the duty to register?

HOLDING AND DECISION: (Douglas, J.) No. One may not be punished for failure to register as a convicted felon (consistent with the requirement of due process) unless the state can show either circumstances that might move one to inquire as to the necessity of registration or actual knowledge of the duty to register. The circumstances of this case show absolutely nothing that should have alerted Lambert (D) to the need for registration, effectively denying her the opportunity to avoid the consequences of the law or to defend any prosecution brought under it. Unless Lambert (D) can be shown to have had actual knowledge of the duty to register, this result would conflict with the requirements of notice that are found in the Due Process Clause of the Fourteenth Amendment. Reversed.

DISSENT: (Frankfurter, J.) Criminal provisions often result in conviction of persons who were unaware of their wrongdoing. Precedent supports such convictions. It is equally fair to imprison a person for five years for narcotics when that person was completely unaware of the laws being broken as it is to convict a person for violation of the local registration laws after she was placed on probation for three years on condition of payment of $250. It is possible that a sanction can be so disproportionate to the law's requirements as to be a violation of the Eighth Amendment prohibition against cruel and unusual punishment. Here, however, the Court questions the State's requirement of doing versus not doing, which violates years of precedent.

▶ ANALYSIS

The student should be careful to keep the holding of this case appropriately narrow. The Supreme Court held that ignorance of the law covering the conduct in question will be a defense only when: (1) we are dealing with an omission to act or (2) the omission to act is under circumstances that would not move one to inquire as to the need to act. Therefore, if the state made a law that criminalized failure to aid a choking or drowning person, a defendant would not be able to claim that he was unaware of the law because there were circumstances that should have alerted him. In general, a defendant will not be able to use this ignorance of the law defense whenever the omission runs counter to established notions of morality or common sense.

■═■

Quicknotes

PROCEDURAL DUE PROCESS The constitutional mandate that if the state or federal government acts so as to deny a citizen of a life, liberty or property interest the individual is first entitled to notice and the right to be heard.

■═■

Regina v. Faulkner

Government (P) v. Thief (D)

Ct. of Crown Cases Reserved, Ireland, 13 Cox C.C. 550 (1877).

NATURE OF CASE: Appeal of arson conviction.

FACT SUMMARY: Faulkner (D), trying to steal rum from a ship, accidently started a fire, destroying the entire ship.

> 🏛 **RULE OF LAW**
> One is criminally liable for a crime collateral to an intended crime only when it is a natural and probable consequence of the intended crime.

FACTS: Faulkner (D) boarded a ship to steal rum. During the course thereof he accidentally started a fire which destroyed the ship. Faulkner (D) was tried and convicted of both the attempted theft and the fire. Faulkner (D) appealed the **arson conviction.**

ISSUE: Is one criminally liable for a crime collateral to an intended crime only when it is a natural and probable consequence of the intended crime?

HOLDING AND DECISION: (Per curiam) No. One is not criminally liable for a crime collateral to an intended crime only when it is a natural and probable consequence of the intended crime. Reversed.

CONCURRENCE: (Barry, J.) To hold one criminally liable for all consequences of his criminal acts is too broad a proposition.

CONCURRENCE: (Fitzgerald, J.) Only those consequences which are natural and probable from a crime should be chargeable to a defendant.

CONCURRENCE: (O'Brien, J.) Had Faulkner (D) acted recklessly, a conviction might be proper, but no such instruction was presented to the jury.

DISSENT: (Keogh, J.) The jury properly ruled on intention and malice.

▶ ANALYSIS

The statute under which Faulkner (D) was prosecuted required malice for a conviction. This was probably the element lacking, yet the court and the concurrences did not discuss it. The concurrence of Justice O'Brien might be read to equate malice with recklessness, but the opinion is silent as to whether that was what he was thinking.

■▬■

Quicknotes

ARSON The unlawful burning of a building or structure.

MALICE The intention to commit an unlawful act without justification or excuse.

■▬■

Regina v. Prince

Government (P) v. Abductor (D)

Ct. for Crown Cases Reserved, L.R. 2 Crim. Cas. Res. 154 (1875).

NATURE OF CASE: Appeal of conviction for "taking" a girl under 18.

FACT SUMMARY: Prince (D) went away with a 16-year-old girl, believing her to be 18.

🏛 RULE OF LAW
Where a statute does not make mens rea an element of a crime, knowledge of the pertinent facts is irrelevant.

FACTS: Prince (D) abducted a willing 16-year-old girl from the custody of her father, in violation of a statute making such abduction of girls under 18 illegal. Prince (D) reasonably believed her to be 18 or older. The statute proscribing such acts was written as a strict liability offense. Prince (D) was convicted under the statute and appealed.

ISSUE: When a statute does not make mens rea an element of a crime is knowledge of the pertinent facts relevant?

HOLDING AND DECISION: (Blackburn, J.) No. When a statute does not make mens rea an element of a crime knowledge of the pertinent facts is irrelevant. Where the statutory language omits the mental element of a crime and no indication of contrary intention exists, it is to be assumed that knowledge was not to be an element of the crime. One violating such a statute does so at his peril. Here, the statute had no element of mens rea, and hence Prince's (D) erroneous belief was irrelevant. Affirmed.

CONCURRENCE: (Bramwell, J.) Where the act involved is wrong, here the taking of a girl from her father, a defendant's lack of knowledge of aggravating circumstance should not exonerate him from the aggravated crime.

CONCURRENCE: (Denman, J.) Taking a girl of any age from her father is wrong, and Prince (D) assumed the risk of a greater crime in taking a minor girl.

DISSENT: (Brett, J.) There should be no conviction of a crime without a mens rea.

▶ ANALYSIS

The most interesting opinion was that of Justice Bramwell. He seemed to be saying that once the threshold of criminality was crossed, knowledge or the lack thereof of facts making the crime worse was irrelevant as a defense to the greater charge. Perhaps, by negative implication, the opinion can be read to mean that lack of mens rea might have been a defense to the original threshold of criminality. An example in this instance might be that, had Prince (D)

believed the girl not to be in anyone's custody, his actions might not have been criminal in Justice Bramwell's eyes.

■=■

Quicknotes

MENS REA Criminal intent.

STRICT LIABILITY Liability for all injuries proximately caused by a party's conducting of certain inherently dangerous activities without regard to negligence or fault.

■=■

People v. Ryan

State (P) v. Drug possessor (D)

N.Y. Ct. App., 82 N.Y.2d 497, 626 N.E.2d 51, 605 N.Y.S.2d 235 (1993).

NATURE OF CASE: Appeal from conviction for drug possession.

FACT SUMMARY: Ryan (D) claimed that he was convicted of felony drug possession even though he did not know how much weight of the drug he had.

RULE OF LAW
Laws against drug possession include a mens rea element for the weight of the drugs.

FACTS: Ryan (D) asked his friend Hopkins to order and receive a shipment of hallucinogenic mushrooms on his behalf. The police were tipped off to Hopkins's receipt of the drugs, and an investigator delivered the drugs to Hopkins. After Hopkins was arrested, he informed on Ryan (D) and taped a conversation in which he told Ryan (D) that there were two pounds of mushrooms. Ryan (D) was convicted of felony drug possession for having more than 625 milligrams of a hallucinogen after evidence showed that the package delivered to Hopkins contained well over that amount. Ryan (D) appealed, claiming that he did not knowingly possess that amount of drugs.

ISSUE: Do laws against drug possession include a mens rea element for the weight of the drugs?

HOLDING AND DECISION: (Kaye, C.J.) Yes. Laws against drug possession include a mens rea element for the weight of the drugs. The statute at issue provides that a person is guilty for knowingly and unlawfully possessing a certain amount of drugs. The language of the law demonstrates that "knowingly" applies to the weight element as well as to the possession element. This reading is supported by the rule that statutes defining crimes include a mens rea requirement for all material elements unless there is a clear intent to create a strict liability crime. Therefore, if a single mens rea is set forth in a criminal law, it presumptively applies to all elements of the offense unless there is a contrary legislative intent. In the present case, the purpose of the knowledge requirement is partially to avoid over penalizing a person who unwittingly possesses a larger amount of a controlled substance than anticipated. Since Ryan (D) knew only that he possessed two pounds of mushrooms, he did not knowingly possess the requisite amount of hallucinogens, in absence of evidence that two pounds of mushrooms usually contain that amount of hallucinogen. Reversed.

▶ ANALYSIS

The court's decision allows the use of inferences to prove the knowledge requirement. Thus, knowledge of the weight of substances can be inferred from the defendant's handling of the material. The court also noted that many drugs are measured by aggregate weight, which includes cutting agents.

■■■■

Quicknotes

KNOWINGLY Intentionally; willfully; an act that is committed with knowledge as to its probable consequences.

MATERIAL ELEMENT OF CRIME A part of a crime which must be demonstrated by the prosecution in order to convict a defendant.

MENS REA Criminal intent.

STRICT LIABILITY Liability for all injuries proximately caused by a party's conducting of certain inherently dangerous activities without regard to negligence or fault.

■■■■

People v. Bray

State (P) v. Felon (D)

Cal. Ct. App., 52 Cal. App. 3d 494, 124 Cal. Rptr. 913 (1975).

NATURE OF CASE: Appeal of conviction for illegal possession of firearm.

FACT SUMMARY: Not certain whether a previous conviction constituted a felony, Bray (D) purchased a gun, stating he had no felony convictions.

🏛 RULE OF LAW
In a non-strict liability crime, lack of knowledge of facts necessary for criminal intent exculpates the defendant.

FACTS: Bray (D) was convicted of being an accessory to a crime. He was given probation. Years later, having obtained a job as a security officer, Bray (D) purchased a firearm. Prior to purchasing a gun, Bray (D) was required to affirm that he had no prior felony convictions. Bray (D) stated he had none, not believing his prior conviction to be a felony. Bray (D) was charged and convicted of falsifying his record by not listing the conviction. Bray (D) appealed.

ISSUE: In a non-strict liability crime, does lack of knowledge of facts necessary for criminal intent exculpate a defendant?

HOLDING AND DECISION: (Brown, J.) Yes. In a non-strict liability crime, lack of knowledge of facts necessary for criminal intent exculpates a defendant. One cannot form an intent without knowledge of the underlying relevant facts. Here, Bray (D) in fact did not know that he was a felon, and the fact that he was given no jail time makes this lack of knowledge quite reasonable. Reversed.

▶ ANALYSIS

It is an old axiom of the law that "ignorance of the law is no excuse." However, as this case demonstrates, ignorance of the facts sometimes is. However, it can sometimes be a problem figuring out whether a certain lack of knowledge was of law or facts.

■■■

Quicknotes

FELONY A criminal offense of greater seriousness than a **misdemeanor;** felonies are generally defined pursuant to statute as any crime that is punishable by death or by a term of imprisonment exceeding one year.

STRICT LIABILITY Liability for all injuries proximately caused by a party's conducting of certain inherently dangerous activities without regard to negligence or fault.

■■■

United States v. Baker

Federal government (P) v. Watch dealer (D)

807 F.2d 427 (5th Cir. 1986).

NATURE OF CASE: Appeal from conviction for trafficking in counterfeit goods.

FACT SUMMARY: Baker (D) claimed that he was not guilty of trafficking in counterfeit watches because he did not know that Congress had enacted a new law criminalizing his conduct.

 RULE OF LAW
Ignorance of the law is no excuse.

FACTS: In 1984 Congress enacted the Trademark Counterfeiting Act, which criminalized conduct that had formerly been subject to civil penalties only. It penalized anyone who intentionally trafficked in goods and knowingly used a counterfeit mark. Baker (D) intentionally and knowingly dealt in counterfeit Rolex watches and was convicted. Baker (D) appealed, claiming that he did not know that trafficking in counterfeiting goods was a crime.

ISSUE: Is ignorance of the law an excuse?

HOLDING AND DECISION: [Reavley, J.] No. Ignorance of the law is no excuse. While this principle is often overstated, it remains true that criminal law does not require knowledge that an act is illegal. A defendant may not avoid prosecution by simply claiming that he had not brushed up on the law. In the present case, Baker's (D) conduct met the required mental state because he admittedly had knowledge of dealing in counterfeiting goods. His knowledge of the new law is irrelevant. Affirmed.

▶ **ANALYSIS**

LaFave and Scott's criminal law treatise points out that it is important to distinguish between the defendant's mental state required for the commission of a crime and a claim of ignorance that certain conduct was proscribed by law. In other words, ignorance of certain factual conditions specified by the governing law may lead to acquittal, but ignorance of which conditions are actually contained in that law will not. This principle dates back to the beginning of English common law.

■═■

Quicknotes

MISTAKE OF LAW An error involving a misunderstanding or incorrect application of law.

■═■

Cheek v. United States

Tax evader (D) v. Federal government (P)

498 U.S. 192 (1991).

NATURE OF CASE: Appeal from conviction for income tax evasion.

FACT SUMMARY: Cheek (D) claimed that he was not guilty of willful tax evasion because he believed that income taxes were unconstitutional, that wages were not income, and that he was not a taxpayer within the meaning of the Internal Revenue Code.

🏛 RULE OF LAW
A subjective misunderstanding about the law is a defense to willful evasion of taxes.

FACTS: Cheek (D) failed to file federal income tax returns between 1980 and 1986. The federal government (P) charged Cheek (D) with willfully attempting to evade his tax obligations. These offenses were specific intent crimes that require the defendant to have acted willfully. During the period in question, Cheek (D) was active in anti-tax movements and testified that he believed that the federal income tax was unconstitutional. Cheek (D) argued that since this belief was sincere, he lacked the willfulness required for conviction. At trial, the court instructed the jury that an honest but unreasonable belief was not a defense that negates willfulness. Cheek (D) was convicted and subsequently appealed.

ISSUE: Is a subjective misunderstanding about the law a defense to willful evasion of taxes?

HOLDING AND DECISION: (Revealey, C.J.) Yes. A subjective misunderstanding about the law is a defense to willful evasion of taxes. Willfulness requires that the government prove that the defendant voluntarily and intentionally violated a duty imposed by law. The government cannot prove knowledge of the duty if the defendant was ignorant of it, misunderstood it, or believed it did not exist. This belief must be held in good faith but does not need to be objectively reasonable. Since the tax system is complex, proof of knowledge of the law is required to show willfulness. However, claims that the tax laws are unconstitutional do not arise from innocent mistakes caused by the complexity of the Internal Revenue Code. Instead, these claims reveal full knowledge and a conclusion, however wrong, that the provisions are invalid. Thus, a defendant's view about the validity of the law is irrelevant. Accordingly, Cheek's (D) claims about his view that the law was unconstitutional were properly excluded from consideration by the jury. However, it was error for the trial court to instruct the jury that Cheek's (D) subjective beliefs that wages were not income and that he was not a taxpayer within the meaning of the Code and should not be considered by the jury in determining willfulness. Remanded.

▶ ANALYSIS

This decision has not been extended by other courts outside the tax law context. However, the Supreme Court reached a similar decision in *Ratzlaf v. United States*, 501 U.S. 135 (1994), interpreting a banking law. Congress immediately revised the law by removing the willful requirement.

■━■

Quicknotes

SPECIFIC INTENT The intent to commit a specific unlawful act which is a required element for criminal liability for certain crimes.

SUBJECTIVE A belief that is personal to an individual.

WILLFULLY An act that is undertaken intentionally, knowingly, and with the intent to commit an unlawful act without a justifiable excuse.

■━■

Commonwealth v. Twitchell

State (P) v. Parents (D)

Mass. Sup. Jud. Ct., 416 Mass. 114, 617 N.E.2d 609 (1993).

NATURE OF CASE: Appeal from convictions for involuntary manslaughter.

FACT SUMMARY: Christian Scientist parents (D) did not seek medical treatment for their child's illness and the child died.

> 🏛 **RULE OF LAW**
> Mistake of law can be a defense when the government official charged with enforcing that law has issued a mistaken or misleading ruling about the law upon which the defendants relied.

FACTS: Christian Scientist parents (D) did not seek medical treatment for their child for an illness that is usually successfully treated by surgery. The parents did obtain official religious counseling about their responsibilities as parents and relied on documents prepared by their denomination. These religious papers had relied on a misleading interpretation of the law written by the Attorney General of Massachusetts. Following their convictions for involuntary manslaughter, the parents (D) appealed, claiming their mistake of law should excuse their conduct.

ISSUE: Can mistake of law ever be a defense to charges of involuntary manslaughter?

HOLDING AND DECISION: (Wilkins, J.) Yes. In very narrow circumstances mistake of law can be a defense to charges of involuntary manslaughter. These circumstances include instances where the mistake of law grows out of the misleading or false opinion provided by the government official charged with interpreting the law. In the instant case, the parents (D) based their conduct in part on the misleading opinion of the Attorney General. Reversed and remanded for new trial.

intent to kill or to commit a felony, which may be reasonably expected to result in death or serious bodily injury; involuntary manslaughter is characterized by reckless conduct in the commission of a lawful act, or by the commission of an unlawful act that is not a felony, but which leads to the killing of another.

MISTAKE OF LAW An error involving a misunderstanding or incorrect application of law.

■══■

▶ ANALYSIS

The defense of entrapment by estoppel rests on the principles of fairness and the Due Process Clause of the Fifth Amendment. The theory is that if a person tried to determine the law and consulted the official interpretation of the law, he should not be liable for false official government pronouncement. The person must be actually misinformed or misled by the interpretation given by the government official charged with interpreting the law.

■══■

Quicknotes

INVOLUNTARY MANSLAUGHTER The killing of another person without premeditation or deliberation or with the

Hendershott v. People

Assailant (D) v. State (P)

Col. Sup. Ct., 653 P.2d 385 (1982).

NATURE OF CASE: Appeal from third degree assault conviction.

FACT SUMMARY: Hendershott (D) contends that it was unconstitutional to prohibit him from presenting evidence of impaired mental condition showing lack of requisite culpability for third degree assault.

🏛 RULE OF LAW
Opinion evidence of a mental impairment due to mental disease or defect may be admitted to negate the mens rea for a nonspecific intent crime such as third degree assault.

FACTS: Hendershott (D) was living in the rooming house of Styskal, whom he had dated occasionally for three years. Problems developed in their relationship due to Hendershott's (D) excessive drinking. One evening, Ms. Styskal told Hendershott (D) that he would have to move out. Later that evening, Hendershott (D) accused her of having been out with another man. He then struck, kicked, and began to choke her. She escaped and called the police. The police found Hendershott (D) unconscious in Ms. Styskal's home and immediately arrested and charged him with third degree assault. In the course of pretrial discovery, the district attorney filed a pretrial motion to exclude evidence of Hendershott's (D) mental condition offered to establish lack of requisite culpability of "knowingly" or "recklessly" causing bodily injury, an element essential to proving the crime. The county court ruled the evidence inadmissible as a matter of law in prosecution for crimes not requiring specific intent. Both the county and district courts convicted Hendershott (D). Hendershott (D) appealed.

ISSUE: May opinion evidence of a mental impairment due to a mental disease or defect be admitted to negate the mens rea for a nonspecific intent crime such as third degree assault?

HOLDING AND DECISION: (Quinn, J.) Yes. Opinion evidence of a mental impairment due to mental disease or defect may be admitted to negate the mens rea for a nonspecific intent crime such as third degree assault. Evidence that the defendant suffered from a mental disease or defect is admissible whenever it is relevant to prove that the defendant did or did not have a state of mind which is an element of the offense. It would be a violation of due process to require the prosecution to establish the culpable mental state beyond a reasonable doubt, while, at the same time, to prohibit a defendant from presenting evidence to contest this issue. Such a prohibition assumes all the features of an impermissible presumption of culpability. An accused is not only entitled to the presumption of innocence on all elements of a charge but also is protected against conviction unless the prosecution establishes the requisite mens rea by proof beyond a reasonable doubt. The trial court's exclusion of the mental impairment evidence rendered the prosecution's evidence uncontestable as a matter of law on the issue of mens rea, thus adversely implicating the constitutional presumption of innocence. A reasonable doubt as to guilt may arise not only from the prosecution's case, but also from defense evidence casting doubt upon what previously may have appeared certain. Denying the defendant any opportunity to controvert the prosecution's case by reliable and relevant evidence of mental impairment downgrades the prosecution's burden to something less than that mandated by due process of law. Reversed and remanded.

▌ ANALYSIS

Only ten states allow evidence of psychological impairment to negate the mental element of all crimes. A greater number of states allow such evidence to negate specific intent crimes only. Other states do not permit it to negate mens rea at all.

■══■

Quicknotes

ASSAULT The intentional placing of another in fear of immediate bodily injury.

DISCOVERY Pretrial procedure during which one party makes certain information available to the other.

DUE PROCESS The constitutional mandate requiring the courts to protect and enforce individuals' rights and liberties consistent with prevailing principles of fairness and justice and prohibiting the federal and state governments from such activities that deprive its citizens of a life, liberty or property interest.

MENS REA Criminal intent.

SPECIFIC INTENT The intent to commit a specific unlawful act which is a required element for criminal liability for certain crimes.

■══■

State v. Cameron

State (P) v. Assailant (D)

N.J. Sup. Ct., 104 N.J. 42, 514 A.2d 1302 (1986).

NATURE OF CASE: Appeal of reversal of conviction of assault, illegal weapon possession, and resisting arrest.

FACT SUMMARY: Cameron (D) wished to invoke voluntary intoxication as a defense to a charge of assault, illegal weapon possession, and resisting arrest.

🏛 **RULE OF LAW**
Voluntary intoxication may be a defense to a charge of assault, illegal weapon possession, and resisting arrest.

FACTS: Cameron (D) became involved in an altercation with several individuals, which resulted in charges of assault, illegal weapon possession, and resisting arrest. At trial, the court refused to permit her to raise the defense of voluntary intoxication, and Cameron (D) was convicted. A state court of appeals reversed, ruling that the defense should have been permitted. The state supreme court granted review.

ISSUE: May voluntary intoxication be a defense to a charge of assault, illegal weapon possession, and resisting arrest?

HOLDING AND DECISION: (Clifford, J.) Yes. Voluntary intoxication may be a defense to a charge of assault, illegal weapon possession, and resisting arrest. At common law, voluntary intoxication could be a defense to a "specific intent" crime but not a "general intent" crime. New Jersey has statutorily changed the culpability element of criminal law, so that mens rea now has four categories: "knowing," "purposeful," "reckless," and "criminally negligent." By statute, voluntary intoxication may be raised as a defense to crimes involving the first two mental states. Here, the assault, illegal weapon possession, and resisting arrest all fall with the first two categories, so the defense would be applicable. [The court went on to rule that, as a matter of law, evidence of intoxication here was insufficient to go to a jury, so the conviction was reinstated.]

▌ *ANALYSIS*

Voluntary intoxication used to be both a complete and an incomplete defense. In the latter situation, it could reduce a charge, such as the diminished capacity defense might. The trend in recent years has been to permit it to be a complete defense only, to be used when it negates an element of the offense in question.

■══■

Quicknotes

GENERAL INTENT The intention to conduct unlawful activity, as opposed to a particular unlawful act.

MENS REA Criminal intent.

SPECIFIC INTENT The intent to commit a specific unlawful act which is a required element for criminal liability for certain crimes.

VOLUNTARY INTOXICATION The voluntary consumption of substances that the defendant knows or should know will obscure his judgment; voluntary intoxication may be considered when determining whether the defendant possessed the requisite intent.

■══■

Montana v. Egelhoff

State (P) v. Intoxicated killer (D)

518 U.S. 37 (1996).

NATURE OF CASE: Appeal from conviction for purposely or knowingly causing death.

FACT SUMMARY: [Facts not stated in casebook excerpt.]

🏛 RULE OF LAW
State legislation defining mens rea to eliminate the exculpatory value of voluntary intoxication is not unconstitutional.

FACTS: [Factual background not stated in casebook excerpt.] At trial, the jury was instructed to ignore Egelhoff's (D) "intoxicated condition" in considering his requisite mental state for the offense of "purposely or knowingly" causing a death. The jury convicted and Egelhoff (D) appealed. The Montana Supreme Court reversed on the basis that his intoxication was relevant to the mental element of the crime charged. The United States Supreme Court reversed in a four-justice plurality opinion. Justice O'Connor argued that excluding such evidence violated due process because it presumes mens rea. Justice Scalia argued the state could exclude exculpatory evidence relevant to mens rea. Justice Ginsburg filed the "swing" opinion.

ISSUE: Is state legislation defining mens rea to eliminate the exculpatory value of voluntary intoxication unconstitutional?

HOLDING AND DECISION: (Ginsburg, J.) No. State legislation defining mens rea to eliminate the exculpatory value of voluntary intoxication is not unconstitutional. States enjoy wide latitude in defining the elements of criminal offenses. When a state's power to define criminal conduct is challenged under the Due Process Clause, we inquire only whether the law offends some principle of justice so rooted in the traditions and conscience of our people as to be ranked as fundamental. Defining mens rea to eliminate the exculpatory value of voluntary intoxication does not offend a fundamental principle of justice, given the lengthy common-law tradition, and the adherence of a significant minority of the states to that position today. Other state courts have upheld similar statutes. Legislation of this order, if constitutional in Arizona, Hawaii, and Pennsylvania, ought not be declared unconstitutional by this Court when enacted in Montana. Reversed.

▶ ANALYSIS

Justice Ginsberg delivered the controlling "swing" opinion for a divided court. Justice O'Connor, in a four-justice plurality, took the view that excluding evidence relevant to the mens rea of an offense violated due process by presuming culpability over innocence. Justice Scalia and three other justices took the view that a state could exclude exculpatory evidence relevant to mens rea.

■▬■

Quicknotes

DUE PROCESS CLAUSE Clauses found in the Fifth and Fourteenth Amendments to the United States Constitution providing that no person shall be deprived of "life, liberty, or property, without due process of law."

MENS REA Criminal intent.

VOLUNTARY INTOXICATION The voluntary consumption of substances that the defendant knows or should know will obscure his judgment; voluntary intoxication may be considered when determining whether the defendant possessed the requisite intent.

■▬■

Causation

Quick Reference Rules of Law

Regina v. Martin Dyos

Government (P) v. Alleged murderer (D)

Cent. Crim. Ct., Crim. L. Rev. 660-662 (1979).

NATURE OF CASE: Criminal proceeding for murder.

FACT SUMMARY: Martin Dyos (D) had caused an injury to the right forehead of RM, but no evidence could be offered as to the cause of a second injury to RM or which injury was the cause of death.

🏛 RULE OF LAW
One's act cannot be held to be the cause of death of another if the death would, or could, have occurred without the act.

FACTS: A number of persons, including Martin Dyos (D), faced criminal charges as the result of a fight that occurred between two groups of youths after a dance. Martin Dyos (D) was charged with murder and grievous bodily harm. Evidence was offered that he had caused injury to the right forehead of RM by means of a brick and that RM, who died nine days later from his injuries, had also received an injury behind his right ear. There was no evidence as to the cause of this later injury. The pathologist concluded that both wounds were potentially fatal and either could "very probably" cause death, and that there was a "reasonable and sensible" possibility that RM might have recovered from the first injury, whichever that was.

ISSUE: Can one's act be held to be the cause of death of another if the death would, or could, have occurred without the act?

HOLDING AND DECISION: (Cantley, J.) No. One is not the cause of another's death in the legal sense unless the death was a natural and probable consequence of his act. Thus, one's act is not the legal cause of death if the death would, or could, have occurred without the act. In this case, the Crown had to exclude the possibility that death was caused by an injury other than the one caused by Martin Dyos (D). Since another injury did occur that may reasonably have been the cause of death of RM and for which Martin Dyos (D) has not been shown to be responsible, the count of murder cannot go to the jury. [After the ruling, Dyos pled guilty to two of the lesser counts.]

▌ ANALYSIS

Commentators have dubbed the causation requirement highlighted in this case the "but for" causation principle. It is also often referred to as the factual cause, the de facto cause, or the scientific cause, and should be distinguished from "cause" in another sense, i.e., "proximate" cause or "legal" cause. When looking at the notion of "but for" causation, it should be remembered that an omission can be a "but for" cause of a result.

■=■

Quicknotes

"BUT FOR" TEST For purposes of determining tort liability, the test for the element of causation is whether the plaintiff would have suffered the injury "but for" the defendant's conduct.

PROXIMATE CAUSE The natural sequence of events without which an injury would not have been sustained.

■=■

R. v. Benge

Queen (P) v. Crew foreman (D)

Maidstone Cr. Ct., 4 F. & F. 504 (1865).

NATURE OF CASE: Trial for manslaughter.

FACT SUMMARY: Benge (D) foreman of a crew, inadvertently ordered the removal of certain rails just before a train was due, resulting in an accident in which lives were lost.

🏛 RULE OF LAW

Criminal liability may be imputed where the causal chain is dependent upon negligent omissions of others.

FACTS: Benge (D), foreman of a construction crew, ordered the removal of certain rails just before a train was due. He had inadvertently looked at the wrong date on his train schedule. As a precaution, he ordered a crewman to place a warning flag 1,000 yards up the track, but the crewman only went 540 yards. It was established at trial that: (1) the train's engineer could have seen the flag 500 yards away (1,040 total) and stopped within 1,000 yards, but (2) he was inattentive and did not see it until he was abreast of the crewman. Benge (D) was indicted for manslaughter. At trial, he admitted his mistake.

ISSUE: May criminal liability be imputed where the causal chain is dependent upon negligent omissions of others?

HOLDING AND DECISION: (Pigott, J.) Yes. Criminal liability may be imputed where the causal chain is dependent upon negligent omissions of others. The chain of criminal causation is not broken where culpable negligence has substantially caused an accidental harm, merely because if other persons had not been negligent, it might possibly have been avoided. Any question of contributory negligence is immaterial. Any other analysis would result in the absurd conclusion that no one was responsible because many were responsible. Here, since the jury found, as a matter of fact, that Benge's (D) negligence was the substantial cause of death, the mere fact that other company precautions were not observed does not reduce responsibility. The underlying rationale here is that justice requires that negligent persons be held for the natural and probable consequences of their acts. Guilty.

▶ ANALYSIS

This case points up an extreme but valid example of the general rule that contributory conduct (negligence or intentional acts) is immaterial to the determination of criminal causation. This is because the focus of the criminal law is upon deterrence of the conduct of each accused. Note, here, that culpability has been precluded for the other negligent participants in this causal chain. This is best explained in terms of proximate cause, since it clearly would be unjust to hold either of them responsible when the circumstance which initiated the chain was unknown to them. It may also be explained on cause-intact grounds on the theory that it cannot be said that "but for" their negligence the accident would not have occurred. (Engineer might not have seen the sign at all, even if it had been properly in place. Further, he had ample time to stop even at 540 yards, if he had seen the sign sooner.) Note, finally, that a mistake-of-fact defense is not available here. Such defense is only available where the mistake negates the mental element of a crime.

■══■

Quicknotes

CAUSATION The aggregate effect of preceding events that bring about a tortious result; the causal connection between the actions of a tortfeasor and the injury that follows.

CONTRIBUTORY NEGLIGENCE Behavior on the part of an injured plaintiff falling below the standard of ordinary care that contributes to the defendant's negligence, resulting in the plaintiff's injury.

PROXIMATE CAUSE The natural sequence of events without which an injury would not have been sustained.

■══■

Hubbard v. Commonwealth

Manslaughter defendant (D) v. State (P)

Ky. Ct. App., 202 S.W.2d 634 (1947).

NATURE OF CASE: Appeal from a voluntary manslaughter conviction.

FACT SUMMARY: When Hubbard (D) was convicted for the voluntary manslaughter of a jailor who suffered a fatal heart attack while attempting to subdue Hubbard (D), the latter argued that his actions were not the legally proximate cause of the death.

RULE OF LAW

Criminal liability for death arises only where death or serious bodily harm was the probable and natural consequence of the accused's act.

FACTS: Robert Hubbard (D) was arrested for being drunk in a public place and was taken before the county judge. Being too drunk to be tried, he was ordered to jail but refused to go peaceably. Dyche, the jailor, tried to subdue him in a scuffle. Hubbard (D) was finally persuaded to get off the floor, and he, a deputy, and Dyche left the courthouse for jail. Dyche suffered a fatal heart attack as he left the courthouse. Hubbard (D) had never struck Dyche, and Dyche never received a physical injury from the scuffle. Hubbard (D) was charged with, and convicted of, voluntary manslaughter. He appealed, arguing that his act of initially resisting being taken from the courthouse was not the legally proximate cause of Dyche's heart attack and subsequent death.

ISSUE: Does criminal liability for death arise only where death or serious bodily harm was the probable and natural consequence of the accused's act?

HOLDING AND DECISION: (Stanley, Commn.) Yes. Criminal liability for death arises only where death or serious bodily harm was the probable and natural consequence of the accused's act. Where the cause of death was not due to a corporal blow or injury (essential under the early common law) or to some hostile demonstration or overt act directed toward the person of the decedent, there is no criminal liability unless the death was the natural and probable consequence of an indirect, unlawful act of the accused. If there is reasonable doubt as to this point, as here, it would be unjust to punish the accused. Here, Hubbard's (D) misdemeanor must be regarded as too remote—not in time, but as to cause. The deceased, knowing he had a serious heart condition, undertook a task which he knew would excite him or create an emotional state of mind, which he also well knew he should have avoided. His intervening act in rolling and tumbling in pain on the courthouse yard, instead of lying quiet and still, was probably as much responsible for his ensuing death as was the initial excitement caused by Hubbard's (D) conduct. It would be too speculative to say that Hubbard's (D) misdemeanor act of resisting arrest was sufficiently proximate to impose criminal homicide liability upon him in this factual setting. Reversed.

ANALYSIS

One cannot escape culpability simply because factors other than their act contributed to the death of another or hastened it. Under most modern decisions, death caused or accomplished through fright, fear, or nervous shock may form a basis for criminal responsibility. On the other hand, it is held that to warrant a conviction for homicide, the act of the accused must be the proximate cause of death; that if there was an intervening cause for which the accused was not responsible and but for which death would not have occurred, the accused is blameless.

Quicknotes

INTERVENING ACT An event whose occurrence breaks the causal chain between the tortfeasor's acts and the resulting injury.

MISDEMEANOR Any offense that does not constitute a felony, which is generally less severe and for which a lesser punishment is imposed.

VOLUNTARY MANSLAUGHTER The killing of another person without premeditation, deliberation or malice aforethought, but committed while in the "heat of passion" or upon some adequate provocation, thereby reducing the charge from murder to manslaughter.

Commonwealth v. Rhoades

State (P) v. Arsonist (D)

Mass. Sup. Jud. Ct., 401 N.E.2d 342 (1980).

NATURE OF CASE: Appeal from conviction for murder.

FACT SUMMARY: Rhoades (D) was found guilty of second-degree murder after the judge charged the jury that Rhoades (D) was liable for second-degree murder if the victim died "as a result" of his act, or if his act "in any way contributed to hasten, or was part of the proximate cause of the death."

🏛 RULE OF LAW
One is criminally liable for the death of another only if his action was the proximate cause of death, i.e., a cause which, in the natural and continuous sequence, produced the death, and without which the death would not have occurred.

FACTS: Captain Trainor was among the firefighters responding to the fire that Rhoades (D) set. Trainor went inside the burning building to rescue persons thought to be trapped inside. He encountered intense heat and experienced difficulty in getting air through his face mask. He collapsed on the roof of the building, a medical expert finding that he died as the result of a coronary thrombosis precipitated by the combination of cold weather, stress, and smoke inhalation. Rhoades (D) was found guilty of second-degree murder after the judge instructed the jury that he was liable for second-degree murder if Captain Trainor died "as a result" of his act, or if his act "in any way contributed to hasten, or was part of the proximate cause of," Trainor's death. Rhoades (D) appealed, claiming the instruction was in error.

ISSUE: Must one's action have been the proximate cause of the death of another in order for one to be held criminally liable for said death?

HOLDING AND DECISION: [Judge not stated in casebook excerpt.] Yes. One's action must be the proximate cause of another's death before he can be held criminally liable for said death. The jury instruction at issue in this case exposed Rhoades (D) to potential liability for events not proximately caused by his felonious act in setting the fire. It left the jury with the impression that if his act in setting the fire in any way constituted a link, no matter how remote, in the chain of events leading to Trainor's death, Rhoades (D) should be convicted. It failed to explain the need to find that his action was the proximate cause of death, i.e., a cause which, in the natural and continuous sequence, produced the death, and without which the death would not have occurred. Reversed and remanded.

▶ ANALYSIS

Section 2.03 of the Model Penal Code addresses the issue of the causal relationship between conduct and result. It provides, in pertinent part, that conduct "is the cause of a result when: (a) It is an antecedent but for which the result in question would not have occurred; and (b) the relationship between the conduct and result satisfies any additional causal requirements plainly imposed by law."

Quicknotes

PROXIMATE CAUSE The natural sequence of events without which an injury would not have been sustained.

SECOND-DEGREE MURDER The unlawful killing of another person, without premeditation, and characterized by either an intent to kill or by a reckless disregard for human life.

Commonwealth v. Root

State (P) v. Driver (D)

Pa. Sup. Ct., 403 Pa. 571, 170 A.2d 310 (1961).

NATURE OF CASE: Appeal from conviction for involuntary manslaughter.

FACT SUMMARY: Root's (D) conviction for involuntary manslaughter was reviewed to determine if his unlawful and reckless conduct in participating in an automobile race on a highway was a sufficiently direct cause of the death of the competing driver to warrant his being charged with criminal homicide.

🏛 RULE OF LAW
The tort liability concept of proximate cause has no proper place in prosecutions for criminal homicide and more direct causal connection is required for conviction.

FACTS: Root (D) and another person were participants in an automobile race on a rural three-lane highway one night. Root (D) was in the lead. The other party attempted to pass him when a truck was closely approaching from the opposite direction. In so doing, he swerved to the wrong side of the road and slammed head-on into the oncoming truck. He died as a result, and Root (D) was convicted of involuntary manslaughter. The conviction was affirmed on appeal, but the Supreme Court of Pennsylvania reviewed the important question whether Root's (D) unlawful and reckless conduct was a sufficiently direct cause of the death to warrant his being charged with criminal homicide.

ISSUE: Does the tort liability concept of proximate cause have any proper place in prosecutions for criminal homicide?

HOLDING AND DECISION: (Jones, C.J.) No. One essential element of the crime of involuntary manslaughter is that the unlawful or reckless conduct charged to the defendant was the direct cause of the death in issue. Although precedent is to be found for application of the tort law concept of "proximate cause" in fixing responsibility for criminal homicide, the want of any rational basis for its use in determining criminal liability can no longer be disregarded. Thus, utilizing that concept in this case was improper. Reversed.

DISSENT: (Eagen, J.) Root's (D) conduct was a direct cause of the death. The victim was responding to a situation Root (D) helped create, his reaction should have been expected, and it was clearly foreseeable.

▶ ANALYSIS

Since only the other participating racer was killed, the question comes to mind whether the court's view would be different if the innocent truck driver had been killed. A Florida case involving just such a scenario suggests that the result would indeed be different. *Jacob v. State*, 184 So. 2d 711, 716, 717 (Fla. 1966).

◼━◼

Quicknotes

INVOLUNTARY MANSLAUGHTER The killing of another person without premeditation or deliberation or with the intent to kill or to commit a felony, which may be reasonably expected to result in death or serious bodily injury; involuntary manslaughter is characterized by reckless conduct in the commission of a lawful act, or by the commission of an unlawful act that is not a felony, but which leads to the killing of another.

PROXIMATE CAUSE The natural sequence of events without which an injury would not have been sustained.

RECKLESSNESS The conscious disregard of substantial and justifiable risk.

◼━◼

United States v. Hamilton

Federal government (P) v. Assailant (D)

182 F. Supp. 548 (D.D.C. 1960).

NATURE OF CASE: Trial on a charge of murder in the second degree.

FACT SUMMARY: Victim, who was recuperating in hospital after being severely beaten by Hamilton (D), died of asphyxiation when he had a convulsion and pulled out life support tubes attached to his throat.

🏛 RULE OF LAW
A person is guilty of homicide where, even though a wound he inflicts on another is not in and of itself fatal, he thereby sets in action a chain of causation which results in the victim's death.

FACTS: Hamilton (D) severely beat the victim during a quarrel. The victim fell to the ground, but Hamilton (D), in an uncontrollable rage, continued to pummel him about the head and face. While in a semi-comatose, violent condition and in shock, the victim was rushed to the hospital where tubes were attached to his throat to keep his airways clear of blood. Three days later, the victim fell into convulsions after restraints were removed from his hands, immediately pulled out the tubes with his own hands, and died of asphyxiation. Hamilton (D) was charged with second-degree murder.

ISSUE: Is a person guilty of homicide where, even though a wound he inflicts on another is not in and of itself fatal, he thereby sets in action a chain of causation which results in the victim's death?

HOLDING AND DECISION: (Holtzoff, J.) Yes. A person is guilty of homicide where, even though a wound he inflicts on another is not in and of itself fatal, he thereby sets in action a chain of causation which results in the victim's death. Here, the victim pulled out the life support tubing, which was affirmative action which contributed to his own death. That action, however, is immaterial. It has no effect on Hamilton's (D) liability if it could be shown that, but for pulling out the tubes, which may have been a conscious, deliberate act, the victim would have lived. In other decisions, liability for a homicide has been imposed on the assailant where the victim, who has been dealt a serious but not mortal, blow, takes his own life shortly thereafter. The victim's death was a natural and probable consequence of Hamilton's (D) unlawful and criminal treatment. The court must determine whether Hamilton (D) is guilty of homicide or assault with a dangerous weapon. Based on the injuries inflicted and the applicable law, Hamilton (D) is guilty of homicide.

▶ ANALYSIS

Liability for a homicide is clearest when the victim's reaction is instinctive, as where B, in order to escape A's murderous approach, hurls himself out a window, and falls to his death. Less clear cut are those cases, as here, where the victim's intervening act is more voluntary. However, even in apparently extreme situations, courts have imposed liability for a homicide. In one such case, the victim could have saved himself if he had submitted to an operation for the amputation of his leg; he refused, and gangrene was the listed medical cause of death. Nonetheless, the original act of assault was held to be the legal cause of death. The court reasoned that, although the victim's response—his refusal to undergo the amputation—was unreasonable, it was not abnormal.

Quicknotes

INTERVENING CAUSE A cause, not anticipated by the initial actor, which is sufficient to break the chain of causation and relieve him of liability.

MANSLAUGHTER The killing of another person without premeditation, deliberation or with the intent to kill or to commit a felony, which may be reasonably expected to result in death or serious bodily injury; manslaughter is characterized by reckless conduct or by some adequate provocation on the part of the actor, as determined by a subjective standard.

SECOND-DEGREE MURDER The unlawful killing of another person, without premeditation, and characterized by either an intent to kill or by a reckless disregard for human life.

Stephenson v. State

Abductor (D) v. State (P)

Ind. Sup. Ct., 179 N.E. 633 (1932).

NATURE OF CASE: Appeal from conviction for second-degree murder.

FACT SUMMARY: Stephenson (D) abducted a woman who poisoned herself and later died.

RULE OF LAW
Persons are responsible for all consequences resulting from a single criminal program.

FACTS: Stephenson (D) abducted Oberholtzer and assaulted and attempted to rape her over the next several days. Oberholtzer obtained bichloride of mercury when Stephenson (D) allowed her out and later ingested this poison when Stephenson (D) was out of the room. When Oberholtzer became ill, Stephenson (D) refused to take her to a hospital but returned her home, where she received medical treatment. Although her wounds healed, Oberholtzer died ten days later. The doctor ascribed her death to a combination of poison, loss of food and rest, and the general impact of her abduction. Stephenson (D) was convicted of murder but appealed, claiming that he had not caused Oberholtzer's death.

ISSUE: Are persons responsible for all consequences resulting from a single criminal program?

HOLDING AND DECISION: (Per curiam) Yes. Persons are responsible for all consequences resulting from a single criminal program. Persons who engage in criminal enterprises are charged with all of the natural results of that enterprise. The required causal connection between a criminal act and the result encompasses the entire criminal program and all natural and probable consequences. In the present case, Oberholtzer was controlled and entrapped by Stephenson (D) during the entire abduction. Therefore, Stephenson (D) is properly responsible for all of the natural consequences of Oberholtzer's abduction and Stephenson's (D) treatment of her. The evidence was sufficient for the jury to determine that Oberholtzer was distracted and mentally irresponsible due to her abduction and this led to the poisoning. Accordingly, there is a causal connection between Stephenson's (D) conduct and her death. Affirmed.

ANALYSIS

Much of Stephenson's (D) argument was based not on the lack of a causal connection between Oberholtzer's death and the abduction as a whole, but rather on the fact that Stephenson (D) had not actually abducted her since she had voluntarily returned after buying the poison. However, the prosecution (P) argued that she was not a free agent since she had been accompanied to the store by Stephenson's (D) chauffeur and had already tried twice to escape, unsuccessfully. Once the jury and the appellate court accepted the continuous abduction scenario, Stephenson (D) had a very weak argument.

■=■

Quicknotes

SECOND-DEGREE MURDER The unlawful killing of another person, without premeditation, and characterized by either an intent to kill or by a reckless disregard for human life.

■=■

People v. Kevorkian

State (P) v. Doctor (D)

Mich. Sup. Ct., 447 Mich. 446, 527 N.W.2d 714 (1994).

NATURE OF CASE: Appeal to dismiss murder charges.

FACT SUMMARY: Dr. Kevorkian (D) was charged with murder for assisting a suicide.

🏛 RULE OF LAW
Providing the means for another's suicide is not murder.

FACTS: Dr. Kevorkian (D) assisted in the deaths of two women in Michigan prior to the enactment of the state's assisted suicide law. One woman was hooked to his so-called "suicide machine" and instructed by Kevorkian (D) on how to activate the device to release the deadly drugs. The other opened a gas valve on a carbon monoxide cylinder attached to a mask fitted to her face by Kevorkian (D). Michigan charged Dr. Kevorkian (D) with murder. The trial court granted Kevorkian's (D) motion to dismiss the charges, but a court of appeals reversed. Kevorkian (D) appealed.

ISSUE: Is providing the means for another's suicide chargeable as murder?

HOLDING AND DECISION: (Cavanagh, C.J.) No. Providing the means for another's suicide is not murder. Under the common law, murder is the unlawful killing of a person with malice aforethought. Previous decisions in Michigan have held that providing the means by which another commits suicide is sufficient for a murder conviction. However, recent decisions draw a distinction between active participation in a suicide and mere involvement in the events leading up to the suicide. Courts have generally held that a person may be prosecuted for murder if his conduct goes beyond the conduct the assisted suicide statutes were intended to cover. Furthermore, other newer decisions have held that a closer nexus between an act and a death is required to meet the causation requirement. It should be noted that if a person recklessly or negligently provides the means for suicide, he can be guilty of involuntary manslaughter. Therefore, Kevorkian (D) may not be charged with murder. Reversed and remanded.

DISSENT: (Boyle, J.) A person who participates in the death of another may be charged with murder, irrespective of the consent of the deceased. At the time these acts were committed, the Michigan state legislature had not shown any intent to depart from the common-law definition of murder as including assisted suicide.

▌ ANALYSIS

The dissenting opinion makes a valid point about separating subsequent actions of the legislature from the state of the law when Kevorkian (D) assisted the suicides at issue in this case. Although the majority claims that there is now a distinction between active participation in a suicide and providing the means for suicide, it is difficult to see where this line should be drawn. By all accounts, Kevorkian (D) not only provided the means but was present and even inserted the needle into one woman's arm.

■■■

Quicknotes

INVOLUNTARY MANSLAUGHTER The killing of another person without premeditation or deliberation or with the intent to kill or to commit a felony, which may be reasonably expected to result in death or serious bodily injury; involuntary manslaughter is characterized by reckless conduct in the commission of a lawful act, or by the commission of an unlawful act that is not a felony, but which leads to the killing of another.

MURDER Unlawful killing of another person either with deliberation and premeditation or by conduct demonstrating a reckless disregard for human life.

■■■

Commonwealth v. Levesque

State (P) v. Homeless person who accidently started a fire (D)

Mass. Sup. Jud. Ct., 436 Mass. 443m 766 N.E.2d 50 (2002).

NATURE OF CASE: Appeal of trial court's granting of defendants' motion to dismiss charges for lack of evidence to support involuntary manslaughter based on wanton and reckless conduct for failure to report a fire.

FACT SUMMARY: Levesque (D) and Julie Ann Barnes (D), were homeless and living in a vacant factory building. After accidentally starting a fire, Levesque (D) failed to report the incident and six firefighters died battling the blaze. Having been charged with involuntary manslaughter, the trial court granted the defendants' motion to dismiss based on insufficient evidence.

🏛 RULE OF LAW
A duty of reasonable care is imposed on a criminal defendant who creates a life-threatening risk to another.

FACTS: Levesque (D) and Julie Ann Barnes (D) were homeless and living in a vacant factory building. A candle they were using accidentally tipped over and caused a fire. Unable to put out the blaze, the defendants left the warehouse and did not report the fire to the authorities, despite having time and passing several occupied locations where public telephones were available. The fire was not reported until later that evening. Upon arriving on the scene, fire fighters were advised that there might be homeless persons inside the warehouse. The fire fighters entered the warehouse to locate any persons that might have been inside and to evaluate their tactics to combat the fire. During these efforts six firefighters died. The trial court granted the defendants' motion to dismiss finding that there was no legal duty to report the fire and the failure to act did not satisfy the standard of wanton and reckless conduct required for manslaughter charges. The Commonwealth appealed, and the Supreme Judicial Court of Massachusetts granted the application for direct appellate review.

ISSUE: Is a duty of reasonable care imposed on a criminal defendant who creates a life-threatening risk to another?

HOLDING AND DECISION: (Cowin, J.) Yes. A duty of reasonable care is imposed on a defendant who creates a life-threatening risk to another. A conviction will be based on any failure to act or omission. Wanton or reckless conduct usually consists of an affirmative act "like driving an automobile or discharging a firearm," *Commonwealth v. Welansky*, 316 Mass. 383, 397, 55 N.E.2d 902 (1944). An omission, however, may form the basis of a manslaughter conviction where the defendant has a duty to act. It is true that, in general, one does not have a duty to take affirmative action; however, a duty to prevent harm to others arises when one creates a dangerous situation, whether that situation was created intentionally or negligently. Both civil and criminal law, imposes on people a duty to act reasonably. It is consistent with society's general understanding that certain acts need to be accompanied by some kind of warning by the actor. In applying this principle to the present case: Where one's actions create a life-threatening risk to another, there is a duty to take reasonable steps to alleviate the risk. Where a defendant's failure to exercise reasonable care to prevent the risk he created is reckless and results in death, the defendant can be convicted of involuntary manslaughter. Levesque (D) and his co-defendant started the fire and then increased the risk of harm from that fire by allowing it to burn without taking adequate steps either to control it or to report it to the proper authorities. Whether a defendant has satisfied this duty will depend on the circumstances of the particular case and the steps that the defendant can reasonably be expected to take to minimize the risk. Although, in this case, the defendants apparently could not have successfully put out the fire, they could have given reasonable notice of the danger they created. Reversed and remanded.

▶ ANALYSIS

Involuntary manslaughter requires evidence of wanton or reckless conduct. The motion's judge reasoned that because the Commonwealth conceded that the fire was started accidentally, and because Massachusetts courts have not found a duty to report or extinguish a fire, the defendant's failure to do so was merely negligent. The Supreme Court, however, rejected this finding by stating that individuals have a duty to prevent harm to others when they create a dangerous situation, whether that situation was created intentionally or negligently. Because the defendants' failure to exercise reasonable care to prevent the risk they created was reckless and resulted in death, they could ultimately be convicted of involuntary manslaughter.

■■■

Quicknotes

INVOLUNTARY MANSLAUGHTER The killing of another person without premeditation or deliberation or with the intent to kill or to commit a felony, which may be reasonably expected to result in death or serious bodily injury;

Continued on next page.

involuntary manslaughter is characterized by reckless conduct in the commission of a lawful act, or by the commission of an unlawful act that is not a felony, but which leads to the killing of another.

MANSLAUGHTER The killing of another person without premeditation, deliberation or with the intent to kill or to commit a felony, which may be reasonably expected to result in death or serious bodily injury; manslaughter is characterized by reckless conduct or by some adequate provocation on the part of the actor, as determined by a subjective standard.

RECKLESS CONDUCT Conduct that is conscious and that creates a substantial and unjustifiable risk of harm to others.

WILLFUL AND WANTON CONDUCT Unlawful intentional or reckless conduct without regard to the consequences.

■═■

CHAPTER 5

Intentional homicide

Quick Reference Rules of Law

Francis v. Franklin

[Parties not identified.]

471 U.S. 307 (1985).

NATURE OF CASE: Appeal of murder conviction.

FACT SUMMARY: Franklin (D), a convict, apparently accidentally shot an individual while escaping from prison.

🏛 RULE OF LAW
A jury instruction may not imply that a defendant must disprove intent to kill.

FACTS: Franklin (D) escaped from custody during a routine dental visit, seizing the gun of a guard. He entered the house of the decedent, demanding a vehicle. The decedent stated he had no vehicle and slammed the door. The door hit Franklin's (D) gun, and it discharged. The bullet went through the door, killing the decedent. At Franklin's (D) murder trial, the jury was instructed that the law presumes that a person intends the natural consequences of his acts. Franklin (D) was convicted, and he appealed.

ISSUE: May a jury instruction imply that a defendant must disprove intent to kill?

HOLDING AND DECISION: (Brennan, J.) No. A jury instruction may not imply that a defendant must disprove intent to kill. The prosecution has the burden of proving this essential element of a murder charge, and any jury instruction which implies the contrary is prejudicial. Here, the instruction could reasonably have implied to the jury that it was presumed that Franklin (D) intended to kill, and for that reason the conviction must be reversed.

▶ ANALYSIS

Basic to a murder conviction is the requirement of an intent to kill. This is what separates murder from manslaughter. Intent can either be an actual desire to kill (usually classified as murder one) or extremely reckless behavior (usually classified as murder two).

■■■■

Quicknotes

MANSLAUGHTER The killing of another person without premeditation, deliberation or with the intent to kill or to commit a felony, which may be reasonably expected to result in death or serious bodily injury; manslaughter is characterized by reckless conduct or by some adequate provocation on the part of the actor, as determined by a subjective standard.

MURDER Unlawful killing of another person either with deliberation and premeditation or by conduct demonstrating a reckless disregard for human life.

■■■■

United States v. Watson

Federal government (P) v. Driver (D)

D.C. Ct. App., 501 A.2d 791 (1985).

NATURE OF CASE: Appeal of conviction of murder.

FACT SUMMARY: Watson (D) was convicted of murder even though no one witnessed the few moments prior to Watson's (D) firing a gun at the victim.

🏛 RULE OF LAW
Murder may be proved absent evidence of what occurred in the few moments prior to the fatal assault.

FACTS: A police officer chased Watson (D) into his home, having seen him driving a stolen car. In the home were three girls. The officer demanded that Watson (D) surrender. He responded by fighting back. Watson (D) was able to knock away the officer's gun. Watson (D) grabbed the gun and having the officer pinned down, pointed the gun at his chest. At this point the girls ran to the other rooms. A few words were exchanged between Watson (D) and the officer, and a shot was fired. The officer later died. Watson (D) was charged with murder. The jury rejected his manslaughter defense and found him guilty of murder. Watson (D) appealed.

ISSUE: May murder be proved absent evidence of what occurred in the few moments prior to the fatal assault?

HOLDING AND DECISION: (Rogers, Assoc. J.) Yes. Murder may be proved absent evidence of what occurred in the few moments prior to the fatal assault. Murder requires premeditation, which, in the context of a homicide arising out of an altercation, requires deliberation. The homicide must not arise out of the heat of the fight but must be a conscious choice. To prove such deliberation, however, no direct evidence of the fatal moment is necessary. A jury may find, from all the circumstances, that deliberation did occur. Here, the jury was given evidence of a fight in which Watson (D) had trained the gun on the officer for a significant period of time prior to the pulling of the trigger. While time does not necessarily prove deliberation, it is probative thereof. The jury could reasonably find Watson (D) to have deliberated. Affirmed.

▶ ANALYSIS

Some have criticized the legal definition of premeditation. It is argued that the definition permits both scenarios in the same category of crime, although most would agree the latter crime to be much more morally reprehensible. In some states, a difference between the situations is drawn so that only certain aggravated examples of first-degree murder can give rise to the death penalty.

Quicknotes

DELIBERATION Reflection; the pondering and weighing of the consequences of an action.

FIRST-DEGREE MURDER The willful killing of another person with deliberation and premeditation; first-degree murder also encompasses those situations in which a person is killed within the perpetration of, or attempt to perpetrate, specified felonies.

MANSLAUGHTER The killing of another person without premeditation, deliberation or with the intent to kill or to commit a felony, which may be reasonably expected to result in death or serious bodily injury; manslaughter is characterized by reckless conduct or by some adequate provocation on the part of the actor, as determined by a subjective standard.

PREMEDITATION The contemplation of undertaking an activity prior to action; any length of time is sufficient.

People v. Walker

State (P) v. Convicted murderer (D)

Ill. Ct. App., 204 N.E.2d 594 (1965).

NATURE OF CASE: Appeal of conviction for murder.

FACT SUMMARY: Walker (D), having killed a man during an altercation, contended that it was done in the heat of passion and therefore was, at most, manslaughter.

🏛 RULE OF LAW

A homicide occurring while the killer is in an excited, irrational state is properly charged as manslaughter.

FACTS: Walker (D) was with some acquaintances when Stenneth, a stranger, came up to them and demanded that they gamble. When the group refused, Stenneth pulled a knife. He made several lunges at Walker, to little effect. Stenneth then succeeded in lacerating Walker (D). Walker (D) responded by hurling a brick at Stenneth, which knocked him down. Walker (D) then grabbed the knife, still in Stenneth's hand, and cut his throat. The entire episode lasted five to ten minutes, with no pauses. Walker (D) was charged with murder. He was convicted, and he appealed.

ISSUE: Is a homicide occurring while the killer is in an excited, irrational state properly charged as manslaughter?

HOLDING AND DECISION: (Drucker, J.) Yes. A homicide occurring while the killer is in an excited, irrational state is properly charged as manslaughter. When a killing occurs without deliberation, the law provides that the malice aforethought necessary to sustain a murder charge has not arisen. A serious and highly provoking injury is considered sufficient to produce the excited state necessary for manslaughter to exist. Here, Stenneth did inflict a knife injury on Walker (D). Walker's (D) subsequent killing of Stenneth, while not occurring immediately thereafter, occurred in the same sequence of events. In view of this, as a matter of law, Walker's (D) killing of Stenneth was an act of manslaughter. [The court remanded the matter with instructions that the murder conviction be changed to manslaughter.]

▶ ANALYSIS

The crucial aspect of manslaughter is lack of deliberation. Time is necessarily an important factor in this analysis, but it is not determinative. A brief pause between provocation and homicide may be sufficient to negate heat of passion. Reflection takes only a moment.

■==■

Quicknotes

HEAT OF PASSION DEFENSE A defense utilized in order to reduce a charge of murder to manslaughter, based on the theory that the perpetrator was under adequate provocation so that he was incapable of forming the premeditation necessary for first-degree murder.

HOMICIDE The killing of another individual.

MANSLAUGHTER The killing of another person without premeditation, deliberation or with the intent to kill or to commit a felony, which may be reasonably expected to result in death or serious bodily injury; manslaughter is characterized by reckless conduct or by some adequate provocation on the part of the actor, as determined by a subjective standard.

■==■

Ex parte Fraley

State (P) v. Father (D)

Okla. Crim. Ct. of App., 109 P. 295 (1910).

NATURE OF CASE: Application for habeas corpus based on denial of bail.

FACT SUMMARY: Fraley (D) shot and killed a man who he believed had killed his son nine or ten months before.

🏛 RULE OF LAW
An objective standard will be used in gauging the "cooling down" period for murder versus manslaughter.

FACTS: Fraley (D) shot and killed a man. Testimony demonstrated that Fraley (D) walked up to the decedent, shot him, and then said, "I told you I'd kill you." The man had apparently killed Fraley's (D) son nine or ten months before and had been acquitted of wrongdoing. Fraley (D) argued that he killed in the heat of passion, and that therefore he could only be guilty of manslaughter. When the court denied bail, Fraley (D) applied for habeas corpus.

ISSUE: Will an objective standard be used in gauging the "cooling down" period for murder versus manslaughter?

HOLDING AND DECISION: (Richardson, J.) Yes. An objective standard will be used for gauging the "cooling down" period for murder versus manslaughter. A killing in the heat of passion is manslaughter, not murder, However, there must be a point at which the law will not give a defendant the benefit of this rule, even if he has in fact not "cooled down." Here, we are talking about nine or ten months, a period far longer than the law can possibly allow. Bail denied.

▶ ANALYSIS

As stated in the opinion, a "reasonable man" standard is used in determining a "cooling down" period. A subjective standard is also used, but if the actor's subjective state of mind remains agitated too long, the "reasonable man" standard takes over. Actually one has to question the validity of this in that the argument can be made that reasonable men don't lose their heads to the point of killing.

■■■

Quicknotes

COOLING PERIOD A sufficient period, after provocation, for an individual to regain his composure and after which he is presumed to understand the consequences of his actions.

HABEAS CORPUS A proceeding in which a defendant brings a writ to compel a judicial determination of whether he is lawfully being held in custody.

HEAT OF PASSION DEFENSE A defense utilized in order to reduce a charge of murder to manslaughter, based on the theory that the perpetrator was under adequate provocation so that he was incapable of forming the premeditation necessary for first-degree murder.

MANSLAUGHTER The killing of another person without premeditation, deliberation or with the intent to kill or to commit a felony, which may be reasonably expected to result in death or serious bodily injury; manslaughter is characterized by reckless conduct or by some adequate provocation on the part of the actor, as determined by a subjective standard.

MURDER Unlawful killing of another person either with deliberation and premeditation or by conduct demonstrating a reckless disregard for human life.

OBJECTIVE STANDARD A standard that is not personal to an individual but is dependent on some external source.

SUBJECTIVE STANDARD A standard that is based on the personal belief of an individual.

■■■

Rowland v. State

Spouse (D) v. State (P)

Miss. Sup. Ct., 35 So. 826 (1904).

NATURE OF CASE: Appeal of conviction for murder.

FACT SUMMARY: Rowland (D) killed his wife immediately after seeing her commit adultery.

🏛 RULE OF LAW
The proper charge against one killing a spouse in reaction to witnessing adultery is manslaughter, not murder.

FACTS: Rowland (D) witnessed his wife getting out of bed with another man. Rowland (D), in a fit of rage, shot at the man, but hit his wife instead, killing her. Rowland (D) was indicted for murder. He was convicted, and he appealed.

ISSUE: Is the proper charge against one killing a spouse in reaction to witnessing adultery manslaughter rather than murder?

HOLDING AND DECISION: (Truly, J.) Yes. The proper charge against one killing a spouse in reaction to witnessing adultery is manslaughter, not murder. The law provides that a homicide committed in the heat of passion is properly chargeable as manslaughter, not murder. Because of the inherently provocative nature of adultery, the law presumes that any homicide committed in such a situation would be manslaughter, not murder. Here, Rowland (D) was charged with murder, and this was improper. Reversed.

▌ ANALYSIS

Jurisdictions vary as to how proximate to the "act" an observation of adultery must be for a homicide not to be chargeable as murder. A few jurisdictions at common law required actually viewing intercourse. The more prevalent view was that any observation which would leave one to conclude with reasonable certainty that adultery had occurred was sufficient.

■═■

Quicknotes

ADULTERY Sexual intercourse between a married person and another who is not that person's spouse, or between a person and another who is married.

HEAT OF PASSION DEFENSE A defense utilized in order to reduce a charge of murder to manslaughter, based on the theory that the perpetrator was under adequate provocation so that he was incapable of forming the premeditation necessary for first-degree murder.

MANSLAUGHTER The killing of another person without premeditation, deliberation or with the intent to kill or to commit a felony, which may be reasonably expected to result in death or serious bodily injury; manslaughter is characterized by reckless conduct or by some adequate provocation on the part of the actor, as determined by a subjective standard.

MURDER Unlawful killing of another person either with deliberation and premeditation or by conduct demonstrating a reckless disregard for human life.

■═■

People v. Berry

State (P) v. Husband (D)

Cal. Sup. Ct., 18 Cal. 3d 509, 556 P.2d 777 (1976).

NATURE OF CASE: Appeal from a first-degree murder conviction.

FACT SUMMARY: Berry (D) strangled his wife after she had repeatedly frustrated him sexually and tormented him with tales of her involvement with another man.

🏛 RULE OF LAW

A party who kills his victim in the heat of passion induced by a prolonged period of taunting and provocation can be guilty only of voluntary manslaughter.

FACTS: Berry (D), a 46-year-old cook, married a 20-year-old woman named Rachel. Three days after their marriage, Rachel returned to her native Israel for a period of about two weeks. When she came back, she told Berry (D) that she had fallen in love with a man named Yako, with whom she had been involved sexually. About ten days later, Berry (D) choked Rachel. She went to a hospital and also notified the police, who caused a warrant to be issued for Berry's (D) arrest. He had, in the interim, left the couple's apartment and spent a short time with a friend. Two days after the original choking incident, Berry (D) returned to the couple's apartment, but Rachel did not appear until the following morning. He told Rachel that he wanted to talk with her, but she began screaming and when he was unable to stop her, Berry (D) strangled her to death with a telephone cord. At his murder and assault trial, Berry (D) did not deny the killing. Instead, he testified to a two-week period of torment during which his wife had sometimes demanded immediate sexual gratification and other times refused to have relations at all, constantly taunting Berry (D) with threats of leaving to live with Yako, and regaling him with stories of her affair. Berry (D) claimed that the killing had occurred in the heat of passion. A psychiatrist corroborated this testimony, adding that Rachel had been suicidal and had deliberately driven Berry (D) to kill her. Despite this testimony, the trial judge refused to charge the jury concerning voluntary manslaughter. Berry (D) was convicted of first-degree murder, but he appealed.

ISSUE: May a party be convicted of murder if he killed in the heat of passion produced by a long period of taunts and provocation?

HOLDING AND DECISION: (Sullivan, J.) No. A party who kills his victim in the heat of passion induced by a prolonged period of taunting and provocation can be guilty only of voluntary manslaughter. According to the oft-cited case of People v. Logan, the issue of whether or not a killing occurred in the heat of passion should at least be submitted to the jury. It is up to the jurors to decide whether or not the circumstances were such as would naturally have aroused an ordinary and reasonable person to a passionate state. "Heat of passion" defies precise definition, but verbal taunts and admissions of infidelity have been held sufficient to justify the finding of such a condition. The State (P) argues that Berry's (D) night alone was a sufficient cooling-off period to diminish his rage, but this overlooks the fact that the killing was but the culmination of a protracted period of continual torment and passion. The testimony of Berry (D) and the psychiatrist amply establishes that Berry's (D) state of mind at the time of the killing was such that he should have been convicted only of voluntary manslaughter. Reversed.

▶ ANALYSIS

As *People v. Berry* illustrates, a party's state of mind may be a sufficient mitigating factor to reduce the extent of his liability even though it may not justify an outright acquittal. Certain familiar fact patterns are traditionally deemed sufficient to reduce a charge from first-degree murder to voluntary manslaughter. Circumstances which typically provoke one sufficiently to reduce his culpability include being threatened with unlawful arrest, finding one's wife (but not necessarily husband) engaged in an adulterous act, or being assaulted viciously. In most jurisdictions, words are usually not adequate to provide the necessary provocation. Enlightened jurisdictions are gradually accepting the proposition that circumstances justifying provocation are not limited to fixed fact patterns, but may encompass virtually an infinite number of situations.

■■■

Quicknotes

FIRST-DEGREE MURDER The willful killing of another person with deliberation and premeditation; first-degree murder also encompasses those situations in which a person is killed within the perpetration of, or attempt to perpetrate, specified felonies.

HEAT OF PASSION DEFENSE A defense utilized in order to reduce a charge of murder to manslaughter, based on the theory that the perpetrator was under adequate provocation so that he was incapable of forming the premeditation necessary for first-degree murder.

Continued on next page.

VOLUNTARY MANSLAUGHTER The killing of another person without premeditation, deliberation or malice aforethought, but committed while in the "heat of passion" or upon some adequate provocation, thereby reducing the charge from murder to manslaughter.

■━■

People v. Wu

State (P) v. Mother (D)

Cal. Ct. App., 235 Cal. App. 3d 614, 286 Cal. Rptr. 868 (1991).

NATURE OF CASE: Appeal from conviction for murder.

FACT SUMMARY: Wu (D) sought to introduce evidence of her cultural background to explain her mental state when she killed her son.

🏛 RULE OF LAW
Evidence of a defendant's cultural background is relevant on the issue of the mental state required for murder.

FACTS: Helen Wu (D), an immigrant from China, had a difficult on-and-off-again relationship with Gary Wu. The two had a son, Sidney, who became a pawn in their battles. Helen (D) strangled Sidney and then attempted to kill herself so she could care for him in the afterlife. She claimed that she was unconscious during the killing. Helen (D) was charged and convicted of second-degree murder after the prosecution (P) argued that she killed her son to take revenge on Gary. Helen (D) attempted to argue to the jury that she was in an intense emotional upheaval because she believed that Sidney would be mistreated by Gary's family because he had been born out of wedlock. The trial court rejected a proposed jury instruction that noted to the jury that they could consider Helen's (D) cultural background in deciding on her mental state. Helen Wu (D) appealed.

ISSUE: Is evidence of a defendant's cultural background relevant on the issue of the mental state required for murder?

HOLDING AND DECISION: (Timlin, Acting P.J.) Yes. Evidence of a defendant's cultural background is relevant on the issue of the mental state required for murder. The essential mental states at issue for murder are: (1) premeditation; (2) malice aforethought; and (3) specific intent to kill. Generally, all relevant evidence is admissible. Evidence of a defendant's cultural background is relevant on the issue of premeditation. In the present case, the prosecution (P) argued that Wu's (D) statements in the days before the killing indicated planning. However, the evidence of Wu's (D) Chinese background provided an alternative theory—that Wu (D) intended to kill herself and that when Wu (D) discovered that Sidney was being mistreated, it triggered an emotional response. Thus, Wu's (D) cultural background could have shown the existence of heat of passion at the time of the killing. Since the requested jury instruction was a correct statement of law and was the basis of the defense, the conviction is reversed.

▶ ANALYSIS

The court also ruled that the trial court should have given an instruction on unconsciousness. Helen Wu (D) had presented evidence that the act of strangulation was committed while she was in an unconscious state. Generally, acting while unconscious negates the mental state required for crimes.

Quicknotes

HEAT OF PASSION DEFENSE A defense utilized in order to reduce a charge of murder to manslaughter, based on the theory that the perpetrator was under adequate provocation so that he was incapable of forming the premeditation necessary for first-degree murder.

PREMEDITATION The contemplation of undertaking an activity prior to action; any length of time is sufficient.

SECOND-DEGREE MURDER The unlawful killing of another person, without premeditation, and characterized by either an intent to kill or by a reckless disregard for human life.

SPECIFIC INTENT The intent to commit a specific unlawful act which is a required element for criminal liability for certain crimes.

CHAPTER 6

Unintentional Homicide

Quick Reference Rules of Law

Commonwealth v. Welansky

State (P) v. Nightclub owner (D)

Mass. Sup. Jud. Ct., 55 N.E.2d 902 (1944).

NATURE OF CASE: Appeal of manslaughter conviction.

FACT SUMMARY: A fire erupted at a nightclub belonging to Welansky (D), and many patrons were killed because emergency exits were blocked.

🏛 RULE OF LAW
Considered disregard for the safety of others is sufficient for the sort of recklessness which may support a manslaughter conviction.

FACTS: Welansky (D) operated a Boston nightclub. The club consisted of several different lounges over two stories. The club had five exits which were ostensibly to be used for emergency purposes. These had, however, either been hidden for aesthetic purposes or otherwise did not work properly. On a crowded evening a fire swept through the club, and many patrons were killed when the exits proved unpassable. Welansky (D) was charged with manslaughter and convicted. He appealed.

ISSUE: Is considered disregard for the safety of others sufficient for the sort of recklessness which may support a manslaughter conviction?

HOLDING AND DECISION: (Lummus, J.) Yes. Considered disregard for the safety of others is sufficient for the sort of recklessness which may support a manslaughter conviction. While recklessness usually consists of an affirmative act, it need not be. When one is charged with the safety of others and makes a conscious decision to do the unsafe thing, inaction may constitute negligence. Here, Welansky (D) intentionally failed to make the emergency exits passable, and this certainly could be called reckless. Affirmed.

▶ ANALYSIS

The critical issue here was not the acts of Welansky (D), but rather his state of mind. The court rejected the idea that mere carelessness on Welansky's part could have supported a conviction. The determinative fact was that Welansky (D) weighed the alternatives before acting (or failing to act). As the court said, negligence is usually not a crime.

■■■

Quicknotes

MANSLAUGHTER The killing of another person without premeditation, deliberation or with the intent to kill or to commit a felony, which may be reasonably expected to result in death or serious bodily injury; manslaughter is characterized by reckless conduct or by some adequate provocation on the part of the actor, as determined by a subjective standard.

NEGLIGENCE Conduct falling below the standard of care that a reasonable person would demonstrate under similar conditions.

RECKLESSNESS The conscious disregard of substantial and justifiable risk.

■■■

State v. Williams

State (P) v. Parents (D)

Wash. Ct. App., 484 P.2d 1167 (1971).

NATURE OF CASE: Appeal of manslaughter conviction.

FACT SUMMARY: Mr. and Mrs. Williams (D) failed to obtain medical aid for their 17-month-old child and he died as a result.

🏛 RULE OF LAW
Where the failure of a person to act while under a duty to do so is the proximate cause of the death of another, that person may be convicted of involuntary manslaughter, even though his conduct was no more than ordinary negligence.

FACTS: Mrs. Williams (D) had a son by a previous marriage before she married Mr. Williams (D). When the lad, only 17 months old, developed a toothache, neither she nor her husband considered it serious enough to seek out medical help. As the tooth became worse and abscessed, however, the Williamses (D) became apprehensive but did not seek medical or dental care for the boy, fearing that the welfare department might take him away if they saw how bad he looked. Eventually, the boy developed gangrene from which the smell was clearly noticeable, and pneumonia, from which he died about ten days later. The Williamses (D) were convicted of manslaughter on these facts. They appealed.

ISSUE: May ordinary negligence serve as the basis for convicting someone of involuntary manslaughter?

HOLDING AND DECISION: (Horowitz, C.J.) Yes. Where the failure of a person to act while under a duty to do so is the proximate cause of the death of another, that person may be convicted of involuntary manslaughter, even though his conduct was no more than ordinary negligence. There is no question but that the Williamses (D) were under a duty to obtain medical care for their seriously ill son, and their fear of the welfare department does not excuse this duty. The tough question here is whether the seriousness of the child's illness became sufficiently apparent to them early enough for their failure to do anything about it to be declared the proximate cause of the boy's death. Medical experts, however, testified that the gangrenous condition of the boy's cheek must have been apparent both by sight and smell to his parents for some ten days before he died. Clearly they were on notice as to the seriousness of their son's illness in time to prevent him from dying of it. Conviction affirmed.

▶ ANALYSIS

This case points up a modern departure from the common-law rule that involuntary manslaughter required an act of gross negligence (i.e., criminal negligence). Ordinary negligence may arise either by act or, as above, by omission while under a duty to act. As in tort, its general formulation is the "failure of a man of reasonable prudence to exercise due care under the circumstances." Note, however, that this "objective" standard (i.e., what a reasonable man would do) runs the risk of undermining individualized justice by sanctioning punishment regardless of the subjective knowledge of the wrongdoer. In Williams, supra, for example, it appeared that the parents were illiterates—wholly ignorant of the most rudimentary principles of health care—who honestly did not know their son was in trouble.

Quicknotes

GROSS NEGLIGENCE The intentional failure to perform a duty with reckless disregard of the consequences.

INVOLUNTARY MANSLAUGHTER The killing of another person without premeditation or deliberation or with the intent to kill or to commit a felony, which may be reasonably expected to result in death or serious bodily injury; involuntary manslaughter is characterized by reckless conduct in the commission of a lawful act, or by the commission of an unlawful act that is not a felony, but which leads to the killing of another.

OBJECTIVE STANDARD A standard that is not personal to an individual but is dependent on some external source.

PROXIMATE CAUSE The natural sequence of events without which an injury would not have been sustained.

Mayes v. People

Husband (D) v. State (P)

Ill. Sup. Ct., 106 Ill. 306, 46 Am. Rep. 698 (1883).

NATURE OF CASE: Appeal of conviction for murder.

FACT SUMMARY: Mayes (D) was convicted of murder following a charge to the jury that said, in effect, that an act done with an abandoned and malignant heart causing death may be murder, even if death was not intended.

🏛 RULE OF LAW
An act done with an abandoned and malignant heart causing death may be murder, even if death is not intended.

FACTS: Mayes (D) came home after an evening at a saloon. Unfriendly words were exchanged between him and his wife. The wife then told Mayes (D) that she and their daughter were retiring for the night. At this point, Mayes (D) threw a glass as his wife. It struck an ignited oil lamp she was carrying, splattering burning oil all over her. Her burns proved fatal. Mayes (D) was charged with murder. The court instructed the jury that an act done with an abandoned and malignant heart causing death to occur may be murder, even if death was not intended. Mayes (D) was convicted, and he appealed.

ISSUE: May an act done with an abandoned and malignant heart causing death be murder, even if death is not intended?

HOLDING AND DECISION: (Scholfield, J.) Yes. An act done with an abandoned and malignant heart causing death may be murder, even if death is not intended. Murder requires malice, but malice does not require an intent to kill. When an unlawful action is committed with deliberation in a situation such that great bodily harm is likely to result, such malice may be inferred. Hence, Mayes (D) unlawfully threw an object at his wife under circumstances likely to cause great bodily harm. That he may not have intended death is of no import. He is responsible for the consequences at his acts. Affirmed.

▶ ANALYSIS

The type of conduct which gives rise to murder of this type might be described as aggravated recklessness or extreme recklessness. "Recklessness," in itself, is synonymous with "foolhardiness," and this is not sufficient for murder (involuntary manslaughter is the more proper charge). The

standard might be best described as a "conscious disregard for human life."

■=■

Quicknotes

INVOLUNTARY MANSLAUGHTER The killing of another person without premeditation or deliberation or with the intent to kill or to commit a felony, which may be reasonably expected to result in death or serious bodily injury; involuntary manslaughter is characterized by reckless conduct in the commission of a lawful act, or by the commission of an unlawful act that is not a felony, but which leads to the killing of another.

MALICE The intention to commit an unlawful act without justification or excuse.

MURDER Unlawful killing of another person either with deliberation and premeditation or by conduct demonstrating a reckless disregard for human life.

RECKLESSNESS The conscious disregard of substantial and justifiable risk.

■=■

State v. Martin

State (P) v. Murderer (D)

N.J. Sup. Ct., 537 A.2d 1359 (1990).

NATURE OF CASE: Appeal from murder conviction based on felony-murder doctrine.

FACT SUMMARY: When Martin (D) was convicted of felony murder, he argued that the trial court erred in instructing the jury that it did not matter whether the act which caused the death was committed recklessly or unintentionally or accidently.

🏛 RULE OF LAW

A defendant is liable for felony murder only if the death is not too remote, accidental in its occurrence, or too dependent on another's volitional act to have a just bearing on the defendant's culpability.

FACTS: Daniel Martin (D) and four other persons attended a late night party at which all participants were intoxicated and using marijuana. An altercation arose and all participants left the building except one woman. Shortly thereafter, the building was on fire. The woman who remained had passed out in the apartment from intoxication and died from smoke inhalation from the fire. As Martin (D) had left the apartment, he set the fire by lighting a paper bag containing trash, saying that he intended only to "make a mess of things," but that "I didn't mean to hurt nobody." Martin (D) was convicted of felony murder resulting from his arson. He appealed, arguing that the trial court erred in instructing the jury that it did not matter whether the act which caused the death was committed recklessly or unintentionally or accidently.

ISSUE: Is a defendant liable for felony murder only if the death is not too remote, accidental in its occurrence, or too dependent on another's volitional act to have a just bearing on the defendant's culpability?

HOLDING AND DECISION: (Pollock, J.) Yes. A defendant is liable for felony murder only if the death is not too remote, accidental in its occurrence, or too dependent on another's volitional act to have a just bearing on the defendant's culpability. To the extent that the felony-murder rule holds an actor liable for a death irrespective of the actor's mental state, the rule cuts across the grain of criminal law. Generally, people are not criminally culpable for the consequences of their acts unless those consequences were intended, contemplated, or foreseeable. Because the felony-murder rule runs counter to normal rules of criminal culpability, it received careful attention from the drafters of the Model Penal Code who objected to the rule as "a form of strict liability to which we are opposed." The New Jersey statute, on the other hand, while rejecting the Model Penal Code approach and keeping the felony-murder rule, provides that when causing a particular result is a material element of an offense for which absolute liability is imposed by law, the element is not established unless the actual result is a "probable consequence" of the actor's conduct. In effect, the New Jersey statute provides that the actual result—death, in the case of felony murder—is not established unless it is the probable consequence of the commission of the felony. The term "probable consequence" manifests legislative intent that some deaths are simply too remotely related to the commission of the felony to justify holding the actor responsible not only for the death but for commission of the felony. Accordingly, here the trial court erred in instructing the jury that under the felony-murder rule it did not matter whether the act which caused death is committed recklessly or unintentionally or accidently. Reversed and remanded.

▶ ANALYSIS

Instead of treating felony murder as an absolute-liability offense, the Model Penal Code created a presumption of recklessness when a homicide occurred in the course of the commission of certain felonies. If not rebutted, that presumption would support a conviction for murder.

■=■

Quicknotes

FELONY MURDER The unlawful killing of another human being while in the commission of, or attempted commission of, specified felonies.

■=■

People v. Hickman

State (P) v. Burglar (D)

Ill. Ct. App., 12 Ill. App. 3d 412, 297 N.E.2d 582 (1973).

NATURE OF CASE: Appeal of trial court's refusal to apply the felony-murder rule to a homicide.

FACT SUMMARY: During the course of a burglary by Hickman (D) and others, one police officer fatally shot another.

🏛 RULE OF LAW
The felony-murder rule applies when a homicide is committed by an arresting officer.

FACTS: Hickman (D) and several others were surprised by police when emerging from a burglary. The police gave chase, and one officer shot and killed another whom he believed to be one of the suspects. The trial court refused the State's (P) request that the jury be instructed as to felony murder. The State (P) appealed.

ISSUE: Does the felony-murder rule apply when a homicide is committed by an arresting officer?

HOLDING AND DECISION: (Scott, J.) Yes. The felony-murder rule applies when a homicide is committed by an arresting officer. While the language of the statute does not mandate such a conclusion, it is well-founded in logic. It is natural and probable that a crime will be met by resistance, and the possibility that one resisting the crime will kill another is ever-present. Since the chain of events leading to the death was set in motion by the felons, the responsibility therefore is theirs. Reversed and remanded for sentencing.

▎ *ANALYSIS*

The rule announced here is not universal. Some courts have come to a different conclusion. Some, such as New York, have statutes providing otherwise. Whether or not the rule announced here is consistent with the rationales for the felony-murder rule is a matter of some debate.

■═■

Quicknotes

FELONY MURDER The unlawful killing of another human being while in the commission of, or attempted commission of, specified felonies.

HOMICIDE The killing of another individual.

■═■

People v. Gladman

State (P) v. Robber (D)

N.Y. Ct. App., 41 N.Y.2d 124, 359 N.E.2d 420 (1976).

NATURE OF CASE: Appeal of a first-degree felony-murder conviction.

FACT SUMMARY: After robbing a delicatessen, Gladman (D) was approached by an officer in a nearby lot, whereupon Gladman (D) shot the officer.

🏛 RULE OF LAW
Whether a killing occurs during the immediate flight from a felony, and therefore may constitute felony murder, must be decided from a consideration of all relevant circumstances.

FACTS: Gladman (D) robbed a delicatessen. His description was shortly broadcast over the police radio. In a parking lot about one-half mile away, Gladman (D) was approached by a police officer. This was about 15 minutes after the robbery. Gladman (D) shot and killed the officer. Gladman (D) was charged with first-degree felony murder in that it occurred during immediate flight from the robbery. Gladman (D) was convicted, and he appealed.

ISSUE: Must the issue of whether a killing occurs during the immediate flight from a felony, therefore possibly constituting felony murder, be decided from a consideration of all relevant circumstances?

HOLDING AND DECISION: (Jasen, J.) Yes. Whether a killing occurs during the immediate flight from a felony, therefore constituting felony murder, must be decided from a consideration of all relevant circumstances. Courts have at various times placed rather arbitrary boundaries of where a crime began and ended, for purposes of applying the felony-murder rule. These often lead to distinctions without purpose. It is better to submit the issue and the facts to a jury it the facts at all warrant it. Here, the shooting occurred less than 15 minutes after the robbery, and Gladman (D) was still obviously concerned with his safety. This was sufficient evidence to submit the issue to the jury. Affirmed.

▶ ANALYSIS

The reason why the felony-murder issue was important here was that it was the basis for first-degree murder. In most jurisdictions that employ the felony-murder rule, certain egregious felonies are murder one felonies and the rest are murder two felonies. In New York, robbery was a murder one felony, and hence the conviction for first-degree murder.

Quicknotes

FELONY MURDER The unlawful killing of another human being while in the commission of, or attempted commission of, specified felonies.

FIRST-DEGREE MURDER The willful killing of another person with deliberation and premeditation; first-degree murder also encompasses those situations in which a person is killed within the perpetration of, or attempt to perpetrate, specified felonies.

People v. Cavitt

State v. Convicted murderer

Cal. Sup. Ct., 33 Cal. 4th 187, 14 Cal. Rptr. 3d 281 (2004).

NATURE OF CASE: Appeal from felony-murder convictions.

FACT SUMMARY: Cavitt (D) and Williams (D) participated in the burglary-robbery of Betty McKnight's home with the help of McKnight's stepdaughter, Mianta. Cavitt (D) and Williams (D) left McKnight bound and injured. They tied Mianta up to make it look like she was not part of the crime. McKnight died sometime after Cavitt (D) and Williams (D) left, but it was not clear if she died from being bound and hooded or if Mianta suffocated her.

🏛 **RULE OF LAW**
The crime of felony murder requires a logical nexus between the killing and the felony but does not require the killing to have furthered the purpose of the felony.

FACTS: James Cavitt (D) and Robert Williams (D) plotted with Mianta McKnight to rob Mianta's stepmother, Betty McKnight. On December 1, 1995, Cavitt (D) and Williams (D) entered 58-year-old Betty's home with Mianta's assistance. The men threw a sheet over Betty's head and tied it with rope and duct tape to her wrists and ankles. They took jewelry and other valuables from Betty's bedroom. Betty was left bound, face-down on the bed, beaten, and her breathing was labored. Cavitt (D) and Williams (D) pretended to tie up Mianta too. Mianta called her father to report the burglary-robbery after the men left. By that time, Betty had died. At trial, Cavitt (D) and Williams (D) admitted to the burglary-robbery but argued Mianta deliberately suffocated Betty for reasons unrelated to the burglary-robbery after they were gone. The jury convicted Cavitt (D) and Williams (D) of felony murder in separate trials. The men appeal their convictions.

ISSUE: Does the crime of felony murder require a logical nexus between the killing and the felony rather than require the killing to have furthered the purpose of the felony?

HOLDING AND DECISION: (Baxter, J.). Yes. The crime of felony murder requires a logical nexus between the killing and the felony but does not require the killing to have furthered the purpose of the felony. The defense presented evidence at trial that Mianta may have killed Betty for personal reasons and now asserts the court erred in failing to instruct the jury that the felony-murder rule would not apply because of the alternate theory of death. The court must consider the "complicity aspect" of the felony-murder rule, namely, how the rule applies to

nonkiller liability. Cavitt (D) and Williams (D) argue Betty's death was not a result of the commission of the burglary-robbery. The Attorney General (P) argues the causal relationship is unnecessary because it is enough that Betty died at the same time as the felony. Neither interpretation is correct. The court must clarify the Penal Code section 189's language that the felony-murder rule requires a causal relationship and a temporal relationship between the killing and the underlying felony. The causal relationship is established through proof of a logical nexus, beyond coincidence in time and place, between the attempted or completed underlying felony and the homicidal act. The temporal relationship is established through proof that the underlying felony and the killing consisted of one ongoing action. Cavitt (D) and Williams (D) assert the State (P) must prove Mianta intended to kill Betty to advance the underlying burglary-robbery for liability to attach to them as nonkillers. To the contrary, the felony-murder rule is intended to avoid considering killer intent. 125-year-old precedent does not support the defendants' argument. Other jurisdictions, such as New York, have felony-murder statutes that require the killing to have occurred "in furtherance" of the felony, but do not require evidence that the killing aided or furthered the felony. "In furtherance" should not be interpreted to mean the killing was necessary to the success of the felony. The court similarly requires only a logical nexus between the killing and the felony. Here, the jury found "the killing occurred during" by "persons engaged in the commission" of the burglary-robbery. That is sufficient to show the temporal (i.e., during the felony) and causal (i.e., logical nexus) relationships. Mianta's personal animus toward Betty does not absolve Cavitt (D) and Williams (D) of their liability for Betty's death. The jury instructions sufficiently required the jury to find the logical nexus. Affirmed.

▌ *ANALYSIS*

The *Cavitt* court focused on the defendants' intent to commit the underlying felony rather than intent to commit the killing. The offenses listed in Penal Code 189 are only those felonies that would be inherently dangerous or violent, so intent to commit those is sufficient to put the offender on warning that a death could result. Thus, a death resulting from those felonies is first-degree murder regardless of circumstances and even if the co-felon does not participate in the actual killing.

■=■

Continued on next page.

Quicknotes

FELONY MURDER The unlawful killing of another human being while in the commission of, or attempted commission of, specified felonies.

COMPLICITY The act of conspiring to, or participating in, the commission of an unlawful act.

■━━■

State v. Shock

State (P) v. Murderer (D)

Mo. Sup. Ct., 68 Mo. 552 (1878).

NATURE OF CASE: Appeal from murder conviction.

FACT SUMMARY: When Shock (D) was convicted of murder for beating a small boy to death, he argued the trial court had erred in instructing the jury on the felony-murder doctrine.

🏛 RULE OF LAW
The words "other felony" in a felony-murder statute refer to some collateral felony and not to those acts of personal violence to the deceased which constitute an element of the murder itself.

FACTS: Shock (D) severely beat a five-year-old boy to death. He was convicted of first-degree murder. Shock (D) appealed, arguing that the trial judge had erred in instructing the jury that if it believed that it was not the intention of Shock (D) to kill the child, but that he did intend to do him great bodily harm, and in so whipping him, death ensued, Shock (D) would be guilty of murder in the first degree.

ISSUE: Do the words "other felony" in a felony-murder statute refer to some collateral felony and not to those acts of personal violence to the deceased which constitute an element of the murder itself?

HOLDING AND DECISION: (Hough, J.) Yes. The words "other felony" in a felony-murder statute refer to some collateral felony and not to those acts of personal violence to the deceased which constitute an element of the murder itself, and are, therefore, merged into it, and which do not, when consummated, constitute an offense distinct from the homicide. Since this legislation includes only such murders as were murders at common law, it may well be doubted whether the words "other felony" can be held to include offenses which were not felonies at common law. The statute evidently contemplates such "other felony" as could be consummated, although the murder should also be committed. The arson, rape, robbery, and burglary may each be perpetrated and the murder also be committed. But when great bodily harm has been inflicted, and death immediately or speedily ensues therefrom, no felony has been committed, either at common law or under statutes, in addition to the murder. Here, the jury might properly have been instructed as to the law of first degree murder on the theory of a willful, deliberate, and premeditated killing, and also as to the law of manslaughter. Reversed and remanded.

CONCURRENCE: (Henry, J.) The meaning of the felony-murder statute in relation to crimes and punishments is that every homicide committed in the perpetration of arson, rape, robbery, burglary, or other felony, was not intended to enlarge the class of constructive murders, but only to recognize those designated and assign them their places in the classification made by the section.

DISSENT: (Norton, J.) The felony committed in inflicting great bodily harm, under unjustifiable and inexcusable circumstances, is no more merged in the killing of the decedent than would the felony in committing, for example, a rape resulting in death.

▶ ANALYSIS

Without some kind of independent felony or merger limitation, every manslaughter would be murder.

Quicknotes

COMMON LAW A body of law developed through the judicial decisions of the courts as opposed to the legislative process.

FELONY MURDER The unlawful killing of another human being while in the commission of, or attempted commission of, specified felonies.

FIRST-DEGREE MURDER The willful killing of another person with deliberation and premeditation; first-degree murder also encompasses those situations in which a person is killed within the perpetration of, or attempt to perpetrate, specified felonies.

MANSLAUGHTER The killing of another person without premeditation, deliberation or with the intent to kill or to commit a felony, which may be reasonably expected to result in death or serious bodily injury; manslaughter is characterized by reckless conduct or by some adequate provocation on the part of the actor, as determined by a subjective standard.

CHAPTER 7

Capital Murder and the Death Penalty

Quick Reference Rules of Law

Olsen v. State

Murderer (D) v. State (P)

Wy. Sup. Ct., 67 P.3d 536 (2003).

NATURE OF CASE: Appeal from sentence of death.

FACT SUMMARY: When Olsen (D) was sentenced to death for murders he committed, he argued that the jury instructions as to mitigating circumstances did not correctly state the law.

🏛 RULE OF LAW
When jury instructions as to mitigating circumstances do not correctly state the law, a sentence of death will be set aside.

FACTS: Martin Olsen (D) entered a bar, instructed two patrons to lie down on the floor and robbed the bar. After ordering the bartender to also lie face down on the floor, he shot all three in the back of the head, firing a fourth shot seconds later when it appeared that one victim was not dead. He was tried and found guilty of three counts of premeditated first-degree murder and three counts of first-degree felony murder. At the penalty phase of his trial, the jury sentenced Olsen (D) to death. Olsen (D) appealed, arguing that the jury instructions as to mitigating circumstances did not correctly state the law.

ISSUE: When jury instructions as to mitigating circumstances do not correctly state the law, will a sentence of death be set aside?

HOLDING AND DECISION: (Golden, J.) Yes. When jury instructions as to mitigating circumstances do not correctly state the law, a sentence of death will be set aside. Here, there were errors in the sentencing phase in the form of (1) insufficient evidence that the murders were especially atrocious or cruel; (2) insufficient evidence that Olsen (D) knowingly created a great risk of death to two or more persons; and (3) improper jury instructions on the law of mitigating circumstances and the decision making process. There was no sufficient evidence of physical or mental torture. It was insufficient, under this aggravated circumstance, to argue simply that the victims suffered anguish because of uncertainty as to their ultimate fate. Nor was there sufficient evidence of great risk of death since the lives of bystanders, other than the intended victims, were not directly endangered during Olsen's (D) crimes. Furthermore, Olsen's (D) sentencing jury received inconsistent instructions as to how it should consider mitigating circumstances in that it was not clearly instructed that it was to consider mitigating circumstances even where all the mitigating evidence was not thoroughly proven. It is not sufficient "simply to allow" the defendant to present mitigating evidence to the sentencer. The sentencer "must also be able to consider and give effect" to that evidence in imposing sentence. The Wyoming death penalty statute intends the jury's consideration to be a mental balancing process, "a reasoned judgment," and a consideration of the "substantiality and persuasiveness" of all the circumstances, not the mere numbers of aggravating as opposed to mitigating circumstances. The weighing of aggravating and mitigating circumstances does not mean a mere mechanical counting of factors on each side of an imaginary scale, or the arbitrary assignment of weights to any of them. Additionally, the jury should have been instructed that, under the death penalty statute, a sentence of life imprisonment means that Olsen (D) would never be eligible for parole. Reversed and remanded.

▶ ANALYSIS

The United States Supreme Court requires that a jury's discretion in sentencing defendants to death must be genuinely narrowed. However, once that is accomplished, the jury must be allowed the widest possible discretion to not choose death. Aggravating circumstances must meet certain requirements: (1) the circumstance may not apply to every defendant convicted of murder; (2) it must apply only to a subclass of defendants convicted of murder (genuine narrowing); and (3) the circumstance must not be unconstitutionally vague. The selection decision determines whether an eligible defendant should receive the death penalty and requires an "individualized determination" on the basis of the character of the individual and the circumstances of the crime.

■═■

Quicknotes

JURY INSTRUCTIONS A communication made by the court to a jury regarding the applicable law involved in a proceeding.

MITIGATING CIRCUMSTANCES OR EVIDENCE Circumstances which may be considered as extenuating or reducing the degree of moral culpability. Although they do not constitute a justification or excuse for the offense in question they are considered in light of fairness and mercy.

■═■

Tison v. Arizona

Escapee's sons (D) v. State (P)

481 U.S. 137 (1987).

NATURE OF CASE: Review of convictions of first-degree felony murder.

FACT SUMMARY: Rick and Raymond Tison (D) were convicted under the felony-murder rule despite a lack of evidence that they intended that a death result.

> 🏛 **RULE OF LAW**
> A felony-murder conviction may be based on engaging in a felonious enterprise carrying a high degree of risk of harm, even if no intent to kill exists.

FACTS: Rick and Raymond Tison (D) engaged, with several others, in an operation aimed to "spring" their father from prison. After having carried a cache of guns into prison, they made their getaway. After their car broke down on an open desert highway, they flagged down a passing vehicle. While Rick (D) and Raymond (D) watched without protest, another member of the party gunned down the occupants. The party was later apprehended. Rick (D) and Raymond (D) were charged with first-degree felony murder and convicted. The Arizona Supreme Court held the deaths to have been foreseeable and affirmed the lower court's decision. The United States Supreme Court granted review.

ISSUE: May a felony-murder conviction be based on engaging in a felonious enterprise carrying a high degree of risk of harm, even if no intent to kill exists?

HOLDING AND DECISION: (O'Connor, J.) Yes. A felony-murder conviction may be based on engaging in a felonious enterprise carrying a high degree of risk of harm, even if no intent to kill exists. The purpose behind the felony-murder rule is to deter dangerous conduct, so it is proper to permit the rule to be applied to felonious conduct which, although not involving an intent to kill, presents a serious danger to human life. A review of jurisdictions around the country reveals that very few require such an intent, so to refuse to impose one is consistent with contemporary standards. Here, Rick (D) and Raymond (D) Tison were not merely peripheral participants. They had smuggled guns into a prison, and assisted in a breakout, and stood by as innocent victims were brutally murdered. It is precisely this sort of complicity to which felony murder is meant to apply and the rule was quite properly applied. Vacated and remanded.

▌ *ANALYSIS*

The previous ruling on felony murder was less deferential. In *Edmund v. Florida*, 458 U.S. 782 (1982), the Court refused to permit the rule to be applied to a minor participant in a felonious undertaking that had resulted in a death. The Court distinguished *Edmund* by noting that the defendants herein were much more active in the undertaking.

■═■

Quicknotes

FELONY MURDER The unlawful killing of another human being while in the commission of, or attempted commission of, specified felonies.

FIRST-DEGREE MURDER The willful killing of another person with deliberation and premeditation; first-degree murder also encompasses those situations in which a person is killed within the perpetration of, or attempt to perpetrate, specified felonies.

■═■

McCleskey v. Kemp

Convicted murderer (P) v. State (D)

481 U.S. 279 (1987).

NATURE OF CASE: Review of order dismissing habeas corpus petition.

FACT SUMMARY: McCleskey (P) contended that statistics demonstrating that capital punishment was more severely applied against blacks made capital punishment unconstitutional.

🏛 RULE OF LAW
Statistical evidence of racial bias in the imposition of capital punishment does not make capital punishment unconstitutional.

FACTS: McCleskey (P), a black, was convicted of murder in the course of robbery and sentenced to death. This was affirmed on appeal. In a federal habeas proceeding, McCleskey (P) introduced evidence of statistical studies showing that capital punishment was more likely to be applied when the perpetrator was black and/or the victim was white. McCleskey (P) argued that this made the death penalty unconstitutional as cruel and unusual punishment and a violation of equal protection. The district court dismissed the habeas petition, and the Eleventh Circuit Court of Appeals affirmed. The United States Supreme Court granted review.

ISSUE: Does statistical evidence of racial bias in the imposition of capital punishment make capital punishment unconstitutional?

HOLDING AND DECISION: (Powell, J.) No. Statistical evidence of racial bias in the imposition of capital punishment does not make capital punishment unconstitutional. To show an equal protection violation, a party challenging such a sentence must show a discriminatory intent. Statistics show, at best, a result. This does make an equal protection violation. With respect to McCleskey's (P) Eighth Amendment claim, this court's decisions have held that, for a violation to occur, a state system of meting out death sentences must be arbitrary in such a fashion as to there being no rhyme or reason as to application of the punishment. A system that sets clear guidelines, but at the same time permits discretion as to aggravation and leniency, will not violate the Eighth Amendment. Some bias will almost naturally result from a system permitting discretion, but this does not raise a constitutional violation. Here, Georgia's system for implementing the death penalty falls well within accepted parameters, and no constitutional violation has been shown. Affirmed.

▶ ANALYSIS

The Court's test for what constitutes an unacceptable death penalty system was largely announced in *Furman v. Georgia*, 408 U.S. 238 (1972). At that time, Georgia had no guidelines for when death could or could not be imposed on a convict. This sort of unbridled discretion the Court could not reconcile with the Eighth Amendment.

■═■

Quicknotes

CAPITAL PUNISHMENT Punishment by death.

EIGHTH AMENDMENT Prohibits the imposition of excessive bail, fines and cruel and unusual punishment.

EQUAL PROTECTION A constitutional guarantee that no person shall be denied the same protection of the laws enjoyed by other persons in life circumstances.

HABEAS CORPUS A proceeding in which a defendant brings a writ to compel a judicial determination of whether he is lawfully being held in custody.

■═■

CHAPTER 8

Defensive Force, Necessity, and Duress

Quick Reference Rules of Law

People v. La Voie

State (P) v. Driver (D)

Colo. Sup. Ct., 395 P.2d 1001 (1964).

NATURE OF CASE: Appeal of directed verdict dismissing a murder charge.

FACT SUMMARY: La Voie (D), in apparent imminent peril from a group of strangers, shot and killed one of them.

RULE OF LAW
One reasonably in fear for his safety may use deadly force against the source of the fear.

FACTS: La Voie (D) was driving home from work early one morning. His car was forced off the road from the rear by another vehicle. Four men got out making threatening remarks to La Voie (D). As they approached, La Voie (D) pulled out his gun, which he had a license to carry, and shot one of the group, who later died. La Voie (D) was charged with murder. After trial, the court granted a directed verdict for the defense. The State (P) appealed.

ISSUE: May one reasonably in fear for his safety use deadly force against the source of the fear?

HOLDING AND DECISION: (Moore, J.) Yes. One reasonably in fear for his safety may use deadly force against the source of the fear. When a person has reasonable grounds for believing, and does actually believe, that danger of great bodily harm is imminent, he may act on that fear and defend himself, even to the point of using deadly force, provided that such force is not disproportionate to the threat. Here, La Voie (D) was forced off the road and approached by four strange men, who threatened him. This certainly was sufficient to establish a fear of imminent bodily harm in his mind, and he was entitled to protect himself. Affirmed.

▌ ANALYSIS

Self-defense has both objective and subjective components. Subjectively, a person must actually be in fear for his safety. Objectively, the fear must be reasonable. The objective analysis is a bit like the "reasonable man" standard in tort law.

■■■■

Quicknotes

DEADLY FORCE That degree of force which is likely to result in death or great bodily injury.

DIRECTED VERDICT A verdict ordered by the court in a jury trial.

SELF-DEFENSE The right to protect an individual's person, family or property against attempted injury by another.

■■■■

People v. Gleghorn

State (P) v. Assault and battery defendant (D)

Cal. Ct. App., 193 Cal. App. 3d 199, 238 Cal.Rptr. 82 (1987).

NATURE OF CASE: Appeal from assault and battery conviction.

FACT SUMMARY: When Gleghorn (D) was convicted of assault and battery, he argued that he was simply using justified deadly force to repel deadly force.

🏛 RULE OF LAW
If an attacked person defends himself so successfully that the attacker is rendered incapable of inflicting injury, there is no justification for further retaliation.

FACTS: In the early morning hours, Kelsey Gleghorn (D) entered a garage rented by Michael Fairall as his dwelling and began beating with a stick the rafters where Fairall slept. He then set fire to the rafters, and yelled he wanted to kill Fairall, whereupon Fairall shot Gleghorn (D) in the back with an arrow from his bow. At this point, Gleghorn (D), greatly angered, began beating Fairall, who had descended from the rafters, and did so with such severity that Fairall nearly died. Gleghorn (D) was convicted of assault and battery with the infliction of serious bodily injury. He appealed, contending that since the jury found his acts prior to being shot constituted only a simple assault, Fairall was not justified in replying with deadly force, which therefore entitled Gleghorn (D) to "defend himself" with equally deadly force. Thus, he argued, he could not be convicted of battery with the intention to inflict serious bodily injury.

ISSUE: If an attacked person defends himself so successfully that the attacker is rendered incapable of inflicting injury, is there justification for further retaliation?

HOLDING AND DECISION: (Stone, J.) No. If an attacked person defends himself so successfully that the attacker is rendered incapable of inflicting injury, there is no justification for further retaliation. Not every assault gives rise to the right to kill in self-defense. To repel a simple assault, the person assaulted is not authorized to resort to unduly violent measures. Gleghorn (D) contends that since he initially committed only a simple assault, he was legally justified as a matter of law in standing his ground, even though he was the attacker, and justified in utilizing lethal force against his adversary. Gleghorn's (D) argument, however, is misplaced since the right of self-defense is based upon the appearance of imminent peril to the person attacked. The right to defend one's person or home with deadly force depends upon the circumstances as they reasonably appeared to that person. That right cannot depend upon Gleghorn's (D) supposedly nonfelonious

secret intent. Similarly, justification does not depend upon the existence of actual danger, but rather upon appearances, namely, if a reasonable person would be placed in fear for his or her safety, and defendant acted out of that fear. Here, the jury could reasonably infer from the evidence that Fairall acted reasonably upon the appearance this his life was in danger, or, even if he acted unreasonably in shooting Gleghorn (D) with an arrow, Gleghorn (D) was unjustified in further attacks upon Fairall. Affirmed.

▶ ANALYSIS

As illustrated in the *Gleghorn* case, generally if one makes a felonious assault upon another, or has created appearance of imminent peril justifying the other to launch a deadly counterattack in self-defense, the original assailant cannot slay the adversary in self-defense unless he has first, in good faith, declined further combat, and has fairly notified him that he has abandoned the affray. On the other hand, however, when the victim of simple assault responds in a sudden and deadly counterassault, the original aggressor need not attempt to withdraw and may use reasonable necessary force in self-defense.

■■■

Quicknotes

ASSAULT AND BATTERY Any unlawful touching of another person without justification or excuse.

DEADLY FORCE That degree of force which is likely to result in death or great bodily injury.

■■■

State v. Leidholm

State (P) v. Wife (D)

N.D. Sup. Ct., 334 N.W.2d 811 (1983).

NATURE OF CASE: Appeal from conviction for manslaughter.

FACT SUMMARY: Leidholm (D) contended she acted in self-defense in stabbing her husband to death.

🏛 RULE OF LAW
A person acts in self-defense if, under the circumstances perceived by that person, such acts appeared necessary to protect him from imminent harm.

FACTS: Leidholm (D) was involved in a stormy marriage marked by frequent violent altercations. On August 6, 1981, after a violent fight, she and her husband went to bed, and she stabbed him while he slept. She was charged with murder. She contended that she acted in self-defense, responding to the years of abuse and her expectation of further abuse. The trial court instructed the jury that self-defense must be judged on the basis of what a reasonable person, regardless of subjective perceptions, would believe to be imminent danger. Leidholm (D) was convicted and appealed.

ISSUE: Does a person act in self-defense if, under the circumstances perceived by that person, such acts appeared necessary to protect him from imminent harm?

HOLDING AND DECISION: (Vande Walle, J.) Yes. A person acts in self-defense if, under the circumstances perceived by that person, such acts appeared necessary to protect him from imminent harm. The evidence clearly showed a subjective belief by Leidholm (D) that she was in imminent danger. Thus she acted in a subjective manner adequate to allow her defense of self-defense to go to the jury. This court must also address the expert testimony on "battered woman syndrome." The elements of the syndrome include low self-esteem and "learned helplessness" on the part of an abused woman. An abused woman cannot bring herself to leave her batterer. This syndrome was offered as part of a proposed jury instruction for the jury to consider whether Leidholm's husband had abused her prior to her stabbing him and her accompanying mindset. This separate jury instruction is not necessary. The jury must consider the existence and reasonableness of Liedholm's imminent fear, so the expert testimony on battered woman syndrome is included in that analysis. Reversed and remanded.

▶ ANALYSIS

This case illustrates a rejection of the objective test of self-defense and the application of a subjective test. The trial court instructed the jury on an objective test. This requires the jury to disregard peculiar sensitivities of a particular defendant. The subjective test allows consideration of such sensitivities and requires an evaluation of the perception of the actor.

■■■

Quicknotes

MANSLAUGHTER The killing of another person without premeditation, deliberation or with the intent to kill or to commit a felony, which may be reasonably expected to result in death or serious bodily injury; manslaughter is characterized by reckless conduct or by some adequate provocation on the part of the actor, as determined by a subjective standard.

REASONABLE PERSON STANDARD The standard of care exercised by a hypothetical person who possesses the intelligence, education, knowledge, attention, and judgment required by society of its members when governing behavior; the standard applies to a person's judgment when determining breach of a duty under the theory of negligence.

SELF-DEFENSE The right to protect an individual's person, family or property against attempted injury by another.

SUBJECTIVE STANDARD A standard that is based on the personal belief of an individual.

■■■

People v. Goetz

State (P) v. Subway passenger (D)

N.Y. Ct. App., 68 N.Y.2d 96, 497 N.E.2d 41 (1986).

NATURE OF CASE: Appeal from dismissal of counts from an indictment on charges of attempted murder, assault, and illegal weapons possession.

FACT SUMMARY: Goetz (D) shot four unarmed teenagers on a subway train because he believed they were attempting to rob him.

RULE OF LAW
A person's use of force in self-defense must be objectively reasonable.

FACTS: In 1984, Goetz (D) was riding a subway in New York City when he was approached by a group of four teenagers. Believing they were going to rob him, Goetz (D) pulled out a handgun and shot all four boys. According to statements made by Goetz (D), he fired another shot at one of the boys, Cabey, although he was already lying on the ground defenseless. Goetz (D) was indicted for attempted murder but appealed, claiming that the prosecutor (P) had erroneously introduced an objective element in consideration of Goetz's (D) claim of self-defense. An appeals court ruled for Goetz (D), and New York (P) appealed.

ISSUE: Must a person's use of force for self-defense be objectively reasonable?

HOLDING AND DECISION: (Wachtler, C.J.) Yes. A person's use of force in self-defense must be objectively reasonable. New York Penal Law § 35.15 states that a person may act in self-defense when and to the extent that he reasonably believes it is necessary to defend himself against what he reasonably believes to be the use of imminent use of force. The language of this statute clearly shows an intent that self-defense at least be objectively reasonable, although incorrect in actuality. New York intentionally did not follow the Model Penal Code's rule with regard to self-defense, which allows a defense for the subjective belief in the necessity of defense. Instead, New York chose to follow the rule that a person's actions must be objectively reasonable under the circumstances. The situation and circumstances may include all relevant evidence, of course, including prior experiences that lead to reasonable beliefs. Accordingly, the prosecution's (P) use of the "reasonable man" during the indictment proceedings was proper. Reversed.

▶ ANALYSIS

When Goetz (D) subsequently went to trial the jury acquitted him of all charges except illegal gun possession. The jury's decision was probably influenced by the prevailing community feelings at the time about street crime. More recently, a New York jury ruled for one of the four boys in a civil trial against Goetz (D).

■══■

Quicknotes

OBJECTIVE STANDARD A standard that is not personal to an individual but is dependent on some external source.

SELF-DEFENSE The right to protect an individual's person, family or property against attempted injury by another.

■══■

Tennessee v. Garner

State (P) v. Father of felon (D)

471 U.S. 1 (1985).

NATURE OF CASE: Appeal from a dismissal of an action for unnecessary use of deadly force.

FACT SUMMARY: Tennessee (D) contended its statute allowing the use of deadly force on unarmed nonviolent fleeing suspects was constitutional.

🏛 RULE OF LAW
Deadly force may not be used to prevent escape unless the officer harbors a good-faith belief that the suspect poses a significant threat of death or serious injury to the officer or others.

FACTS: Garner was shot and killed by a Tennessee police officer while fleeing the scene of a felony. The officer saw Garner was unarmed, yet shot him to prevent escape. Garner's father sued, contending the use of deadly force in this situation, pursuant to Tennessee statute, was unconstitutional. The trial court entered judgment for Tennessee (D), holding the statute constitutional, the district court affirmed, and the court of appeals reversed. The State of Tennessee (D) appealed.

ISSUE: May deadly force be used to prevent escape of an unarmed, nonviolent felon?

HOLDING AND DECISION: (White, J.) No. Deadly force may not be used to prevent escape unless the officer harbors a good-faith belief that the suspect poses a significant threat of death or serious injury to the officer or others. The seizure, in a case of a nonviolent felon, occurs when he is ordered to stop and relinquish himself to police. The use of deadly force when that order is ignored goes beyond the constitutional bounds of reasonableness, unless deadly force has been threatened. Thus, the statute allowing for such force is unconstitutional. Affirmed.

▌ANALYSIS

At common law, deadly force would be allowed in this situation. This is so because most felonies were punishable by death. Thus, the consequences, although obtained without trial, equaled those facing the felon. Today, this is outdated and the court recognized this in its decision.

■═■

Quicknotes

DEADLY FORCE That degree of force that is likely to result in death or great bodily injury.

■═■

People v. Ceballos

State (P) v. Property owner (D)

Cal. Sup. Ct., 12 Cal. 3d 470, 526 P.2d 241 (1974).

NATURE OF CASE: Appeal from conviction for assault with a deadly weapon.

FACT SUMMARY: Ceballos (D) was convicted of assault with a deadly weapon when a trap gun he set up in his garage fired into the face of a teenage boy who broke open the garage door.

🏛 RULE OF LAW
A person may be held criminally or civilly liable under statutes proscribing homicide if he sets upon his premises a deadly mechanical device and that device kills or injures another.

FACTS: Ceballos (D) lived in his apartment over his garage. One month some tools were stolen from his garage. Later, he noticed the lock had been bent and that there were pry marks on the door. Ceballos (D) then set up a trap gun which would fire when someone opened the garage. Two boys, Robert, 15, and Stephen, 16, both unarmed, pried off the lock. When Stephen opened the door, he was shot in the face by the trap gun.

ISSUE: May a person be held criminally or civilly liable under statutes proscribing homicide if he sets upon his premises a deadly mechanical device and that device kills or injures another?

HOLDING AND DECISION: (Burke, J.) Yes. A person may be held criminally or civilly liable under statutes proscribing homicides with intent to injure if he sets upon his premises a deadly mechanical device and that device kills or injures another. An exception has been recognized where the intrusion is, in fact, such that the person, were he present, would be justified in taking life or inflicting the bodily harm with his own hands. But if the actor is present there is the possibility that he will realize that deadly force is not necessary, while a device lacks that discretion. Deadly devices should be discouraged because, even though the law of torts recognizes an exception as stated above, that exception is not appropriate to criminal law, for it does not prescribe a workable standard of conduct; liability depends on fortuitous results. While burglary is a dangerous crime at common law, by statute that crime has a much wider scope, so where the character and manner of a burglary would not create a fear of great bodily harm, there is no use of deadly force. Affirmed.

▶ ANALYSIS

Defense of property relies on the theory that a man's home is his castle. Deadly force may be used where it appears reasonable and necessary to prevent an unlawful trespass

apparently committed to harm the occupants or commit a felony therein. A mere trespass without felonious intent or not creating a serious threat of danger to the occupants will not justify the use of deadly force. Notice that the exception being argued on appeal is a rule of tort law and that the court noted that its decision was against the position of the Restatement Second of Torts. The tort rule simply did not state a clear enough standard to be applicable to criminal situations.

Quicknotes

ASSAULT The intentional placing of another in fear of immediate bodily injury.

BURGLARY Unlawful entry of a building at night with the intent to commit a felony therein.

DEFENSE OF PROPERTY An affirmative defense to criminal liability for the use of force in the protection of one's property.

TRESPASS Unlawful interference with, or damage to, the real or personal property of another.

The Queen v. Dudley & Stephens

Government (P) v. Shipwreck survivors (D)

Queen's Bench Division, 14 Q.B.D. 273 (1884).

NATURE OF CASE: Judicial review of murder indictment.

FACT SUMMARY: Dudley (D) and Stephens (D), while shipwrecked, killed Parker and ate him in order to avoid starving to death.

🏛 RULE OF LAW
It is not legal justification to kill another to save oneself in the absence of self-defense.

FACTS: Dudley (D), Stephens (D), Brooks, and Parker were cast away when their ship was caught in a storm. They were floating on a small boat for several days without food or water. To avoid starving to death, Dudley (D) and Stephens (D) agreed that Parker, the youngest and weakest, and who had no dependent family, should be sacrificed to save the others. Brooks dissented, and Parker was not consulted. Dudley (D) killed Parker and the remaining three lived off the body until help came. Dudley (D) and Stephens (D) were indicted for murder, and the jury found that all would have died if the act had not been committed. The jury sought judicial advice as to whether the acts constituted murder.

ISSUE: Is it legally justified to take another's life to save oneself in the absence of self-defense?

HOLDING AND DECISION: (Per curiam) No. It is not legally justified to kill another to save oneself in the absence of self-defense. In this case, the acts performed were in no way justified by law, even though any other human being probably would have acted the same way. There is no unqualified justification for self-preservation. Thus, the killing constituted murder. Dudley (D) and Stephens (D) are sentenced to death.

▶ *ANALYSIS*

The Crown subsequently commuted the sentences to six months' imprisonment. This indicates the difficulty society had, and still has, with this factual situation. Commentators have suggested that, had Parker assented to the killing, the result would have been different as the defense of consent might have been available.

■■■

Quicknotes

MURDER Unlawful killing of another person either with deliberation and premeditation or by conduct demonstrating a reckless disregard for human life.

NECESSITY DEFENSE A defense to liability for unlawful activity where the conduct is unavoidable and is justified by preventing the occurrence of a more serious harm.

SELF-DEFENSE The right to protect an individual's person, family or property against attempted injury by another.

■■■

People v. Unger

State (P) v. Escapee (D)

Ill. Sup. Ct., 362 N.E.2d 319 (1977).

NATURE OF CASE: Appeal from criminal escape conviction.

FACT SUMMARY: Unger (D) escaped from a minimum security honor farm to allegedly avoid homosexual assaults and threats of death.

🏛 RULE OF LAW

The defenses of necessity and compulsion are available in escape cases and the jury should be so instructed where evidence adduced at trial is sufficient to raise the defense.

FACTS: Unger (D) was repeatedly sexually assaulted and threatened with death and physical injury at a minimum security honor farm. Unger (D) left the farm and was apprehended several days later. Unger (D) alleged that his escape was not voluntary and had been caused by compulsion (the acts of others) and necessity (outside forces, e.g., natural conditions). The court refused to instruct the jury that these facts were a defense to the charge. Rather, the court instructed the jury that Unger's (D) reasons for escaping were immaterial. The jury convicted Unger (D) of criminal escape and Unger (D) was sentenced to 3–9 years consecutive with the term he was currently serving for auto theft. On appeal, the conviction was reversed and remanded for a new trial. The first jury trial resulted in a hung jury. The second jury convicted Unger (D), and he appealed.

ISSUE: Are compulsion or necessity defenses to an escape charge?

HOLDING AND DECISION: (Ryan, J.) Yes. While escape situations do not fit within the traditional ambit of either compulsion or necessity defenses, they have been recognized by several jurisdictions in similar situations. Since compulsion requires an imminent threat of great bodily harm, many commentators suggest that the situation fits within the necessity defense. The prisoner is forced to choose between the lesser of two evils. We, likewise, find that compulsion and necessity are defenses to a charge of escape. Where the defendant raises sufficient evidence at trial, the jury should be instructed as to the availability of the defense. It is a limited defense and the jury may consider factors such as whether the defendant's fears were justified, whether the threat was imminent and sufficiently severe, whether there was time to resort to either the courts or prison officials and if this would be effective, and whether the prisoner immediately reported his escape to the police. These factors go to the weight of the defense. A jury might find the defense valid even if one or more of these factors are missing. Reversed.

▶ ANALYSIS

Duress was recognized as a defense to escape in a situation similar to *Unger*. *People v. Harmon*, 53 Mich. App. 482 (1974). The traditional response by most jurisdictions is that the defense should not be available on public policy grounds. Other jurisdictions would allow the defense only on a limited basis if certain conditions existed which are similar to those stated by the majority in *Unger*. *People v. Lovercamp*, 43 Cal. App. 3d 823 (1974).

■═■

Quicknotes

COMPULSION Imminent threat of great bodily harm or death by one party so as to induce the other to commit a criminal offense.

NECESSITY DEFENSE A defense to liability for unlawful activity where the conduct is unavoidable and is justified by preventing the occurrence of a more serious harm.

■═■

State v. Warshow

State (P) v. Demonstrators (D)

Vt. Sup. Ct., 410 A.2d 1000 (1980).

NATURE OF CASE: Appeal from trespass convictions.

FACT SUMMARY: Warshow (D) and other demonstrators contended they were justified in committing criminal trespass because they were fighting the danger of a nuclear accident in entering the complainant's nuclear power plant.

🏛 RULE OF LAW
Necessity will justify criminal behavior only where the danger sought to be avoided is imminent.

FACTS: Warshow (D) and others, while protesting nuclear power, demonstrated on property owned by a private company upon which was operated a nuclear power plant. They were arrested and convicted of criminal trespass. They appealed, contending that they were justified in their actions by the necessity of preventing a nuclear disaster.

ISSUE: Will necessity justify criminal behavior only where the danger sought to be avoided is imminent?

HOLDING AND DECISION: (Barney, C.J.) Yes. Necessity will justify criminal behavior only where the danger sought to be avoided is imminent. There clearly was no emergency forcing Warshow (D) et al. to protest in order to save life immediately in danger. Their evidence showed long-range potential danger which is an insufficient necessity. Affirmed.

CONCURRENCE: (Hill, J.) The evaluation of competing evils justifies the result reached.

DISSENT: (Billings, J.) The defendants offered to prove their imminent danger theory. They had expert testimony ready to produce demonstrating the immediate danger of nuclear reaction within seven seconds of the plant starting up. They also offered to prove that reaction would have resulted in severe radiation damage to persons and property. The defendants asserted they had no other alternative to prevent the start up of the plant. The majority wrongly found the defendants did not show imminent danger or that the legislature precluded this theory. The defendants should be permitted to offer the defense of necessity.

▶ ANALYSIS

This case illustrates that the defense of justification based upon necessity is not broadly applied. The danger necessitating the activity must be shown to be immediate, actual, and imminent before criminal activity will be excused. Other acts, such as arson to combat a forest fire in order to save lives, would be considered necessary as a clear choice of evils resulting in the least harmful conclusion.

■═■

Quicknotes

NECESSITY DEFENSE A defense to liability for unlawful activity where the conduct is unavoidable and is justified by preventing the occurrence of a more serious harm.

TRESPASS Unlawful interference with, or damage to, the real or personal property of another.

■═■

State v. Crawford

State (P) v. Robber (D)

Kan. Sup. Ct., 253 Kan. 629, 861 P.2d (1993).

NATURE OF CASE: Appeal of conviction for robbery

FACT SUMMARY: Crawford (D) embarked on a robbery spree that included multiple criminal acts after alleging he had been coerced into committing his crimes by another person to whom he owed money.

🏛 RULE OF LAW
The defense of duress requires an imminent threat to the person being coerced, and that the fear created by that threat be reasonable.

FACTS: Crawford (D), a habitual drug user, frequently purchased his drugs from Bateman on credit. After accruing a debt of nearly $10,000, Crawford (D) was told by Bateman to commit robberies in order to repay the debt or Bateman would injure him. Bateman then drove Crawford (D) to a nearby city and instructed him to approach a woman getting into her car for the purpose of committing a robbery. Crawford (D) complied, accosting the woman and hitting her on the head with his pistol, demanding money and valuables. Crawford (D) then began a series of criminal acts lasting several hours by hijacking a nearby car and its occupant. These acts included robbing two separate homes, loading valuables into a stolen car, eating food from the refrigerator, and forcing one homeowner to access his ATM account and provide Crawford (D) with additional money. Crawford (D) subsequently contacted Bateman, who was dissatisfied with the total value of the items and cash stolen. Bateman then threatened Crawford (D) by suggesting his son would be harmed if he did not commit additional robberies to secure more cash. The homeowner whose car had been initially hijacked eventually freed himself and reported Crawford (D) to the authorities (P), who later arrested him. In his response, Crawford (D) asserted the defense of duress, alleging that Bateman was in fact the primary motivation for his criminal behavior, and that imposing culpability on him would have no deterrent effect.

ISSUE: Does the defense of duress require an imminent threat to the person being coerced, and that the fear created by that threat be reasonable?

HOLDING AND DECISION: (Allegrucci, J.) Yes. The defense of duress requires an imminent threat to the person being coerced, and that the fear created by that threat be reasonable. Duress is a defense because it shifts culpability away from the perpetrator in recognition of his subordinate role and lack of requisite intent, in light of another person who coerces the perpetrator into acting. However, to successfully assert the defense requires that the coercion be imminent, leaving the perpetrator with no means of escaping or withdrawing from the coerced activity. In his defense, Crawford (D) alleges that he was completely dependent on Bateman due to his narcotic addiction. Here, there was no imminence to the threats imposed on Crawford (D) and his son. Crawford (D) engaged in a series of criminal acts that lasted several hours, a period where he was out of touch with Bateman completely. The compulsion imposed by Bateman was therefore not continuous. In addition, Crawford (D) could have escaped and reported the coercive activity to the authorities. This case is distinguishable from similar duress cases because of the dependency present between the perpetrator and the coercing party. However, this dependency does not bear on the imminence of the threat, but the reasonableness of the fear imposed. The facts as presented do not support a finding that the fear experienced by Crawford (D) was reasonable. The threats made by Bateman toward Crawford (D) and his son were indefinite. Furthermore, the argument could be made that Crawford (D) willingly placed himself into the dependent position in the first place by obtaining drugs from Bateman. The defense of duress may therefore not apply. Affirmed.

▌ ANALYSIS

In drafting its opinion, the court relied on another similar case where the perpetrator had in fact escaped from her aggressor and reported the coercion to the police, thereby suggesting that there be no opportunity to withdraw for the threat to fulfill the requirement of imminence. In addition, the defense of duress is an excuse, and not a justification defense, because it furthers the acts of the aggressor rather than resisting them.

■■■■

Quicknotes

DURESS Unlawful threats or other coercive behavior by one person that causes another to commit acts that he would not otherwise do.

ROBBERY The unlawful taking of property from the person of another through the use of force or fear.

■■■■

State v. Hunter

State (P) v. Convicted felon (D)

Kan. Sup. Ct., 740 P.2d 559 (1987).

NATURE OF CASE: Appeal of conviction of felony murder.

FACT SUMMARY: Hunter (D), accused of felony murder, was not permitted to raise the defense of duress.

🏛 RULE OF LAW
Duress is a defense to felony murder.

FACTS: Hunter (D), while hitchhiking, was picked up by two men. A series of events ensued in which several people were kidnapped and robbed and two were killed. Hunter (D) was charged with robbery, battery, kidnapping, and murder under the felony-murder rule. Hunter (D) claimed he had been compelled to join the criminal activity by threats from one of the two men. The court rejected a proffered instruction, holding that duress is not available as a defense to a felony-murder charge. Hunter (D) was convicted, and he appealed.

ISSUE: Is duress a defense to felony murder?

HOLDING AND DECISION: [Judge not stated in casebook excerpt.] Yes. Duress is a defense to felony murder. Duress is available as a defense to all crimes other than voluntary homicide. Since the felony-murder rule imposes homicide liability for actions which were not expected or intended to result in death, it is improper to deny the defense to one who, through fortuity, becomes involved in an enterprise resulting in a death not so expected. Here, Hunter's (D) homicide liability, if any, would be by way of felony murder. Therefore, he should have been able to raise duress as a defense. Reversed.

▌ ANALYSIS

Duress is a universally recognized defense to a criminal charge, although the amount of duress necessary to make the defense available varies. Murder and voluntary manslaughter generally do not afford the defense. The rationale behind this exception is that one is not free to kill another to save his own life.

■■■

Quicknotes

DURESS Unlawful threats or other coercive behavior by one person that causes another to commit acts that he would not otherwise do.

FELONY MURDER The unlawful killing of another human being while in the commission of, or attempted commission of, specified felonies.

■■■

Mental Illness as a Defense

Quick Reference Rules of Law

People v. Serravo

State (P) v. Delusional husband (D)

Colo. Sup. Ct. 823 P.2d 128 (1992).

NATURE OF CASE: State supreme court certiorari of state law defining defense based on insanity.

FACT SUMMARY: Serravo (D) stabbed his wife following a paranoid delusion that he was instructed by God to do so, after which the court issued a jury instruction on a defense of insanity based on the M'Naghten rule that the prosecution later disputed on the grounds that the instruction drew an erroneous distinction between legal and moral wrong.

🏛 RULE OF LAW
A defense of insanity based on the M'Naghten rule is defined by a defendant's inability to distinguish right from moral wrong as opposed to legal wrong.

FACTS: Serravo (D) was a union employee of King Soopers who harbored plans to construct and build a sports complex based on instructions from God. After visiting with several other employees and believing he had received encouragement toward his endeavor, Serravo (D) went home and stabbed his wife, who was hospitalized. Serravo (D) explained to his wife and authorities that an intruder had committed the act, but his wife subsequently discovered letters written by Serravo (D) describing his intentions to stab his wife in an attempt to sever their marriage based on instructions from God. In addition, Serravo (D) later revealed under psychiatric examination that he believed his wife did not support his plan to build the sports complex and that there were inner "evil spirits" troubling him regarding how to deal with his wife's lack of encouragement. After reading his letters, Serravo's (D) wife called the authorities, who arrested him and charged him with attempted first-degree murder and first-degree assault. During trial, psychiatric testimony was offered from both sides. The prosecution's diagnosis was that Serravo (D) experienced a delusional disorder due to brain damage he had sustained in an auto accident some years earlier, but was sane at the time he committed the crime. The defense presented testimony that Serravo (D) was in fact mentally ill at the time of the crime, and that a paranoid delusion about God affected his ability to tell right from wrong. At trial, the court issued a disputed jury instruction that is the basis of this review, which suggested that Serravo (D) would be protected by the defense of insanity if he believed the act he was committing was morally right. The jury returned a not guilty verdict, and the prosecution appealed, asserting that the defense of insanity should be evaluated on legal, not moral grounds. On appeal, the court affirmed the trial court's decision, adding that the moral standard be based on the prevailing societal standard of morality. The

prosecution then petitioned for review by the state supreme court.

ISSUE: Is the defense of insanity based on the M'Naghten rule defined by a defendant's inability to distinguish right from moral wrong as opposed to legal wrong?

HOLDING AND DECISION: (Quinn, J.) Yes. A defense of insanity based on the M'Naghten rule is defined by a defendant's inability to distinguish right from moral wrong as opposed to legal wrong. The state law in question is based on the M'Naghten rule, which defines insanity as an inability to distinguish between right and wrong. We agree with the ruling in M'Naghten suggesting that a person be considered legally sane where a person commits an act which he knows to be morally wrong, regardless of the legal underpinning. Other courts have rejected the view that the term "wrong" as used in M'Naghten refers to an act that is contrary to the laws of the state, or a legal wrong. To base the definition of "wrong" on "legal wrong" removes a critical psychological component from the legal definition of insanity. However, this should not permit a person whose moral views are merely different from the laws of the state to avoid culpability based on insanity. Instead, the distinction this court draws between legal and moral wrong will void culpability in a mentally ill defendant who commits an act which he is aware is contrary to law, but commits anyway. In addition, the definition of morality may either be based objectively on prevailing social standards, or subjectively on the defendant's own moral beliefs. A person's awareness of right and wrong derives from their personal experiences, but is not necessarily limited to the standards endorsed by society. Defining morality on a purely subjective standard thus ignores a part of social morality upon which acceptable behavior is built. We therefore conclude that the term "wrong" as used by M'Naghten and the applicable state statute's definition of insanity refers to moral and not legal wrong. In addition, we affirm the court of appeals' definition of moral wrong based on an objective social standard rather than a subjective one. The finding of not guilty on reason of insanity is therefore affirmed.

▶ ANALYSIS

The opinion bases a part of its analysis on the distinction between subjective and objective moral standards. However, the M'Naghten rule was originally intended to limit a defendant's cognition to the legality of the act, and not to

Continued on next page.

the prevailing moral standard. This ruling now shifts culpability away from persons who may not agree with the established law. Despite the fact that such a person may be insane, the court here did address the decisional balance that must exist to account for both legally and morally culpable perpetrators.

■═■

Quicknotes

CRIMINAL ASSAULT The intentional placing of another in fear of immediate bodily injury; criminal assault does not require that the victim suffer apprehension so long as the defendant has an intent to injure and commits an act in furtherance of that intent.

INSANITY (DEFENSE) An affirmative defense to a criminal prosecution that the defendant suffered from a mental illness, thereby relieving him of liability for his conduct.

M'NAGHTEN RULE A defense to a criminal prosecution that the defendant was not guilty due to a mental disease or defect that rendered him incapable of knowing the nature and quality of his conduct or that such conduct was wrong.

■═■

Smith v. State

Army private (D) v. State (P)

Alaska Sup. Ct., 614 P.2d 300 (1980).

NATURE OF CASE: Appeal of conviction of shooting with intent to kill or to cause great bodily harm.

FACT SUMMARY: A court rejected Smith's insanity plea, although a preponderance of expert medical testimony was to the contrary.

🏛 RULE OF LAW
A fact-finder may hold a defendant to have been legally sane even when a preponderance of expert medical testimony is to the contrary.

FACTS: Smith (D), who was about to be dishonorably discharged from the army due to poor behavior, commandeered an army vehicle at gunpoint and fled the base. Police chased him into a wooded area where he fled on foot. He was eventually captured but not before shooting and seriously wounding a pursuer. He was civilly tried for shooting with intent to kill or cause great bodily harm. Evidence showed a history of aberrant behavior. Two experts testified that Smith (D) suffered from chronic schizophrenia and was legally insane at the time of the incident. One expert testified that while Smith (D) did have schizophrenia, he had not been legally insane. The court, sitting without a jury, held Smith (D) to have been legally sane and convicted him. Smith (D) appealed.

ISSUE: May a fact-finder hold a defendant to have been legally sane even when a preponderance of expert medical testimony is to the contrary?

HOLDING AND DECISION: [Judge not stated in casebook excerpt.] Yes. A fact-finder may hold a defendant to have been legally sane even when a preponderance of expert medical testimony is to the contrary. Under Alaska law, when a defendant claiming the insanity defense produces substantial evidence thereof, the burden shifts to the prosecution to disprove insanity beyond a reasonable doubt. It does not follow, however, that conflicting testimony regarding sanity must be resolved in favor of the accused. A fact-finder is free to give credence to one party's expert and not the others, even if the number of experts on the side not believed is greater than the side believed. Here, the court was convinced by the State's (P) medical expert, and this was not clear error. Affirmed.

DISSENT: (Boochever, J.) The State (P), as a matter of law, did not disprove insanity beyond a reasonable doubt. Smith (D) lacked the capacity to conform his conduct to societal standards.

▶ ANALYSIS

Alaska adopted a two-part test of insanity. A defendant could invoke the defense if (1) he was unable to appreciate the wrongfulness of his conduct, or (2) was incapable of conforming his conduct to societal norms. That the first part was inapplicable was conceded; at issue was the second part of the test. An expert's credibility can be judged by the degree of his experience and whether or not he is in the "business" of being a paid expert witness, among other factors.

■━■

Quicknotes

INSANITY (DEFENSE) An affirmative defense to a criminal prosecution that the defendant suffered from a mental illness, thereby relieving him of liability for his conduct.

■━■

CHAPTER 10

Attempt

Quick Reference Rules of Law

State v. Lyerla

State (P) v. Murderer (D)

S.D. Sup. Ct., 424 N.W.2d 908 (1988).

NATURE OF CASE: Appeal of convictions for murder and attempted murder.

FACT SUMMARY: Lyerla (D) was convicted of attempted second-degree murder.

 RULE OF LAW
There is no crime of attempted second-degree murder.

FACTS: Lyerla (D), driving on an interstate, fired three shots into a pickup truck carrying three girls. One girl was killed and two were injured. Lyerla (D) was charged with murder and attempted murder. The jury found him guilty of second-degree murder with respect to the homicide and attempted second-degree murder with respect to the injured girls. Lyerla (D) appealed.

ISSUE: Is there a crime of attempted second-degree murder?

HOLDING AND DECISION: (Konenkamp, J.) No. There is no crime of attempted second-degree murder. Second-degree murder is based on non-intentional killing; it is the result of acting in an extremely reckless manner, but without an intent to kill. A crime of attempt, on the other hand, by its definition involves an intent to bring about the thing attempted. "Attempted second-degree murder" may be translated as "attempted extreme recklessness," a logical impossibility. Therefore, there is no crime of attempted second-degree murder. Reversed as to the attempt convictions.

DISSENT: (Sabers, J.) Attempted second-degree murder may exist in any situation where, had fortuity not resulted in the victim surviving, a second-degree murder conviction would have been sustainable.

either an intent to kill or by a reckless disregard for human life.

■■■

▌ *ANALYSIS*

The rule announced here would appear to be that of the majority of jurisdictions that have ruled on the issue. The general consensus is that "attempted second-degree murder" in most situations amounts to assault and/or battery. This would be the situation in the instant case.

■■■

Quicknotes

ATTEMPT An intent combined with an act falling short of the thing intended.

SECOND-DEGREE MURDER The unlawful killing of another person, without premeditation, and characterized by

People v. Stone

State (P) v. Drive-by shooter (D)

Cal. Sup. Ct., 46 Cal. 4th 131, 92 Cal. Rptr. 3d 362 (2009).

NATURE OF CASE: Appeal of the intermediate court's reversal of a conviction for attempted premeditated murder for a drive-by shooting where the defendant fired into a crowd but hit no one.

FACT SUMMARY: Stone (D) fired a handgun into a group of rival gang members without hitting anyone. The testimony indicated that Stone (D) shot into the group intending to kill someone, but not knowing or caring which one.

🏛 RULE OF LAW
A person who shoots into a group of people, intending to kill one of the group, but not knowing or caring which one, can be convicted of attempted murder.

FACTS: After two street clashes, Stone (D) returned with a group of others, found the rival gang and through the passenger window fired into the crowd. The testimony was that Stone (D) seemingly aimed at the group but did not point the gun at anyone in particular. No one was injured, and the People (P) charged Stone (D) with attempted premeditated murder of one person in the crowd. Stone (D) was convicted after a jury trial and sentenced to prison. The California Court of Appeal reversed based on the sufficiency of the evidence, specifically focusing on the error of the "kill zone" instruction provided to the jury.

ISSUE: Can a person who shoots into a group of people, intending to kill one of the group, but not knowing or caring which one, be convicted of attempted murder?

HOLDING AND DECISION: (Chin, J.) Yes. A person who shoots into a group of people, intending to kill one of the group, but not knowing or caring which one, can be convicted of attempted murder. The main issue here concerns the nature of the intent-to-kill requirement. Specifically, the question is whether the intent must be to kill a particular person, or whether a generalized intent to kill someone, but not necessarily a specific target, is sufficient. In *People v. Bland*, 28 Cal. 4th 313 (2002), the defendant and a cohort fired multiple shots at three persons in a car, killing the driver and injuring, but not killing, the two passengers. The defendant was convicted of murdering the driver and of attempting to murder the two passengers. The evidence supported a jury finding that the defendant intended to kill the driver, i.e., the one actually killed, but did not specifically target the two who survived. The holding was that a person who intends to kill is guilty of the murder of everyone actually killed, whether or not the person intended to kill each one. However, the situation is different concerning attempted murder.

Someone who in truth does not intend to kill a person is not guilty of that person's attempted murder even if the crime would have been murder if the person were killed. To be guilty of attempted murder, a defendant must intend to kill the alleged victim, not someone else. However, if a person targets one particular person, under some facts a jury could find the person also, concurrently, intended to kill—and thus was guilty of the attempted murder of—other, nontargeted, persons. The fact the person desires to kill a particular target does not preclude finding that the person also, concurrently, intended to kill others within the "kill zone."

This "concurrent intent" or "kill zone" theory is not a legal doctrine requiring special jury instructions. Rather, it is simply a reasonable inference the jury may draw in a given case. In this case, the trial court gave a modified version of the kill zone instruction. The Court of Appeals was correct when it found that the court erred in giving this instruction. The kill zone theory simply does not fit the charge or facts of this case. That theory addresses the question of whether a defendant charged with the murder or attempted murder of an intended target can also be convicted of attempting to murder other, nontargeted, persons. Here, Stone (D) was charged with but a single count of attempted murder. There was no evidence here that he used a means to kill the named victim that inevitably would result in the death of other victims within a zone of danger. The jury instruction might have caused the jury to believe it could convict Stone (D) of attempted murder if it found intent to kill someone, even if not specifically the named victim.

The mental state required for attempted murder differs from that required for murder. Attempted murder requires express malice, i.e., intent to kill. Implied malice, a conscious disregard for life, suffices for murder but not attempted murder. In addition, transferred intent does not apply to attempted murder. A person who intends to kill can be guilty of attempted murder even if the person has no specific target in mind. An indiscriminate would-be killer is just as culpable as one who targets a specific person. Guilt of attempted murder must be judged separately as to each alleged victim. This is true whether the alleged victim was particularly targeted or randomly chosen. A defendant who intends to kill one person will be liable for multiple counts of murder where multiple victims

Continued on next page.

die, but only one count of attempted murder where no one dies. But when no one dies that person will be guilty of attempted murder even if he or she intended to kill a random person rather than a specific one. Reversed.

▶ *ANALYSIS*

Here the court distinguishes actual and attempted murder with relevance to the theory of transferred intent liability. As opposed to murder, where the mental state is required to prove the intent to kill the targeted person, attempted murder only requires a general intent to kill someone. Stated another way, if Stone (D) had decided to kill a specific person and anyone else in the crowd, then the jury could have found that he intended to kill others within the "kill zone." However, the court agreed with the Court of Appeals and found no such "kill zone" evidence. In remanding the case, the California Supreme Court sought to determine if the "kill zone" jury instruction was harmless error if there was sufficient evidence that Stone (D) sought to kill a specific person other than the named victim who just a member of the crowd.

■══■

Quicknotes

ATTEMPTED MURDER An intent to commit murder plus an action taken towards commission of the crime, falling short of completion.

■══■

People v. Murray

State (P) v. Uncle (D)

Cal. Sup. Ct., 15 Cal. 160 (1859).

NATURE OF CASE: Appeal of conviction for attempt to contract an incestuous marriage.

FACT SUMMARY: Murray (D) insisted that his conviction for attempt to contract an incestuous marriage was improper in that his actions had not crossed the line from mere preparation to attempt.

RULE OF LAW

An actual attempt to commit an offense is manifested by acts that would end in the consummation of the particular offense but for the intervention of circumstances independent of the will of the defendant.

FACTS: In appealing his conviction for attempt to contract an incestuous marriage, Murray (D) claimed that he had made certain preparations to attempt to marry his niece, but that he had not crossed the line between that and making an actual attempt to commit the offense. They had eloped for the purpose of marrying, and he had requested one of the witnesses to go for the magistrate to perform the ceremony. That, however, was as far as it went.

ISSUE: Is an actual attempt to commit an offense manifested by acts that would end in the consummation of the particular offense but for the intervention of circumstances independent of the will of the defendant?

HOLDING AND DECISION: (Field, C.J.) Yes. An actual attempt to commit an offense is manifested by acts that would end in the consummation of the particular offense but for the intervention of circumstances independent of the will of the defendant. There exists a wide difference between preparation for an attempt to commit an offense and the attempt itself. Preparation consists in devising or arranging the means or measures necessary for the commission of the offense. The attempt is the direct movement toward the commission after the preparations are made. Thus, in this case, the attempt contemplated by the statute must be manifested by acts which would end in the consummation of the particular offense but for the intervention of circumstances independent of Murray's (D) will. Preparations to attempt the marriage had been made, but until the officer was engaged and the parties stood before him ready to take the marriage vows, it cannot be said, in strictness, that the attempt was made. Clearly, Murray (D) cannot be held to have attempted to contract an incestuous marriage. Reversed and remanded.

ANALYSIS

Model Penal Code § 5.01 contains the rules for determining whether an attempt to commit a crime has been made. An attempt can be established if the defendant, acting with the kind of culpability otherwise required for commission of the crime, purposefully does or omits to do anything that is an act or omission constituting a "substantial step" in the course of conduct planned to culminate in his commission of the crime. Such acts or omissions include lying in wait, searching for, or following the intended victim, and reconnoitering the scene where the crime is to be committed.

Quicknotes

ATTEMPT An intent combined with an act falling short of the thing intended.

OMISSION The failure to perform an act or obligation that one is required to perform by law.

McQuirter v. State

Alleged intending rapist (D) v. State (P)

Ala Ct. App., 63 So. 2d 388 (1953).

NATURE OF CASE: Appeal from conviction for attempt to commit an assault with intent to commit rape.

FACT SUMMARY: McQuirter (D), a black man, followed a white woman down the street and then up the street.

🏛 RULE OF LAW
An attempt to commit assault with intent to commit rape is merely an attempt to commit rape that has not proceeded far enough to constitute an assault.

FACTS: Mrs. Allen, a white woman, and her two children walked down the street at eight p.m. on a summer evening. McQuirter (D) was sitting in a truck as they walked by. He said something unintelligible as they walked past and then got out of the truck and followed her down the street. Allen turned into a friend's house when McQuirter (D) was two or three feet behind her. She waited ten minutes for McQuirter (D) to pass and then she proceeded on her way. She then observed McQuirter (D) walking toward her from behind a telephone pole. Allen sent the children to get another friend. When the friend appeared, McQuirter (D) went across the street and waited there for thirty minutes. He then left and Allen went home. McQuirter (D) testified that he had just been walking up the street to go to another part of town and that Mrs. Allen just happened to be in front of him. When he got to the telephone pole, he waited, trying to decide whether to go on or not. After thinking a few minutes, he went on to the other part of town. He came back after thirty minutes. He denied saying anything or making any gestures toward Allen. A police chief testified that McQuirter (D) told him that he was sitting in the truck, that he wanted a woman, and that he was going to have the first woman that came by whether he had to rape her or not. McQuirter (D) was found guilty of an attempt to commit an assault with intent to commit rape.

ISSUE: Is an attempt to commit assault with intent to commit rape merely an attempt to commit rape that has not proceeded far enough to constitute an assault?

HOLDING AND DECISION: (Price, J.) Yes. An attempt to commit assault with intent to commit rape is merely an attempt to commit rape that has not proceeded far enough to constitute an assault. The jury need only be satisfied that the accused actually intended to rape Mrs. Allen. In determining intent, the jury may look at all the circumstances, including social conditions and customs founded upon racial differences. Here, Mrs. Allen was a white woman and McQuirter (D) was a black man, and the jury may take this into account when deciding whether McQuirter's (D) actions indicated an intent to rape. Conviction affirmed.

▶ ANALYSIS

Attempt to commit rape is a recognized offense which requires only that the defendant have the apparent ability to do so, and intent is proven. As such, proof of conduct which a jury believes to manifest the intent to commit a crime is sufficient to convict. By Hornbook law, assault is the attempted battery (e.g., rape) of another with the apparent ability to succeed. Where no act in furtherance of a battery occurs, however, no assault will arise. However, acts in furtherance of the object of the contemplated assault (e.g., rape) may be sufficient to establish an attempt to accomplish that object (e.g., following Mrs. Allen). Hence, an attempted attempt arises. Note, however, that since such a rule permits criminal liability merely for manifesting an intent in one's actions, this case borders on a violation of the universal criminal law requirement of actus reus.

■━■

Quicknotes

ACTUS REUS The unlawful act that gives rise to criminal liability, as distinguished from the required mental state.

ASSAULT The intentional placing of another in fear of immediate bodily injury.

ATTEMPT An intent combined with an act falling short of the thing intended.

BATTERY Unlawful contact with the body of another person.

RAPE Unlawful sexual intercourse with a woman by a man by means of fear or force and without her consent.

■━■

People v. Rizzo

State (P) v. Attempted robber (D)

N.Y. Ct. App., 246 N.Y. 334, 158 N.E. 888 (1927).

NATURE OF CASE: Appeal from conviction for attempt to commit robbery in the first degree.

FACT SUMMARY: Rizzo (D) and three others set out with the intention to commit a robbery but they were arrested before they found the person they intended to rob.

🏛 RULE OF LAW
An attempt to commit a crime requires an act "tending," but failing, to effect its commission, which encompasses only those acts that are so near to the accomplishment of the crime that in all reasonable probability the crime itself would have been committed but for timely interference.

FACTS: Rizzo (D) and three others set out in a car to rob one Charles Rao of a payroll he was to carry from the bank for the United Lathing Company. Rizzo's (D) job was to point out Rao to the others. In fact, the police were following the four as they rode around looking for Rao. They were arrested at the site of one of the buildings being constructed by United Lathing as they were canvassing the buildings looking for Rao. Neither Rao nor another man, who was supposed to carry a payroll, were at the building at the time of the arrest. Rizzo (D) appealed his conviction for attempt to commit robbery in the first degree, asserting that his conduct had not been sufficient to constitute an "attempt."

ISSUE: Does an attempt to commit a crime require an act "tending," but failing, to effect its commission encompass only those acts which are so near to the accomplishment of the crime that in all reasonable probability the crime itself would have been committed but for timely interference?

HOLDING AND DECISION: (Crane, J.) Yes. An attempt to commit a crime requires an act "tending," but failing, to effect its commission, which encompasses only those acts that are so near to the accomplishment of the crime that in all reasonable probability the crime itself would have been committed but for timely interference. However, the line is drawn between acts which are remote and those which are proximate and near to the consummation. That is, the law considers those acts "tending" to the commission of the crime to be the ones which are so near to its accomplishment that, in all reasonable probability, the crime itself would have been committed but for timely interference. Here, the defendants had not even found or seen the man they intended to rob. Their acts were not so near to the result that the danger of success was very great. Thus, no "attempt" was made to commit the crime. Reversed.

▶ ANALYSIS

It is interesting that the Model Penal Code provision dealing with criminal attempt lists certain acts that shall not be insufficient as a matter of law to constitute an "attempt." The list includes lying in wait, searching for, or following, the contemplated victim of the crime, and reconnoitering the place contemplated for the commission of the crime.

Quicknotes

ATTEMPT An intent combined with an act falling short of the thing intended.

ROBBERY The unlawful taking of property from the person of another through the use of force or fear.

People v. Staples

State (P) v. Attempted burglar (D)

Cal. Ct. App., 6 Cal. App. 3d 61, 85 Cal. Rptr. 589 (1970).

NATURE OF CASE: Appeal from conviction for attempted burglary.

FACT SUMMARY: Staples (D) offered evidence to show he had abandoned any attempt to commit a burglary before he was arrested, contending such abandonment would preclude his being found guilty of attempted burglary.

🏛 RULE OF LAW
Abandonment is no defense to a criminal charge of attempting to commit a particular offense.

FACTS: While his wife was away, Staples (D), a mathematician, rented an office he knew was directly over the vault of a bank. He brought in drilling tools and drilled two groups of holes in the floor, but stopped drilling before they went through the floor. He brought in acetylene gas tanks, a blow torch, a blanket, and linoleum. According to his later confession, he came back to the office a number of times, covered the holes with a linoleum rug, and installed a hasp lock on a closet where he intended to, or did, place his tools. The landlord, who had been coming and going to do repair work, had notified the police of the strange goings on. Staples (D), who was convicted of attempted burglary, made a voluntary oral statement in which he admitted that he kept going back to the office while his wife was away, that he still had not given up his plan to rob the bank, but that his wife came back after two weeks or so and his life as a bank robber seemed more and more absurd. Thus, he claimed, he abandoned the idea of committing the robbery.

ISSUE: Is abandonment a defense to a criminal charge of attempting to commit a particular crime?

HOLDING AND DECISION: (Reppy, J.) No. Abandonment is no defense to a criminal charge of attempting to commit a particular offense. Once it is found that a person attempted to commit a particular offense, there can be no exculpatory abandonment. One of the purposes of criminal law is to protect society from those who intend to injure it. Once it is established that a defendant intended to commit a specific crime and that in carrying out this intention he committed an act that caused harm or sufficient danger of harm, it is immaterial that for some collateral reason he could not complete the intended crime. In the case at bar, the acts committed by Staples (D) reached such a stage of advancement that they could be classified as an attempt. Thus, any later abandonment of his plan is of no significance. Affirmed.

▶ ANALYSIS

The Model Penal Code is different in that it provides in § 5.01(4) for a limited defense of abandonment. It specifically requires "a complete and voluntary renunciation" of criminal purpose by the defendant. It has not been an easy defense for defendants to prove.

■=■

Quicknotes

ABANDONMENT The voluntary relinquishment of a right without the intent of reclaiming it.

BURGLARY Unlawful entry of a building at night with the intent to commit a felony therein.

■=■

People v. Lubow

State (P) v. Solicitor (D)

N.Y. Ct. App., 29 N.Y.2d 58, 272 N.E.2d 331 (1971).

NATURE OF CASE: Appeal from convictions for solicitation to commit a felony.

FACT SUMMARY: Lubow (D) was convicted of solicitation to commit a felony under a state statute.

🏛 RULE OF LAW
One is guilty of statutory criminal solicitation if he "solicits, requests, commands, importunes or otherwise attempts to cause" another person to engage in conduct constituting a crime with the intent that said other person engage in such conduct.

FACTS: Silverman confronted Lubow (D), who owed him a considerable sum on notes covering the purchase of diamonds. Both were in the jewelry business. Lubow (D) suggested that they engage in a scheme whereby they would purchase diamonds partially on credit, sell them for less than cost, and use the proceeds to keep buying and selling until they established a great credit rating for Silverman. At that point, they would claim that Silverman lost the proceeds of the sales gambling and would file for bankruptcy, dividing the proceeds between the three involved in the scheme. Silverman reported it to the district attorney and cooperated in having a recording device planted on him to record incriminating conversations with Lubow (D). Lubow (D) was convicted of solicitation to commit a felony under an applicable state statute making it a crime to solicit, request, command, importune or otherwise attempt to cause another person to engage in conduct constituting a crime, with the intent that he engage in such conduct.

ISSUE: Is one guilty of criminal solicitation if one solicits another to engage in conduct constituting a crime, with the intent that the other person engage in such conduct?

HOLDING AND DECISION: (Bergan, J.) Yes. One is guilty of criminal solicitation if one solicits another to engage in conduct constituting a crime, with the intent that the other person engage in such conduct. The statute speaks in terms of soliciting, requesting, commanding, importuning or otherwise attempting to cause another to engage in conduct constituting a crime. It thus makes communication itself, with the intent that the other person engage in the unlawful conduct, sufficient to uphold a conviction. There need be no corroboration. There is sufficient evidence here to find that Lubow (D) intended that Silverman engage in conduct constituting a felony by means of grand larceny, and that he importuned Silverman

to engage in such conduct. The proof meets the actual terms of the statute. Affirmed.

▶ ANALYSIS

There are instances in which the intent is to communicate with another to solicit the commission of a crime, but there is no actual communication effected. The Model Penal Code treats this situation in § 5.02, which provides that it is immaterial to the criminal solicitation provisions that the actor fails to communicate with the person he solicits to commit a crime if his conduct was designed to effect such communication.

■■■■

Quicknotes

FELONY A criminal offense of greater seriousness than a misdemeanor; felonies are generally defined pursuant to statute as any crime that is punishable by death or by a term of imprisonment exceeding one year.

■■■■

Booth v. State

Buyer (D) v. State (P)

Okla. Ct. Crim. App., 398 P.2d 863 (1964).

NATURE OF CASE: Appeal from conviction for attempting to receive stolen property.

FACT SUMMARY: Booth (D) purchased a coat he believed had been stolen, but which in fact had been recovered by the owner.

🏛 RULE OF LAW
A person cannot be convicted of attempt when the act attempted would not have been criminal if completed.

FACTS: Booth (D) agreed to buy a coat stolen by Stanford. However, Stanford was apprehended before delivery. Stanford agreed with the police to go through with the purported sale. Booth (D) received the coat and was promptly arrested. Booth (D) was charged with, and convicted of, attempting to receive stolen property. Booth (D) appealed.

ISSUE: May a person be convicted of an attempt when the act attempted would not have been criminal if completed?

HOLDING AND DECISION: (Nix, J.) No. A person cannot be convicted of an attempt when the act attempted would not have been criminal if completed. This situation is what is known as "legal impossibility." It is settled law that if one having a criminal intent does an act that is not illegal, no crime exists. It follows that if one is attempting to commit what he believes is an illegal act, but in fact is not illegal, no attempt exists. Here, the coat was no longer stolen property when Booth (D) received it, the coat having been recovered. Since no substantive crime could have been committed, an attempted threat could not have been either. Reversed.

▶ ANALYSIS

Legal impossibility is one of the most confusing areas of criminal law. Legal impossibility occurs when an act, if completed as intended, would not be criminal. This sounds simple in theory, but in practice it can lead to some serious hair-splitting.

■=■

Quicknotes

ATTEMPT An intent combined with an act falling short of the thing intended.

LEGAL IMPOSSIBILITY An activity which the defendant believes to be unlawful, but which does not constitute a crime; legal impossibility is a defense to criminal liability.

■=■

People v. Dlugash

State (P) v. Convicted murderer (D)

N.Y. Ct. App., 41 N.Y.2d 725, 363 N.E.2d 1155 (1977).

NATURE OF CASE: Appeal of reversal of murder conviction.

FACT SUMMARY: Dlugash (D) fired several shots into the head of Geller, already mortally wounded and possibly dead.

🏛 RULE OF LAW
Impossibility is no defense to an attempt conviction.

FACTS: A disagreement arose between Bush, Geller and Dlugash (D). Bush took a .38 pistol and shot Geller three times in the chest. Two to five minutes later Dlugash (D) took a pistol and fired multiple shots into the head of the prostrate Geller. Dlugash (D) was convicted of murder. Medical evidence was unable to prove or disprove that Geller had been alive when Dlugash (D) shot him. Dlugash (D) contended that he believed Geller had been dead when he shot him. The appellate court reversed the conviction, stating that the evidence did not prove that Geller was alive when Dlugash (D) shot him. The State (P) appealed.

ISSUE: Is impossibility a defense to an attempt conviction?

HOLDING AND DECISION: (Jasen, J.) No. Impossibility is not a defense to an attempt conviction. Legal scholars have argued for years over the merits of the impossibility defense. The modern trend, as reflected in the Model Penal Code and adopted by this state, is that the criminal mental state of a defendant is, in itself, a danger to society and should be punished if steps toward the attainment thereof are taken, even if the crime was legally impossible. Here, the state (P) was unable to prove that Dlugash (D) killed Geller, so the murder conviction was properly reversed. However, the lesser included offense of attempted murder was not barred by impossibility. Reversed.

▶ ANALYSIS

The variations on the impossibility doctrine are many. The distinctions between legal and factual impossibility are subtle, and often it seems a situation could be described as involving either. When one considers the confusion engendered by the doctrine and the danger to society of criminal intent, abolishing the doctrine does seem to be the trend.

■■■

Quicknotes

ATTEMPT An intent combined with an act falling short of the thing intended.

IMPOSSIBILITY A doctrine relieving the parties to a contract from liability for nonperformance of their duties thereunder, if the subject matter of the contract ceases to exist, if a person essential to the performance of the contract is deceased, or if the service or goods contracted for has become illegal.

■■■

People v. Thousand

State (P) v. Obscene materials distributor (D)

Mich. Sup. Ct., 631 N.W.2d 694 (2001).

NATURE OF CASE: Appeal of the dismissal of a charge of attempted distribution of obscene materials to a minor.

FACT SUMMARY: When Thousand (D) was charged with attempted distribution of obscene materials to a minor, he argued that because the person to whom he attempted the distribution was an adult police officer, not a child, he could not be guilty of the offense.

🏛 RULE OF LAW
Impossibility is not a defense to a crime of attempt.

FACTS: A deputy sheriff, conducting an undercover investigation for the sheriff department's Internet crimes bureau, made computer contact with Thousand (D) in a chat room. The deputy on line posed as a fourteen-year-old girl. After a series of sexually explicit chat room conversations initiated by Thousand (D), the sheriff, still pretending to be the young girl, agreed to meet with Thousand (D) at a McDonald's. When Thousand (D) arrived, he was arrested and charged with the attempted distribution of obscene materials to a minor. Thousand (D) moved to quash the indictment, arguing that since the existence of a child victim was an element of the charge, the evidence was legally insufficient to support the charges. The trial court agreed and dismissed the charges. The intermediate appellate court affirmed, and the State (P) appealed.

ISSUE: Is impossibility a defense to a crime of attempt?

HOLDING AND DECISION: (Young, J.) No. Impossibility is not a defense to a crime of attempt. Under Michigan statute, an "attempt" consists of (1) an attempt to commit an offense prohibited by law, and (2) any act toward the commission of the intended offense. This court is unable to discern from the words of the attempt statute any legislative intent that the concept of "impossibility" provide any impediment to charging a defendant with, or convicting them of, an attempted crime, notwithstanding any factual mistake—regarding either the attendant circumstances or the legal status of some factor relevant thereto—-that the defendant may harbor. The attempt statute carves out no exception for those who, possessing the requisite criminal intent to commit an offense prohibited by law and taking action toward the commission of that offense, have acted under an extrinsic misconception. Here, Thousand (D) is not charged with the substantive crime of distributing obscene material to a minor. It is unquestioned that he could not be convicted of

that crime, because he allegedly distributed obscene material not to a "minor," but to an adult man. Instead, Thousand (D) is charged with the distinct offense of attempt, which requires only that the prosecution prove intention to commit an offense prohibited by law, coupled with conduct toward the commission of that offense. Because the nonexistence of a minor victim does not give rise to a viable defense to the attempt charge in this case, the circuit court erred in dismissing this charge on the basis of legal impossibility. Reversed.

▶ ANALYSIS

Courts and legal scholars have drawn a distinction between two categories of impossibility: "factual impossibility" and "legal impossibility." At common law, legal impossibility was a defense to a charge of attempt, but factual impossibility was not. However, after struggling unsuccessfully over the years to articulate an accurate rule for distinguishing between categories of "impossibility," the vast majority of American jurisdictions have now simply abolished impossibility as a defense.

■━■

Quicknotes

ATTEMPT An intent combined with an act falling short of the thing intended.

CRIMINAL INTENT An intention to carry out a criminal offense.

FACTUAL IMPOSSIBILITY Refers to a circumstance in which a person commits an act that would otherwise constitute a criminal offense, however, the attendant facts and circumstances unknown to the actor make it impossible to commit the crime; factual impossibility does not constitute a defense to criminal liability.

LEGAL IMPOSSIBILITY An activity which the defendant believes to be unlawful, but which does not constitute a crime; legal impossibility is a defense to criminal liability.

■━■

CHAPTER 11

Complicity

Quick Reference Rules of Law

State v. Ochoa

State (P) v. Protesters (D)

N.M. Sup. Ct., 41 N.M. 589, 72 P.2d 609 (1937).

NATURE OF CASE: Appeal of second-degree murder convictions based on principles of aiding and abetting.

FACT SUMMARY: A riot erupted in which a sheriff was shot to death, although the individual who pulled the trigger was never identified.

🏛 RULE OF LAW
When one in a group altercation becomes aware that deadly force is being used, he becomes an accessory to the use of that force.

FACTS: A group of about 125 people gathered outside a courthouse to support a criminal defendant. The sheriff and his deputies tried to covertly transport the prisoner through the rear entrance. The crowd became aware of this and went around to the back of the building. A melee ensued and shots were fired. The sheriff was killed and several deputies wounded. The shots came from a group including Ochoa (D) and Avitia (D). Evidence showed that Ochoa (D) and Avitia (D) remained in the group while the shots were being fired, beating a downed deputy. Avitia (D), Ochoa (D), and Velarde (D), who had not been in the group, were convicted of second-degree murder, and they appealed.

ISSUE: When one in a group altercation becomes aware that deadly force is being used, does he become an accessory to the use of that force?

HOLDING AND DECISION: (Sadler, J.). Yes. When one in a group altercation becomes aware that deadly force is being used, he becomes an accessory to the use of that force. One is rendered an aider or abettor if a common purpose is shown. In a group altercation situation, it would be unfair to hold one to be an abettor if a common purpose is not shown. Moreover, in a group altercation situation, it would be unfair to hold one to be an abettor in the use of deadly force if he is unaware that his companions plan to use it. However, once the individual becomes aware of the force, he may be held to be an aider. Here, Ochoa (D) and Avitia (D) continued to beat the deputy after they knew that deadly force was being used by the group, so they had the common purpose. There was no evidence of this as to Velarde (D). Reversed as to Velarde (D); affirmed as to the others.

▶ ANALYSIS

Although convicted as aiders and abettors, the defendants were sentenced as would a principal have been. At common law, distinctions in culpability between principals and abettors existed. Many jurisdictions have modified or abolished these distinctions, as had New Mexico.

━■

Quicknotes

ACCESSORY An individual who combines with the main actor in the commission or attempted commission of a criminal offense, either before or after its performance.

AIDING AND ABETTING Assistance given in order to facilitate the commission of a criminal act.

PRINCIPAL A person or entity who authorizes another (the agent) to act on its behalf and subject to its authority to the extent that the principal may be held liable for the actions of the agent.

SECOND-DEGREE MURDER The unlawful killing of another person, without premeditation, and characterized by either an intent to kill or by a reckless disregard for human life.

━■

State v. Tally

State (P) v. Convicted murderer (D)

Ala. Sup. Ct., 102 Ala. 25, 15 So. 722 (1894).

NATURE OF CASE: Appeal of murder conviction grounded on aiding and abetting.

FACT SUMMARY: Tally (D) prevented the transmission of a warning message to Ross, who was subsequently killed by the men about whom the message warned.

> **🏛 RULE OF LAW**
> One who interferes with the relaying of potentially life-saving information is an abettor if a homicide results.

FACTS: A feud had erupted between Ross and the Skeltons. Ross slipped out of town in a coach, unaware that four Skeltons pursued him on horseback. A relative of Ross sent a telegram to Ross at the next town warning him. Tally (D), who knew the telegraph operator in the next town, immediately sent a telegram to the operator requesting he not deliver the message to Ross. When Ross arrived in town, the operator did not give him the message. Ross was ambushed by the Skeltons and was shot to death. Tally (D), who was convicted of aiding and abetting the murder, appealed.

ISSUE: Is one who interferes with the relaying of potentially life-saving information an abettor if a homicide does result?

HOLDING AND DECISION: (McClellan, J.) Yes. One who interferes with the relaying of potentially life-saving information is an abettor if a homicide does occur. To be guilty of aiding a crime, the defendant must do an act in furtherance of the criminal design, the act must contribute to the effectuation of the crime, and the act must actually help bring about the victim's death. The answer on all three counts must be yes, since the relaying of information to Ross that he was being pursued was done with both the intent and effect of helping the Skeltons in their criminal plan. It is hard to conclude that Ross was more vulnerable in his ignorant state than he would have been otherwise. Affirmed.

DISSENT: (Head, J.) Proof beyond a reasonable doubt that Tally's (D) acts contributed to Ross's death does not exist.

▶ ANALYSIS

The court appeared to be of the opinion that any decrease in the victim's chances of survival was sufficient to satisfy the requirement that the act contribute to the crime. The court used the term "depriving him of some disadvantage."

Exactly how much would be sufficient was not stated, but the implication seemed to be that very little is needed since the court noted in passing that there was a strong probability that Ross would have been killed anyway.

Quicknotes

AIDING AND ABETTING Assistance given in order to facilitate the commission of a criminal act.

REASONABLE DOUBT Standard of proof necessary to convict a defendant, requiring the absence of evidence that would cause a reasonable person to hesitate in making an important decision in his personal affairs.

State v. Formella

State (P) v. Convicted accomplice to theft (D)

N.H. Sup. Ct., 158 N.H. 114, 960 A.2d 722 (2008).

NATURE OF CASE: Appeal from conviction of theft as an accomplice.

FACT SUMMARY: Formella (D), who initially served as a lookout for others who stole exams but then decided that participating in the crime was wrong and stopped serving as a lookout before the crime was committed, contended that he could not be convicted of theft as an accomplice since he had withdrawn in time from the crime.

RULE OF LAW
An individual can be held criminally liable as an accomplice where the individual terminates his complicity prior to the commission of the offense but does not wholly deprive the complicity of its effectiveness.

FACTS: Formella (D), a high school student, and his friends were asked by a group of other students to serve as lookouts while the group stole mathematics exams from within the high school. Formella (D) and his friends agreed, and, on their way to their lockers, looked around to "confirm or dispel" whether anyone was there. After getting their books from their lockers, Formella (D) and his friends decided that serving as lookouts was wrong, and they left the school building. The other group succeeded in stealing the exams. Formella (D), who admitted his involvement in the theft, was convicted of theft based on criminal liability for the conduct of another, as an accomplice. Formella (D) appealed, contending that the trial court had erred in failing to make findings of fact relative to the timing of his withdrawal from the theft and the completion of the theft since the accomplice liability statute provides that a person is not an accomplice if he "terminates his complicity prior to the commission of the offense and wholly deprives it of effectiveness in the commission of the offense or gives timely warning to the law enforcement authorities or otherwise makes proper effort to prevent the commission of the offense." The state's highest court granted review.

ISSUE: Can an individual be held criminally liable as an accomplice where the individual terminates his complicity prior to the commission of the offense but does not wholly deprive the complicity of its effectiveness?

HOLDING AND DECISION: (Galway, J.) Yes. An individual can be held criminally liable as an accomplice where the individual terminates his complicity prior to the commission of the offense but does not wholly deprive the complicity of its effectiveness. It is undisputed

that Formella (D) became an accomplice when he agreed to serve as a lookout. The issue, therefore, is whether his later acts terminated his accomplice liability. Formella (D) neither timely warned the police, nor otherwise made a "proper effort" to prevent the offense. The question, therefore, is whether his termination "wholly deprived his complicity of effectiveness." The accomplice statute does not define what is required for a person to wholly deprive his complicity of effectiveness. The State (P) argues that there must be an overt act aimed at undermining the prior complicity, and Formella (D) argues no such act is required. The statute is ambiguous as to this requirement, and the legislative intent must be determined. The Model Penal Code, on which the statute is based, indicates that to deprive complicity such as is involved here of effectiveness, the withdrawing participant must not only withdraw from the commission of the offense, but also must communicate his disapproval to the principals sufficiently in advance of the commission of the crime to allow them time to reconsider as well. Here, even though Formella (D) timely withdrew before the commission of the theft, he nonetheless did not wholly deprive his complicity of its effectiveness because he made no affirmative act, such as communicating his withdrawal to the principals, which would give them a chance to reconsider committing the offense. Instead, the principals remained unaware of his withdrawal. While it is true that Formella (D) no longer served as an effective lookout after he withdrew, he did nothing to counter the effect of his prior complicity. His agreeing to serve as a lookout encouraged the principals to engage in the offense, and it was this encouragement that needed to be undone or undermined. Because there was no evidence that Formella (D) had wholly deprived his complicity of its effectiveness, it was not error for the trial court to refuse to make findings on the timing of the offense because such findings would not have altered the result. Affirmed.

ANALYSIS

As this case demonstrates, a mere change of heart, flight from the crime scene, apprehension by the police, or an uncommunicated decision not to carry out his part of the scheme will not suffice to relieve a withdrawing accomplice of criminal liability. However, as the case also notes, while the terminating accomplice does not actually have to prevent the crime from occurring, he must take some

Continued on next page.

affirmative action that communicates disapproval to the principals in time for them to consider changing course.

∎══∎

Quicknotes

ACCOMPLICE An individual who knowingly, purposefully or voluntarily combines with the main actor in the commission, or attempted commission, of a criminal offense.

ACCOMPLICE LIABILITY Liability of an individual who knowingly, purposefully, or voluntarily combines with the main actor in the commission, or attempted commission, of a criminal offense.

COMPLICITY The act of conspiring to, or participating in, the commission of an unlawful act.

THEFT The illegal taking of another's property with the intent to deprive the owner thereof.

∎══∎

People v. Beeman

State (P) v. Informant (D)

Cal. Sup. Ct., 35 Cal. 3d 547, 199 Cal. Rptr. 60 (1984).

NATURE OF CASE: Appeal from conviction of aiding and abetting a robbery.

FACT SUMMARY: Beeman (D) gave others certain information which was used by them to facilitate the robbery of a relative of Beeman (D), although Beeman (D) claimed he did not want the robbery to occur.

🏛 RULE OF LAW
An aider or abettor must act with knowledge of the criminal purpose and with an intent to facilitate the commission of the offense.

FACTS: Beeman (D) knew Burk and Gray. Burk learned from Beeman (D) of certain valuables owned by Beeman's aunt. Beeman (D) gave Burk other information about the aunt and her possessions. At some point, Burk and Gray decided to rob the aunt, which they did. Charged with aiding the robbery, Beeman (D) contended that the information was given casually, that he never expected that a robbery would occur, and that he later declined an invitation to join in the crime. The jury returned a guilty verdict after being instructed that an aider is one who knowingly aids the commission of a crime. Beeman (D) appealed.

ISSUE: Must an aider or abettor act with knowledge of the criminal purpose and with an intent to facilitate the commission of an offense?

HOLDING AND DECISION: (Reynoso, J.) Yes. An aider or abettor must act with knowledge of the criminal purpose and with an intent to facilitate the commission of an offense. The weight of authority and sound legal principles dictate that to be an aider one must have a concert of mind with the principal. One who gives aid to the commission of a criminal act without wishing to promote the act should not be liable. The jury instruction here did not take that into account. It allows for an interpretation that by giving the information alone, Beeman (D) could have been liable. Reversed.

▶ ANALYSIS

Not all jurisdictions have this requirement, at least not so clearly spelled out. For instance, Model Penal Code § 2.06(3)(a) only requires knowledge that a criminal purpose existed, not a desire that it proceed. This was subsequently changed.

■═■

Quicknotes

AIDING AND ABETTING Assistance given in order to facilitate the commission of a criminal act.

ROBBERY The unlawful taking of property from the person of another through the use of force or fear.

■═■

Wilson v. People

Accessory (D) v. State (P)

Colo. Sup. Ct., 100 Colo. 441, 87 P.2d 5 (1939).

NATURE OF CASE: Appeal of conviction of burglary based on aiding and abetting.

FACT SUMMARY: Wilson (D) "set up" Pierce to commit burglary to exact revenge on Pierce.

🏛 RULE OF LAW
One cannot be an accessory to a crime unless he has the intent that the crime will actually proceed successfully.

FACTS: Wilson (D) met Pierce in a cafe and they spent time drinking together. Pierce talked about some of his criminal acts. At one point, Wilson (D) noticed his watch missing and accused Pierce of stealing it, which Pierce denied. At some point, they developed a plan to rob a drugstore. Wilson (D) boosted Pierce through a window. Wilson (D) then called his father, a prosecutor, who summoned the police. Both Pierce and Wilson (D) were arrested. Wilson (D) was charged with aiding and abetting. Wilson (D) contended that he wanted to "set up" Pierce so that he could be arrested and have Wilson's (D) watch returned. The trial judge did not allow this defense, and Wilson (D) was convicted. He subsequently appealed.

ISSUE: Can one be an accessory to a crime if he does not have the intent that the crime actually proceed successfully?

HOLDING AND DECISION: (Bock, J.) No. One cannot be an accessory to a crime unless he has the intent that the crime actually proceed successfully. An accessory must share the criminal intent with the principal. If he does not share that intent, then he is not an accessory. Here, Wilson (D) contended that he did not want the burglary to succeed, but merely wanted his watch back—an intent hardly concurrent with that of Pierce. This defense should have gone to the jury. Reversed and remanded.

▶ ANALYSIS

The flip side of the issue here is whether someone can be guilty of aiding and abetting when the principal actor is not guilty. An example would be when one aids in the commission of a crime with another who is not mentally competent for criminal liability. Logic would dictate that one could not be liable, but the law gets around this by considering the "abettor" to be the true principal.

■══■

Quicknotes

ACCESSORY An individual who combines with the main actor in the commission or attempted commission of a criminal offense, either before or after its performance.

AIDING AND ABETTING Assistance given in order to facilitate the commission of a criminal act.

BURGLARY Unlawful entry of a building at night with the intent to commit a felony therein.

PRINCIPAL A person or entity who authorizes another (the agent) to act on its behalf and subject to its authority to the extent that the principal may be held liable for the actions of the agent.

■══■

State v. Etzweiler

State (P) v. Car owner (D)

N.H. Sup. Ct., 125 N.H. 57, 480 A.2d 870 (1984).

NATURE OF CASE: Appeal from indictment for negligent homicide.

FACT SUMMARY: Etzweiler (D), knowing that Bailey was intoxicated, loaned him a car with which Bailey caused an accident, killing two people.

🏛 RULE OF LAW
Guilt as a principal requires that the accomplice aid the primary actor in the substantive offense with the purpose of facilitating that offense.

FACTS: Etzweiler (D) and Bailey drove to the plant where they were both employed. Etzweiler (D) went to work and loaned his car to Bailey, who he knew was intoxicated. Ten minutes later, Bailey recklessly collided his car into another, killing two people. The grand jury indicted Etzweiler (D) for negligent homicide, and he appealed.

ISSUE: Does guilt as a principal require that the accomplice aid the primary actor in the substantive offense with the purpose of facilitating that offense?

HOLDING AND DECISION: (Batchelder, J.) Yes. Guilt as a principal requires that the accomplice aid the primary actor in the substantive offense with the purpose of facilitating that offense. At common law, a person had to be present during an offense to be guilty as a principal. However, in New Hampshire, the legislature has enacted the accomplice liability statute, which strikes down the distinctions between principals and accessories. The law provides that a person is an accomplice if he aids another person in committing or planning the offense with the purpose of promoting or facilitating the crime. The best interpretation of this law is that an accomplice's liability does not extend beyond the criminal purpose he shares. In the present case, Etzweiler (D) aided Bailey in the commission of drunk driving. However, Etzweiler (D) did not aid or facilitate Bailey with the purpose of facilitating or promoting negligent homicide. Since the State (P) is unable to establish that Etzweiler's (D) acts were designed to aid Bailey in committing negligent homicide, the indictments must be quashed. Reversed.

▶ ANALYSIS

The provisions of the law at issue in the present case are based upon Model Penal Code § 2.06. It is difficult to figure out what it means to purposefully promote an offense involving negligence. The court in this case decided that it requires that the accomplice have the purpose with respect to the result of the primary actor's conduct.

■=■

Quicknotes

ACCOMPLICE An individual who knowingly, purposefully or voluntarily combines with the main actor in the commission or attempted commission of a criminal offense.

NEGLIGENT HOMICIDE The negligent killing of another person.

PRINCIPAL A person or entity who authorizes another (the agent) to act on its behalf and subject to its authority to the extent that the principal may be held liable for the actions of the agent.

■=■

State v. Christy Pontiac-GMC, Inc.

State (P) v. Corporation (D)

Minn. Sup. Ct., 354 N.W.2d 17 (1984).

NATURE OF CASE: Appeal from a conviction of a corporation for theft by swindle and aggravated forgery.

FACT SUMMARY: After an employee of Christy Pontiac (D) forged the signatures of two customers on rebate applications, Christy Pontiac (D) was charged and convicted of theft by swindle and aggravated forgery.

🏛 RULE OF LAW
A corporation may be held criminally liable for a specific-intent crime.

FACTS: Christy Pontiac (D), a Minnesota corporation, was solely owned by James Christy (D), its president and director. Christy Pontiac (D) made two car sales after a rebate offer from GM had expired. Both customers were told that the salesman would still try to get the rebate for them. Hesli (D), a salesman and fleet manager, forged the signatures of both customers on the rebate applications, and the purchase order forms were backdated to put them within the time frame of the rebate offers. When the purchasers learned of the forged rebate applications, they complained to Christy (D). Charges were filed against Hesli (D), Christy (D), and Christy Pontiac (D). In a separate trial, Hesli (D) was found guilty of theft for the second forgery and was given a misdemeanor disposition. An indictment against Christy (D) was dismissed. Christy Pontiac (D), the corporation, was convicted as charged. This appeal followed.

ISSUE: May a corporation be held criminally liable for a specific-intent crime?

HOLDING AND DECISION: (Simonett, J.) Yes. A corporation may be held criminally liable for a specific-intent crime. Therefore, a corporation may be prosecuted and convicted for the crimes of theft and forgery. Criminal guilt, however, requires that the agent act in furtherance of the corporation's business interests. Moreover, it must be shown that corporate management authorized, tolerated, or ratified the criminal activity. Here, since Christy Pontiac (D) got the GM rebate money, Hesli (D) was acting in furtherance of the corporation's business interests. Hesli (D) himself had middle-management responsibilities for cash rebate applications. Swandy, a corporate officer, signed the backdated retail buyer's order form for the first sale. Christy (D), the president, attempted to negotiate a settlement with the second purchaser. The evidence thus establishes that the theft by swindle and the forgeries constituted the acts of the corporation. Affirmed.

▶ ANALYSIS

The Model Penal Code provides that a corporation may be convicted of an offense if the conduct is performed by an agent of the corporation acting on behalf of the corporation within the scope of his employment. See Model Penal Code 2.07(1). The conduct need not actually benefit the corporation to impart liability. However, if the agent acts only to further his own interests—for example, is embezzling funds from the corporation—such an act is not considered to be "on behalf of the corporation."

■=■

Quicknotes

AGENT An individual who has the authority to act on behalf of another.

FORGERY The false preparation or modification of a written document with an intent to defraud another.

SPECIFIC INTENT The intent to commit a specific unlawful act which is a required element for criminal liability for certain crimes.

■=■

United States v. Hilton Hotels Corp.

Federal government (P) v. Corporation (D)

467 F.2d 1000 (9th Cir. 1972).

NATURE OF CASE: Appeal from a conviction for violation of the Sherman Act.

FACT SUMMARY: Hilton Hotels (D) was convicted of violating the Sherman Act after the judge charged the jury that a corporation is responsible for the acts and statements of its agents, done or made within the scope of their employment, even if contrary to their actual instructions or to the corporation's stated policies.

🏛 RULE OF LAW
As a general rule, a corporation is liable under the Sherman Act for the acts of its agents in the scope of their employment, even though such acts are contrary to general corporate policy and/or express instructions to the agent.

FACTS: Although it was against the corporate policies of Hilton Hotels (D) and constituted a violation of instructions that he take no part in the boycott, the purchasing agent for its hotel in Portland, Oregon, had threatened a supplier with the loss of the hotel's business unless the supplier paid an assessment to an association which the local businesses had organized to attract convention business to Portland. The agreement among the members of the association was that those suppliers who would not pay their assessment would be "boycotted" (i.e., no purchases would be made from them). Hilton Hotels (D) was convicted of violating the Sherman Act, the judge charging the jury that a corporation is responsible for the acts and statements of its agents, done or made within the scope of their employment, even if contrary to their actual instructions or to the corporation's stated policies. On appeal, Hilton Hotels (D) cited this as error.

ISSUE: Is a corporation liable under the Sherman Act for the acts of its agents in the scope of their employment, even though such acts are contrary to general corporate policy and/or express instructions to the agents?

HOLDING AND DECISION: (Browning, J.) Yes. As a general rule, a corporation is liable under the Sherman Act for the acts of its agents in the scope of their employment, even though such acts are contrary to general corporate policy and/or express instructions to the agent. Congress may constitutionally impose criminal liability upon a business entity for acts or omissions of its agents within the scope of their employment, even without proof that the conduct was within the agent's actual authority and even though it may have been contrary to his express instructions or the policies of the corporation. While the Sherman Act does not expressly impose such liability, the construction of the act that best achieves its purpose is that a corporation is liable for the acts of its agents within the scope of their authority, even when done against company orders. Affirmed.

▶ ANALYSIS

Consider the argument that only individuals, not fictional entities, commit crimes. The entity is being held responsible as a group when it was a person's act that resulted in criminal charges. A person may be more likely to engage in criminal behavior if he or she believes the company will have to accept the responsibility and defend against the actions. On the other hand, corporations could always hide behind the veil if not held accountable for the actions of its agents. The entity could have individuals behaving criminally with no one person charged because of the group protection. The debate was silenced with legislation imposing liability on corporations for individual action.

■■■

Quicknotes

AGENT An individual who has the authority to act on behalf of another.

SHERMAN ACT Makes every contract or conspiracy in unreasonable restraint of commerce illegal.

■■■

Conspiracy

Quick Reference Rules of Law

State v. Verive

State (P) v. Conspirator (D)

Ariz. Ct. App., 128 Ariz. 70, 627 P.2d 721 (1981).

NATURE OF CASE: Appeal of conviction of conspiracy to obstruct justice.

FACT SUMMARY: Verive (D) was convicted of both conspiracy to obstruct justice and an attempt to obstruct justice.

🏛 RULE OF LAW
A defendant may be convicted of both conspiracy to obstruct justice and an attempt to obstruct justice.

FACTS: Verive (D) agreed with Woodall that the latter would give the former compensation for Verive's (D) use of force to dissuade one Galvin from testifying against Woodall. Verive (D) went to Galvin's residence and assaulted and beat him. Verive (D) was later indicted for attempting to obstruct justice and conspiracy to obstruct justice. He was convicted of both offenses. He appealed, contending that attempt merged into conspiracy.

ISSUE: May a defendant be convicted of both conspiracy to obstruct justice and an attempt to obstruct justice?

HOLDING AND DECISION: (Haire, J.) Yes. A defendant may be convicted of both conspiracy to obstruct justice and an attempt to obstruct justice. When one transaction is subject to different criminal sanctions, one offense must necessarily merge into the other, if the same acts by the defendant are applicable to the elements of each offense. However, when each offense requires proof of a fact not required by the other, no merger occurs. Hence, the offense of attempt. Further, an attempt offense requires some act beyond mere preparation. Since each conviction requires proof of a fact not required by the other, no merger occurs. Affirmed.

▌ANALYSIS

Conspiracy and attempt, though similar, have different foci. The main concern of conspiracy is the collusive nature thereof; the concern of attempt is the act itself. For that reason, merger is rarely found to occur between conspiracy and attempt.

■■■

Quicknotes

ATTEMPT An intent combined with an act falling short of the thing intended.

CONSPIRACY Concerted action by two or more persons to accomplish some unlawful purpose.

MERGER The acquisition of one company by another, after which the acquired company ceases to exist as an independent entity.

■■■

Griffin v. State

Conspirator (D) v. State (P)

Ark. Sup. Ct., 455 S.W.2d 882 (1970).

NATURE OF CASE: Appeal from conviction for conspiracy.

FACT SUMMARY: Griffin (D) contended that direct evidence of a common design or purpose and of intent to act jointly was necessary to support a conspiracy conviction.

🏛 RULE OF LAW
A conspiracy may be inferred where two or more persons pursued the same unlawful object, each doing a part so that such acts were connected, though independent.

FACTS: Griffin (D) was approached by two police officers after he was involved in a traffic accident. The officers questioned the witnesses and asked who was driving. Griffin (D) became enraged and he violently attacked the officers, as did several members of a crowd which had gathered at the accident site. One of the officers feared he and his partner were going to be killed so he shot Griffin (D) in the chest although the shot was not lethal. The crowd members engaged in both physical and verbal abuse of the officers, yet there was no direct evidence of an agreement between them and Griffin (D) to so act. Griffin (D) was convicted of conspiracy and appealed, contending that such conviction was invalid in the absence of direct evidence of an unlawful agreement.

ISSUE: May a conspiracy be inferred where two or more persons pursued the same unlawful object, each doing a part so that such acts were connected, though independent?

HOLDING AND DECISION: (Fogleman, J.) Yes. A conspiracy may be inferred where two or more persons pursued the same unlawful object, each doing a part so that such acts were connected, though independent. A common intent to injure the officers is manifested by the evidence of the crowd's conduct. Thus, a common pattern of behavior existed sufficient to establish a conspiracy. Affirmed.

▌ ANALYSIS

The court indicated it would be virtually impossible to prove a conspiracy if direct evidence of an actual agreement were required. Often it is necessary to infer such common intent from clear circumstantial evidence. A common avenue of behavior may be sufficient to establish the conspiracy.

Quicknotes

CIRCUMSTANTIAL EVIDENCE Evidence that, though not directly observed, supports the inference of principal facts.

CONSPIRACY Concerted action by two or more persons to accomplish some unlawful purpose.

United States v. Recio

Federal government (P) v. Drug conspirator (D)

270 U.S. 537 (2003).

NATURE OF CASE: Appeal from conviction for conspiracy to distribute drugs.

FACT SUMMARY: When Recio (D) was convicted of having conspired to possess and distribute unlawful drugs, he argued that the Government could not prosecute drug conspiracy defendants unless they had joined the conspiracy before the Government seized the drugs.

🏛 **RULE OF LAW**
A conspiracy does not end automatically when its object becomes impossible to achieve.

FACTS: Police stopped a truck and found and seized a large stash of illegal drugs. With the help of the truck's drivers, the police set up a sting in which the truck was taken to another location and the drivers paged Jimenez Recio (D) and another defendant to come and pick up the truck and the drugs. When Recio (D) and the other defendant arrived, they were arrested. They were convicted of having conspired to possess and distribute unlawful drugs. However, the trial judge determined the jury instructions had been erroneous in failing to inform the jury that it could not convict Recio (D) of the conspiracy unless the jury believed he had joined the conspiracy before the truck was stopped by the police. At the new trial, Recio (D) was again convicted and appealed.

ISSUE: Does a conspiracy end automatically when its object becomes impossible to achieve?

HOLDING AND DECISION: (Breyer, J.) No. A conspiracy does not end automatically when its object becomes impossible to achieve. In *United States v. Cruz*, 127 F.3d 791 (1997), the Ninth Circuit held that the Government could not prosecute drug conspiracy defendants unless they had joined the conspiracy before the Government seized the drugs. The Ninth Circuit thereby held that a conspiracy ends automatically when its object becomes impossible to achieve. In other words, the conspiracy ends through "defeat" when the Government intervenes, making the conspiracy's goals impossible to achieve, even if the conspirators did not know that the Government had intervened and are totally unaware that the conspiracy is bound to fail. In our view, this statement of the law is incorrect. To the contrary, a conspiracy does not automatically terminate simply because the Government, unbeknownst to some of the conspirators, has defeated the conspiracy's object. The essence of a conspiracy is an agreement to commit an unlawful act. That agreement is a "distinct evil" which "may exist and be punished whether or not the substantive crime ensues." To hold otherwise would reach well beyond arguable police misbehavior, potentially threatening the use of properly run law enforcement sting operations. The conspiracy itself poses a threat to the public over and above the threat of the commission of the relevant substantive crime. Reversed.

▶ **ANALYSIS**

The American Law Institute's Model Penal Code § 5.03 (1985) provides that a conspiracy terminates when the crime or crimes that are its object are committed or when the relevant agreement is abandoned. The Model Penal Code would not find "impossibility" a basis for termination.

■■■■

Quicknotes

CONSPIRACY Concerted action by two or more persons to accomplish some unlawful purpose.

■■■■

People v. Lauria

State (P) v. Answering service proprietor (D)

Cal. Ct. App., 251 Cal. App. 2d 471, 59 Cal. Rptr. 628 (1967).

NATURE OF CASE: Appeal from indictment for conspiracy to further prostitution being set aside.

FACT SUMMARY: Lauria (D) knew that some of his answering service customers were prostitutes who used his service for business purposes.

🏛 RULE OF LAW

A supplier does not necessarily become a part of a conspiracy to further an illegal venture by furnishing goods or services that he knows are to be used for criminal purposes, where the crime involved is a misdemeanor.

FACTS: Lauria (D) and three people who used his answering service were arrested for prostitution. Lauria (D) knew that one of the people was a prostitute. He said he did not arbitrarily tell the police about prostitutes who used his service for business purposes. Lauria (D) and three prostitutes were indicted for conspiracy to further prostitution. The trial court set aside the indictment as lacking reasonable or probable cause. The State (P) appeals.

ISSUE: Does a supplier necessarily become a part of a conspiracy to further an illegal venture by furnishing goods or services that he knows are to be used for criminal purposes, where the crime involved is a misdemeanor?

HOLDING AND DECISION: (Fleming, J.) No. A supplier does not necessarily become a part of a conspiracy to further an illegal venture by furnishing goods or services that he knows are to be used for criminal purposes, where the crime involved is a misdemeanor. Both the knowledge of the illegal use of the goods or services and the intent to further that use are necessary to support a conviction for conspiracy. Intent may be inferred from circumstances of the sale which show that the supplier had acquired a special interest in the activity. Or a supplier may be liable on the basis of knowledge alone where he furnishes goods which he knows will be used to commit a serious crime. However, this does not apply to misdemeanors. Here, Lauria (D) was not shown to have a stake in the venture, and he is charged with a misdemeanor. Hence, he could not be charged with conspiracy to further prostitution. Affirmed.

▶ *ANALYSIS*

In *U.S. v. Falcone*, 311 U.S. 205, the sellers of large quantities of sugar, yeast, and cans were absolved from participation in a moonlighting conspiracy. In *Direct Sales Co. v. U.S.*, 319 U.S. 703, a wholesale drug company was convicted of conspiracy to violate the narcotic laws by selling large quantities of drugs to a physician who was supplying them to addicts. The court distinguished these two leading cases on the basis of the character of the goods. The restricted character of the goods in *Direct Sales* showed that the defendant knew of their illegal use and had taken the step from knowledge to intent and agreement.

Quicknotes

CONSPIRACY Concerted action by two or more persons to accomplish some unlawful purpose.

MISDEMEANOR Any offense that does not constitute a felony, which is generally less severe and for which a lesser punishment is imposed.

United States v. Diaz

Federal government (P) v. Conspirator (D)

864 F.2d 544 (7th Cir. 1988).

NATURE OF CASE: Appeal of conviction of conspiracy, among others, to use a firearm in relation to commission of a drug trafficking crime.

FACT SUMMARY: Diaz (D) was convicted of conspiracy to use a firearm in relation to commission of a drug trafficking crime, even though he did not know his accomplice was bringing a gun.

🏛 RULE OF LAW
One may be convicted of conspiracy to use a firearm in relation to commission of a drug trafficking crime even if he did not know his accomplice was bringing a gun.

FACTS: Diaz (D) became involved in a drug deal set up by DEA officers. Diaz (D) was to meet with several accomplices to effect a sale of cocaine to an undercover DEA officer. At the scene of the sale, Peirallo (D), an accomplice, brought a gun. Diaz (D) had no knowledge that Peirallo (D) intended to do so. Diaz (D) and the others were arrested at the scene. Diaz (D) was convicted of conspiracy to distribute cocaine, possession and distribution of cocaine, and conspiracy to use a firearm in relation to commission of a drug trafficking crime. Diaz (D) appealed the firearm conspiracy conviction.

ISSUE: May one be convicted of conspiracy to use a firearm in relation to commission of a drug trafficking crime even if he did not know his accomplice was bringing a gun?

HOLDING AND DECISION: (Ripple, J.) Yes. One may be convicted of conspiracy to use a firearm in relation to commission of a drug trafficking crime even if he did not know his accomplice was bringing a gun. It is a rule that when one enters a conspiracy, he becomes responsible for the acts of every other conspirator done in furtherance of the conspiracy. The only exception to this is when the act is not a foreseeable, reasonable consequence of the conspiracy. In the context of the drug industry, it hardly needs mention that possession of a gun is a foreseeable consequence of a "deal." This being so, the conviction was proper. Affirmed.

▶ ANALYSIS

The leading case in this area is *Pinkerton v. United States*, 328 U.S. 640 (1946). Pinkerton broadly established the rule noted by the opinion. The circuits have varied as to how expansive the rule should be. Some circuits require more agreement as to the offense in question than other circuits.

The Seventh Circuit, by its own admission, takes a broad view of the rule.

Quicknotes

ACCOMPLICE An individual who knowingly, purposefully or voluntarily combines with the main actor in the commission or attempted commission of a criminal offense.

CONSPIRACY Concerted action by two or more persons to accomplish some unlawful purpose.

United States v. Caldwell

Federal government (P) v. Drug dealer Co-conspirator (D)

589 F.3d 1323 (10th Cir. 2009).

NATURE OF CASE: Appeal from conviction for a single conspiracy to distribute drugs.

FACT SUMMARY: Caldwell (D) was charged and convicted of engaging in a single conspiracy with Herrera and Anderson to sell drugs. An introduction by Caldwell (D) of Anderson to Herrera led to Herrera becoming the common source of drugs for both Caldwell (D) and Anderson.

🏛 RULE OF LAW
Having a common drug supplier does not constitute sufficient evidence of a single conspiracy.

FACTS: Caldwell (D) sold drugs, and initially received them only from Herrera. Later, after Caldwell (D) set up an introduction of his friend Anderson (from whom Caldwell had also bought drugs) to Herrera, Caldwell (D) continued to receive drugs from Herrera, but not from Anderson. Ultimately, Caldwell is indicted for conspiring to distribute a large volume of drugs with both Herrera and Anderson as part of one conspiracy. After trial, Caldwell (D) was convicted and imprisoned.

ISSUE: Does having a common drug supplier constitute sufficient evidence of a single conspiracy?

HOLDING AND DECISION: (Lucero, J.) No. Having a common drug supplier does not constitute sufficient evidence of a single conspiracy. A jury convicted the Caldwell (D) of being involved in a single conspiracy with two other individuals (Herrera and Anderson) to distribute drugs. In the present case, Caldwell (D) and Anderson were equal-level purchasers rather than links in a vertical chain. A vertical conspiracy, or "chain-and-link" conspiracy, involves a series of consecutive buyer-seller relationships. The classic vertical conspiracy involves Supplier A selling contraband to Supplier B, who then sells the contraband to Supplier C. But drug distribution organizations often do not fit neatly into the concept of vertical conspiracy.

After Herrera was introduced by Caldwell (D) to Anderson, Herrera became their joint supplier. Neither Caldwell (D) nor Anderson bought or sold marijuana to the other. Instead, each independently sold marijuana to third parties. Thus, their relationship does not evince the characteristics of a vertical conspiracy. This relationship would fit more neatly into the concept of a "hub-and-spoke" conspiracy, in which several separate players all interact with a common central actor, here Herrera.

Herrera's role as a common supplier, Caldwell's (D's) earlier purchase of marijuana from Anderson, and Caldwell's (D's) introduction of Anderson to Herrera do not constitute sufficient evidence of a single conspiracy among the three drug dealers. Instead, the evidence presented at trial demonstrates the existence of separate conspiracies between Caldwell (D) and Anderson, and between Caldwell (D) and Herrera. The sharing of a common supplier, without more, does not demonstrate that two drug dealers are acting together for their shared mutual benefit. Evidence showing that an alleged co-conspirator has an economic stake in the outcome of a drug transaction can demonstrate that a transaction is not merely casual. Of course, direct economic benefit for all individuals involved is not necessarily a prerequisite for a jury to find a single conspiracy. On the other hand, an act that merely facilitates the distribution of drugs may be insufficient to show that two individuals intend to act together for their mutual benefit. The facts surrounding this case demonstrate that it was friendly rather than conspiratorial. There was no evidence that Caldwell (D) received any economic benefit from the introduction, and Anderson testified that Caldwell (D) received no such benefit. Reversed.

▌ ANALYSIS

The charge, and what the jury ultimately convicted Caldwell (D) of, indicated a single, or tripartite, conspiracy that all three (Caldwell, Herrera, and Anderson) acted in conspiratorial coordination. An examination by the court revealed different level of interactions, focusing on what each person did to establish the scope of the alleged conspiracy. However, and the court was quick to note this, Caldwell (D) admitted that he conspired only with Herrera and not Anderson. This distinction was fatal to the charges, which alleged a single conspiracy among all three men, a tripartite conspiracy, which did not occur.

■—■

United States v. Neapolitan

Federal government (P) v. Police officer (D)

791 F.2d 489 (7th Cir. 1986).

NATURE OF CASE: Appeal of conviction under the Racketeering Influenced and Corrupt Organizations Act (RICO).

FACT SUMMARY: Neapolitan (D) was convicted under the RICO statute despite a lack of evidence that he had personally agreed to commit two predicate acts.

🏛 RULE OF LAW
Under the RICO statute, it is not necessary that a defendant had personally agreed to commit two predicate acts.

FACTS: Neapolitan (D), a police officer, was accused of accepting bribes from an auto theft ring. It was alleged that Neapolitan (D) and two other officers would accept cash in exchange for protecting the ring. Neapolitan (D) was charged with several counts of mail fraud and one count of solicitation of bribes. The mail counts were dismissed, and Neapolitan (D) was convicted of the solicitation count and of violating the RICO statute. Neapolitan (D) appealed the RICO violation, contending that he had not been convicted of agreeing to two predicate acts.

ISSUE: Under the RICO statute, is it necessary that a defendant personally agreed to commit two predicate acts?

HOLDING AND DECISION: (Flaum, J.) No. Under the RICO statute, it is not necessary that a defendant had personally agreed to commit two predicate acts. Prosecution under the RICO law requires an agreement with knowledge that the goal of the conspiracy is the commission of a RICO violation, that is, to conduct the affairs of an enterprise through a pattern of racketeering activity. By statute, racketeering activity requires at least two acts. From this definition, Neapolitan (D) argues that an accused must have personally agreed to commit two acts. This is an erroneous interpretation. RICO largely borrows from conspiracy theory. Conspiracy does not require that a participant therein personally agree to commit the acts complained of, but merely that he agree to join in a plan that involves committing the illegal act at issue. Here, while Neapolitan (D) did not personally commit two predicate acts, the enterprise of which he was a part did. Affirmed.

▶ ANALYSIS

RICO was a congressional attempt to defeat organized crime. The perception was that crime chieftains could insulate themselves from prosecution by delegation. RICO was written to make personal involvement unnecessary.

Thus the reliance on conspiracy theory to extend the reach of the law becomes clearer as a public policy choice.

■==■

Quicknotes

CONSPIRACY Concerted action by two or more persons to accomplish some unlawful purpose.

RICO Racketeer Influenced and Corrupt Organization laws; federal and state statutes enacted for the purpose of prosecuting organized crime.

SOLICITATION Contact initiated by an attorney for the purpose of obtaining employment.

■==■

CHAPTER 13

Rape

Quick Reference Rules of Law

Brown v. State

Victim (P) v. Rapist (D)

Wis. Sup. Ct., 127 Wis. 193, 106 N.W. 536 (1906).

NATURE OF CASE: Appeal from rape conviction.

FACT SUMMARY: Brown (D) was alleged to have raped his neighbor, Nethery (P), while she was walking to her grandmother's house.

🏛 RULE OF LAW

To prove rape, a plaintiff must show the most vehement exercise of every physical power to resist the penetration of her person until the offense is consummated.

FACTS: The two parties were children of neighboring farmers who had known each other all their lives. Brown (D) was 20 and Nethery (P) was 16. Nethery (P) was going on the usual path across fields to her grandmother's house to have an aunt try on certain clothing being made for her. The path crossed over the Brown (D) farm. Brown (D) was repairing a fence when Nethery (P) passed by and greeted him. Brown (D) allegedly seized Nethery (D), tripped her to the ground, placed himself over her, and had intercourse with her. Nethery (P) alleges that she tried as hard as she could to get away, that she screamed as loud as possible, but he kept pulling her down to the ground and put his hand on her mouth until she was almost strangled. Brown (D) denied any resistance. There were no marks on his face, hands, or clothing indicating any struggle.

ISSUE: Must a plaintiff show the most vehement exercise of every physical power to resist penetration in order to prove rape?

HOLDING AND DECISION: [Judge not stated in textbook excerpt.] Yes. To prove rape, a plaintiff must show the most vehement exercise of every physical power to resist the penetration of her person until the offense is consummated. This must be in addition to the entire absence of mental consent. Nethery (P) wrongly argues that there is no evidence sufficient to satisfy beyond a reasonable doubt such resistance as the law requires to make out the crime of rape. We need not reiterate these considerations of the ease of assertion of the forcible accomplishment of the sexual act, with the impossibility of defense save by direct denial, or the proneness of the woman when she finds the fact of her disgrace discovered or likely of discovery, to minimize her fault by asserting vis major. Except for one demand by Nethery (P) to let her go and inarticulate screams, Nethery (P) mentions no verbal protests. It is hardly within range of reason that a man should come out of so desperate an encounter as the determined normal woman would make necessary, without signs upon his face, hands, or clothing. Resistance is opposing force to force, not retreating from force. Reversed.

▶ ANALYSIS

To win a rape prosecution, the state would traditionally have to prove very overt force. Force was easier to establish involving encounters between strangers. However, in the majority of cases, which involve non-stranger rapes, courts looked to the victim's resistance as an indicator of the defendant's force and the victim's nonconsent.

■=■

Quicknotes

RAPE Unlawful sexual intercourse with a woman by a man by means of fear or force and without her consent.

■=■

People v. Dorsey

State v. Rapist

N.Y. Sup. Ct., 429 N.Y.S.2d 828 (1980).

NATURE OF CASE: Motion to dismiss.

FACT SUMMARY: Dorsey (D) raped a woman in an elevator, having manipulated the controls to stall the elevator between floors.

🏛 RULE OF LAW
In proving a case of forcible compulsion, a woman has to exert only earnest resistance of a type reasonably to be expected from a person who genuinely refuses to participate in sexual intercourse, deviate sexual intercourse or sexual contact, under all the attendant circumstances.

FACTS: A petite, middle-aged woman entered the lobby of her apartment building after work. She entered the elevator and pressed the button for the tenth floor on which her apartment was located. A large, heavy teenage male entered the elevator after her and pressed the button for another floor. The woman noticed that the elevator had stopped and looked up to see Dorsey (D) manipulating the buttons so that the elevator had stopped between floors; the alarm bell did not go off. Dorsey (D) ordered the woman to take off her clothes. She did not respond, but Dorsey (D) repeated his demand. The woman complied and was subjected to acts of sexual intercourse and sodomy during the next ten to fifteen minutes. Afterwards, Dorsey (D) told the woman to get dressed and started the elevator back up, eventually getting off on the twenty-second floor. As he was leaving the elevator, Dorsey (D) threatened that if anything happened to him in the next couple of days, his friends would get her. The woman got back to her floor, went to her apartment, and immediately called the apartment's security police force who then contacted the New York Police Department. Dorsey (D) was identified and arrested later that evening.

ISSUE: In proving a case of forcible compulsion, does a woman have to exert utmost resistance?

HOLDING AND DECISION: (Schackman, J.) No. In proving a case of forcible compulsion, a woman has to exert only earnest resistance of a type reasonably to be expected from a person who genuinely refuses to participate in sexual intercourse, deviate sexual intercourse or sexual contact, under all the attendant circumstances. The intent of the legislation was set forth in the preamble which stated: "It is the legislature's intention to modify the resistance requirement in the definition of forcible compulsion so that the victim need only offer so much resistance as is reasonable under the circumstances." The reasonable-under-the-circumstances approach, with language to make

clear that the woman need not incur serious risk of death or serious bodily injury, is as low as the standard can be set and remain consistent with fair treatment of defendants. The issue before this court is to determine from the facts of this case whether Dorsey (D) either exerted physical force capable of overcoming this complainant's reasonable, earnest resistance, or whether the complainant was overcome by fear of immediate death or serious physical injury due to threat from the defendant. Both of these questions must be measured by all of the attendant circumstances in this case. Here, instead of being faced with four big men in a lonely place, the complainant was faced with a husky teenager, who was seven inches taller and outweighed her by 70 pounds. She was trapped in a stalled elevator, between floors, with no place to retreat to, or from which help could arrive. The law did not require that she ascertain what the defendant would do to her if she refused to take off her clothes. Nor does it take but a brief recognition of the everyday events in this city to reasonably conclude that a gun, knife or other deadly weapon might quickly and savagely be used if she did not yield to Dorsey (D). Therefore, the court finds, as a matter of law, that the People (P) presented sufficient trial evidence from which the jury could conclude, beyond a reasonable doubt, that Dorsey (D) engaged in sexual acts with the complainant by means of forcible compulsion, in that there was an implied threat which placed the complainant in fear of immediate death or serious physical injury. Motion to dismiss indictment denied.

▶ ANALYSIS

Rape victims were no longer required to demonstrate a show of physical force in resisting the attack although courts still looked for earnest and reasonable resistance. The requirement for fear of or actual force remains even when the sexual activity was nonconsensual. That means, the victim remains the one who has to prove he or she did not quietly acquiesce to escape serious injury even without the judicial requirement of "utmost resistance."

■■■

Quicknotes

RAPE Unlawful sexual intercourse with a woman by a man by means of fear or force and without her consent.

■■■

People v. Barnes

State (P) v. Convicted rapist (D)

Cal. Sup. Ct., 42 Cal. 3d 284, 228 Cal. Rptr. 228 (1986).

NATURE OF CASE: Review of reversal of rape conviction.

FACT SUMMARY: Barnes's (D) rape conviction was reversed on the basis that the alleged victim had not resisted.

🏛 RULE OF LAW
To sustain a rape conviction, evidence of resistance need not be presented.

FACTS: Barnes (D) invited one Marsha M. to his residence. Marsha, wishing to purchase marijuana, came over. According to Marsha, Barnes (D) began demonstrating aberrant behavior, acting belligerent one moment and then rational the next. Barnes (D) made several threats toward her. After several attempts at seduction, Barnes (D) demanded that they have intercourse. Marsha complied, which she later ascribed to fear for her safety. Barnes's (D) version was that she consented, which was his defense at trial. Barnes (D) was convicted. A court of appeals reversed due to the lack of resistance. The California Supreme Court granted review.

ISSUE: Must evidence of resistance be presented to sustain a rape conviction?

HOLDING AND DECISION: (Bird, C.J.) No. Evidence of resistance need not be presented to sustain a rape conviction. In 1980, the California Legislature amended Penal Code § 261, the section defining rape. Rape is now defined as intercourse accomplished against a person's will by means of force or fear of immediate and unlawful bodily injury on the person. Certain references to resistance which existed in the prior law were deleted, and the legislative history makes it clear that these deletions were intentional. This was consistent with the modern trend in the law, which recognizes that resisting a rape puts the victim in danger of further battery. In view of this, the court of appeals incorrectly read a resistance element into the offense, and this was erroneous. Reversed.

▶ ANALYSIS

Rape is one of the more politicized offenses in the legal area. The evidentiary requirements for a rape conviction have been significantly altered. The present case illustrates such a change. Another change is that many states no longer permit evidence of a complainant's sexual history.

■■■

Quicknotes

BATTERY Unlawful contact with the body of another person.

RAPE Unlawful sexual intercourse with a woman by a man by means of fear or force and without her consent.

■■■

State v. Smith

State (P) v. Rapist (D)

Conn. Sup. Ct., 210 Conn. 132, 554 A.2d 713 (1989).

NATURE OF CASE: Prosecution for rape.

FACT SUMMARY: Smith (D) raped a woman after meeting her at a bar, despite her demands for him to stop his advances.

🏛 RULE OF LAW
Whether a complainant should be found to have consented depends upon how her behavior would have been viewed by a reasonable person under the surrounding circumstances.

FACTS: The victim, T, was introduced to Smith (D) by a friend at a bar in West Haven. After a drink, Smith (D) and T went to dinner at a restaurant across the street. Later, Smith (D) invited T to his apartment. Friends were supposed to meet Smith (D) and T at his apartment, but they never arrived. Smith (D) and T began watching television. After some time, Smith (D) put his arm around T and asked for a kiss. She gave him a kiss. Smith (D) then continued to make advances, but T told him to stop. Despite her repeated demands for him to stop, Smith (D) kept insisting, saying that he had not paid for dinner for nothing. T spit in his face and tried to kick Smith (D) off but to no avail because he was too big for her. Smith (D) then threatened her, saying he could make it hard for her or she could make it easy on herself. T, fearing that Smith (D) would hurt her otherwise, agreed "to go along with it." At the point where T ceased resistance, Smith (D) had already pushed her down on the couch and was on top of her. He removed T's clothing, led her to his bedroom, and proceeded to engage in vaginal intercourse with her. After completion of the act, Smith (D) said that he knew T felt she had been raped, but she could not prove it and had really enjoyed herself. After they both dressed, T stayed in the apartment to wait for a cab. However, she placed her pink cigarette lighter underneath the couch, so that she would be able to prove she had been in the apartment. When the cab arrived, she left the apartment and told the cab to take her to the police station because she had been raped. At the station, she gave her account to the police. Smith (D) was then arrested. The police found T's lighter under the couch as she had informed them.

ISSUE: Should a complainant be found to have consented depending upon how her behavior would have been viewed by a reasonable person under the surrounding circumstances?

HOLDING AND DECISION: (Shea, J.) Yes. Whether a complainant should be found to have consented depends upon how her behavior would have been viewed by a reasonable person under the surrounding circumstances. We reject the position of the British and Alaska courts that the state must prove either an actual awareness on the part of the defendant that the complainant had not consented or a reckless disregard of her nonconsenting status. We agree with the California courts that a defendant is entitled to a jury instruction that a defendant may not be convicted of this crime if the words or conduct of the complainant under all the circumstances would justify a reasonable belief that she had consented. Since we have rejected the subjective standard for determining the issue of consent, the question for us is whether the evidence is sufficient to prove that a reasonable person would not have believed that T's conduct under all the circumstances indicated her consent. From our review of the evidence, it is clear that the jury could properly have found beyond a reasonable doubt that T's words and actions could not reasonably be viewed to indicate her consent to intercourse with Smith (D). According to her uncontradicted testimony, she expressly declined his advances. She spat in his face and tried kicking him off. She "gave in" only after Smith (D) had told her that "he could make it hard" for her if she continued to resist. She could have reasonably regarded this statement as a threat of physical injury. The evidence was more than sufficient to support the verdict.

▶ ANALYSIS

While some jurisdictions move more slowly in rape law reform, other jurisdictions go further by eliminating force as well as resistance as an independent requirement and focus on the fact of nonconsent as the crucial element of the crime.

■==■

Quicknotes

RAPE Unlawful sexual intercourse with a woman by a man by means of fear or force and without her consent.

REASONABLE PERSON STANDARD The standard of care exercised by a hypothetical person who possesses the intelligence, education, knowledge, attention, and judgment required by society of its members when governing behavior; the standard applies to a person's judgment when determining breach of a duty under the theory of negligence.

■==■

In the Interest of M.T.S.

State (P) v. Rapist (D)

N.J. Sup. Ct., 129 N.J. 422, 609 A.2d 1266 (1992).

NATURE OF CASE: Prosecution for rape.

FACT SUMMARY: M.T.S. (D) was a houseguest in C.G.'s family's home. After engaging in consensual kissing and heavy petting, M.T.S. (D) engaged in sexual penetration of C.G. to which she had not consented.

🏛 RULE OF LAW
Any act of sexual penetration engaged in by the defendant, without the affirmative and freely given permission of the victim to the specific act of penetration, constitutes the offense of sexual assault.

FACTS: Fifteen-year-old C.G. was living with her family and seven other people, including seventeen-year-old M.T.S. (D) and his girlfriend. One evening, C.G. went upstairs to sleep after watching television with her mother, M.T.S. (D), and his girlfriend. At around 1:15 a.m., M.T.S. (D) entered C.G.'s bedroom as she was walking to the bathroom. C.G. returned from the bathroom, and the two engaged in kissing and heavy petting. According to M.T.S. (D), once they were in bed, they undressed each other and continued to kiss and touch for about five minutes, then proceeded to engage in sexual intercourse. According to M.T.S. (D), who was on top of C.G., he penetrated her three times and the fourth time, she pushed him off of her. As she pushed him off, she said "stop, get off," and he got off immediately. After about one minute, he asked C.G. what was wrong and she replied with a backhand to his face. M.T.S. said that he proceeded to get dressed and told C.G. to calm down, but that she then told him to get away from her and began to cry. He left the room and went to sleep downstairs. The trial court determined that the juvenile was delinquent for committing a sexual assault. The Appellate Division reversed. The State (P) appealed.

ISSUE: Does any act of sexual penetration engaged in by the defendant, without the affirmative and freely given permission of the victim to the specific act of penetration, constitute sexual assault?

HOLDING AND DECISION: (Handler, J.) Yes. Any act of sexual penetration engaged in by the defendant, without the affirmative and freely given permission of the victim to the specific act of penetration, constitutes the offense of sexual assault. The New Jersey Code of Criminal Justice does not refer to force in relation to "overcoming the will", "physical overpowering", or the "submission" of the victim. It does not require the demonstrated non-consent of the victim. In reforming rape laws, the Legislature placed primary emphasis on the assaultive nature of the crime, altering its constituent elements so that they focus exclusively on the forceful or assaultive conduct of the defendant. Thus, by eliminating all references to the victim's state of mind and conduct, and by broadening the definition of penetration to cover not only sexual intercourse between a man and a woman but a range of acts that invade another's body or compel intimate contact, the Legislature emphasized the affinity between sexual assault and other forms of assault and battery. Under the new law, the victim is no longer required to resist and therefore need not have said or done anything in order for the sexual penetration to be unlawful. The alleged victim is not put on trial, and his or her responsive or defensive behavior is rendered immaterial. In a case such as this one, in which the State (P) does not allege violence or force extrinsic to the act of penetration, the fact-finder must decide whether the defendant's act of penetration was undertaken in circumstances that led the defendant reasonably to believe that the alleged victim had freely given affirmative permission to the specific act of sexual penetration. Such permission can be indicated either through words or through actions that, when viewed in the light of all the surrounding circumstances, would demonstrate to a reasonable person affirmative and freely given authorization for the specific act of sexual penetration. In this case, the trial court concluded that the victim had not expressed consent to the act of intercourse, either through her words or actions. Reversed.

▶ ANALYSIS

This case provides a definition of the actus reus of rape as sexual penetration absent some kind of affirmative expression of consent.

■═■

Quicknotes

ACTUS REUS The unlawful act that gives rise to criminal liability, as distinguished from the required mental state.

ASSAULT AND BATTERY Any unlawful touching of another person without justification or excuse.

RAPE Unlawful sexual intercourse with a woman by a man by means of fear or force and without her consent.

■═■

State v. Moorman

State (P) v. Rapist (D)

N.C. Sup. Ct. 320 N.C. 387, 358 S.E.2d 502 (1987).

NATURE OF CASE: Appeal from reversal of rape conviction.

FACT SUMMARY: Moorman (D) raped a woman while she was asleep in her dorm.

🏛 RULE OF LAW
The crime of rape is complete upon the mere showing of sexual intercourse with a person who is asleep, unconscious, or otherwise incapacitated and therefore cannot resist or give consent.

FACTS: Victim was out with friends and returned to her dorm room at 1:00 a.m. She fell asleep fully clothed. The victim dreamed she was engaging in sexual intercourse. She awoke to find Moorman (D) on top of her having vaginal intercourse with her. She tried to sit up, but he pushed her back down. Afraid her attacker might hurt her, she offered no further resistance. Thereafter, Moorman (D) engaged in anal intercourse with the victim. When the victim went to the door and turned on the light, Moorman (D) told her not to call the police. He told her that he was her roommate's friend, and that he thought she was her roommate and that he would not have engaged in the acts if he had known it was her and not her roommate. She did not report the incident until two days later, although she told several friends about the incident. The trial court convicted Moorman (D) of second-degree rape and sentenced him to 12 years in prison. The court of appeals reversed on the grounds that there was a fatal variance between the indictment and proof presented at trial. The State (P) appealed.

ISSUE: Is the crime of rape complete upon the mere showing of sexual intercourse with a person who is asleep, unconscious, or otherwise incapacitated and therefore cannot resist or give consent?

HOLDING AND DECISION: (Exum, C.J.) Yes. The crime of rape is complete upon the mere showing of sexual intercourse with a person who is asleep, unconscious, or otherwise incapacitated and therefore cannot resist or give consent. The court of appeals arrested judgment as to the charge of second-degree rape because it concluded that an indictment for the rape of one who is asleep must proceed on the theory that the victim was "physically helpless" under the N.C.G.S. and not on the theory that the rape was by force and against the will of the victim. The result in the court of appeals was that there is fatal variance between the indictment and the proof presented at trial, and the judgment was arrested. Although the state might have elected to proceed under the first

theory, it was not required to do so. The evidence in this case supports a conviction of rape on theory of force and lack of consent. Therefore, there was no fatal variance between the indictment and the proof. Reversed.

▶ ANALYSIS

Even in jurisdictions that retain force and resistance as independent requirements, a defendant will be guilty of some form of rape or sexual assault where he has sex with a victim who is categorically incapable of offering resistance or giving consent because of disability, unconsciousness at the time of the act, or youth.

■═■

Quicknotes

RAPE Unlawful sexual intercourse with a woman by a man by means of fear or force and without her consent.

■═■

Commonwealth v. Mlinarich

Commonwealth (P) v. Rapist (D)

Pa. Sup. Ct., 518 Pa. 247, 542 A.2d 1335 (1988).

NATURE OF CASE: Appeal from rape conviction.

FACT SUMMARY: Mlinarich (D), victim's adult guardian, threatened to recommit the victim, a fourteen-year old girl, to a juvenile detention facility unless she agreed to sexual intercourse and other sexual acts with him.

🏛 RULE OF LAW
Rape is when a person engages in sexual intercourse with another person not his spouse by forcible compulsion or by threat of forcible compulsion that would prevent resistance by a person of reasonable resolution.

FACTS: Mlinarich (D) was an adult guardian to a fourteen-year-old girl. He threatened to recommit her to a juvenile detention facility unless she agreed to sexual intercourse and other sexual acts with him. Mlinarich (D) was arrested and charged with multiple counts of attempted rape, involuntary deviate sexual intercourse, corruption of a minor, indecent exposure, and endangering the welfare of a minor. A jury convicted him of all the charges. On appeal, the superior court reversed. The prosecution appealed the reversals.

ISSUE: Does a person engaging in sexual intercourse with another person not his spouse by forcible compulsion or by threat of forcible compulsion that would prevent resistance by a person of reasonable resolution constitute rape?

HOLDING AND DECISION: (Nix, C.J.) Yes. Rape is when a person engages in sexual intercourse with another person not his spouse by forcible compulsion or by threat of forcible compulsion that would prevent resistance by a person of reasonable resolution. The critical distinction is where the compulsion overwhelms the will of the victim in contrast to a situation where the victim can make a deliberate choice to avoid the encounter even though the alternative may be an undesirable one. Indeed, the victim in this instance apparently found the prospect of being returned to the detention home a repugnant one. Notwithstanding, she was left with a choice and therefore the submission was a result of a deliberate choice and was not an involuntary act. It does not meet the test of "forcible compulsion" as required by statute. The purpose of the term "forcible compulsion" was to distinguish between assault upon the will and the forcing of the victim to make a choice regardless how repugnant. Certainly difficult choices have a coercive effect but the result is the product of the reason, albeit unpleasant and reluctantly made. The fact cannot be escaped that the victim has made the choice and the act is not involuntary. Affirmed.

DISSENT: (Larsen, J.) Has civilization fallen so far, have our values become so distorted and misplaced, as to leave a fourteen-year-old child without protection when she is forced to make such an awful "choice?" Here, the victim's "choice" was in no way a "deliberate" exercise of her free will and the product of reason.

▌ ANALYSIS

Justice Larsen was rightly incensed by this shocking decision when he wrote in his dissent, "Has civilization fallen so far, have our values become so distorted and misplaced, as to leave a fourteen-year-old child without protection when she is forced to make such an awful 'choice'?"

■══■

Quicknotes

RAPE Unlawful sexual intercourse with a woman by a man by means of fear or force and without her consent.

■══■

Boro v. People

Rapist (D) v. State (P)

Cal. Ct. App., 163 Cal. App. 3d 1224, 210 Cal. Rptr. 122 (1985).

NATURE OF CASE: [Not stated in facts.]

FACT SUMMARY: Boro (D) deceived Ms. R. into sexual intercourse with him by telling her he was a doctor and that her blood tests showed she had a fatal disease which could be cured by having sexual intercourse with an anonymous donor who had been injected with a disease-curing serum.

🏛 RULE OF LAW

Under California statutory law, rape is an act of sexual intercourse with a nonspouse accomplished where the victim is at the time unconscious of the nature of the act.

FACTS: Ms. R., the victim, received a telephone call from a "Dr. Stevens" (D) who said that he worked at Peninsula Hospital. He told Ms. R. that he had results of her blood test and that she had contracted a dangerous, highly infectious and perhaps fatal disease, that she could be sued as a result, and that the disease came from using public toilets. "Dr. Stevens" (D) further explained that there were only two ways to treat the disease. The first was a painful surgical procedure costing $9,000 and requiring her uninsured hospitalization for six weeks. The second alternative, "Dr. Stevens" (D) explained, was to have sexual intercourse with an anonymous donor who had been injected with a serum which would cure the disease. This procedure would cost only $4,500. When the victim replied she lacked sufficient funds, "Dr. Stevens" (D) suggested that $1,000 would suffice. Ms. R. agreed to the nonsurgical alternative and consented to intercourse with the mysterious donor, believing it was the only choice she had. After discussing her intentions with her work supervisor, the victim proceeded to the Hyatt Hotel in Burlingame as instructed, and contacted "Dr. Stevens" (D) by telephone. He was furious that she had informed her employer of the plan, threatened to terminate treatment, and instructed her to inform her employer she had decided not to go through with the treatment. Ms. R. did so, then withdrew $1,000 from her bank, and checked into another hotel and called "Dr. Stevens" to give him her room number. About a half hour later, the "donor" (D) arrived at her room. When Ms. R had undressed, the "donor" (D) had sexual intercourse with her. Boro (D) was apprehended when police arrived at the hotel room, having been called by Ms. R's supervisor. The People (P) contend that at the time of the intercourse, Ms. R. was unconscious of the nature of the act because of the misrepresentation that the act was a medical treatment and not a simple, ordinary act of sexual intercourse. Boro (D) contends that the victim was plainly aware of the nature of the act in which she was voluntarily engaged, so that her motivation is irrelevant.

ISSUE: Under California statutory law, is rape an act of sexual intercourse with a nonspouse accomplished where the victim is at the time unconscious of the nature of the act?

HOLDING AND DECISION: [Judge not stated in textbook excerpt.] Yes. Under California statutory law, rape is an act of sexual intercourse with a nonspouse accomplished where the victim is at the time unconscious of the nature of the act. If deception causes a misunderstanding as to the fact itself (fraud in the factum) there is no legally recognized consent because what happened is not that for which consent was given, whereas consent induced by fraud is as effective as any other consent, so far as direct and immediate legal consequences are concerned, if the deception relates not to the thing done but merely to some collateral matter (fraud in the inducement). In California, the language of the statute is plain. Rape does not include sexual intercourse with a nonspouse that has been brought about by deception. We cannot entertain the slightest doubt that the legislature well understood how to draft a statute to encompass fraud in the factum and how to specify certain fraud in the inducement as vitiating consent. Ms. R. precisely understood the nature of the act, but motivated by a fear of disease and death, succumbed to Boro's (D) fraudulent blandishments. To so conclude is not to vitiate the heartless cruelty of Boro's (D) scheme, but to say that it comprised crimes of a different order than rape under the statute in question.

▶ ANALYSIS

Boro (D), who engaged in the same conduct with several other women, became notoriously known as "Dr. Feelgood" in the California media. He proved unrepentant and repeated this scheme with another victim. In the interim, however, the California legislature had enacted law specifically criminalizing this kind of conduct. In 1987, Boro (D) was prosecuted under the new statute.

■═■

Quicknotes

FRAUD IN THE FACTUM Occurs when a testator is induced to execute a testamentary instrument as a result of a misrepresentation as to the nature of the document or its provisions.

Continued on next page.

FRAUD IN THE INDUCEMENT Occurs when a testator is induced to execute a testamentary instrument as a result of the misrepresentation of certain facts existing at the time of its creation that may have affected the manner in which the testator disposed of his property.

RAPE Unlawful sexual intercourse with a woman by a man by means of fear or force and without her consent.

■══■

Commonwealth v. Fischer

State (P) v. Student rapist (D)

Pa. Super. Ct. 721 A.2d 1111 (1998).

NATURE OF CASE: Appeal on ruling in favor of rape victim on the issue of mens rea.

FACT SUMMARY: Fischer (D), a college student, engaged in intimate contact in a dorm room after which Fischer (D) was charged with and convicted of sexual assault, a decision which he later appealed on the basis that he should not be convicted if he believed the victim had given her consent.

🏛 RULE OF LAW
A defendant's subjective belief that a victim consented to sexual conduct is not a defense to the crime of rape.

FACTS: Fischer (D) and the victim were freshman students at the same college. They went into Fischer's (D) dorm room and engaged in intimate contact for a brief period before parting ways to eat dinner with separate groups of friends. Fischer (D) characterized this encounter as "rough sex" involving intimate contact, while the victim described the activity as light "kissing and fondling." After dinner, the two met again in Fischer's (D) room. Fischer (D) alleges he was encouraged by the victim to continue with the activity from the previous encounter, while the victim asserts that she was forcibly pushed onto the bed after protesting. Fischer (D) was charged with sexual assault. At trial, he asserted that he was sexually inexperienced and believed that the victim was a willing participant in the sexual encounters. In addition, Fischer (D) asserted that the victim's willing conduct did not make his actions "forcible" and that he desisted once the victim protested. The jury found Fischer (D) guilty, after which he filed this appeal, suggesting that his counsel at trial had provided ineffective assistance because he had failed to assert a mistake of fact defense based on Fischer's (D) belief that the victim had given her consent.

ISSUE: Is a defendant's subjective belief that a victim consented to sexual conduct a defense to the crime of rape?

HOLDING AND DECISION: (Beck, J.) No. A defendant's subjective belief that a victim consented to sexual conduct is not a defense to the crime of rape. When an individual uses threats or force to have sex with another person without that person's consent, that individual commits the crime of rape. The issues of consent and forcible compulsion are complex, requiring an analysis of the psychological and physiological dimensions of the encounter. The degree of force required to constitute rape depends on the facts and particular circumstances of each case. Force vitiating consent may include psychological, moral, and intellectual force. In addition, the young age of a victim may void consent regardless of the circumstances. However, we cannot find support for Fischer's (D) assertion that the subjective belief of a defendant that consent has been given is an adequate defense, based on the applicable and binding precedent as enunciated in Commonwealth v. Williams. There, the court refused to create such a defense. This case is distinguishable from Williams because it involves intimate contact between acquaintances, where Williams involved a sexual encounter between a victim and a stranger. However, in both cases the victim alleged physical force and the defendant claimed he reasonably believed he had consent. As with the court in Williams, we do not recognize Fischer's (D) belief as an adequate basis for a defense based on mistake of fact, and are not persuaded that defense counsel performed ineffectively during trial. Affirmed.

▶ ANALYSIS

Although Fisher (D) failed to convince the court otherwise, the opinion does note that courts elsewhere have provided jury instructions regarding the reasonableness of a defendant's belief as to the consent of the victim. The court in the present case found these opinions convincing, but procedurally refused to depart from the specific ruling in Williams, which it found binding based on the aforementioned similarity of facts. As was mentioned in the opinion, the Williams court recognized that creation of laws and defenses were tasks for the legislature, and so refused to create what amounted to a new law. In cognizance of this, the court in the present case affirmed Fischer's (D) conviction because it could not fault Fischer's (D) attorney for failing to predict that such a law should be created.

■━■

Quicknotes

MENS REA Criminal intent.

MISTAKE OF FACT An unintentional mistake in knowing or recalling a fact without the will to deceive.

RAPE Unlawful sexual intercourse with a woman by a man by means of fear or force and without her consent.

SEPARATION OF POWERS The system of checks and balances preventing one branch of government from infringing upon exercising the powers of another branch of government.

■━■

Theft Offenses

Quick Reference Rules of Law

Commonwealth v. Mitchneck

State (P) v. Coal mine owner (D)

Pa. Super. Ct., 130 Pa. Super. 433, 198 A. 463 (1938).

NATURE OF CASE: Appeal from conviction for fraudulent conversion.

FACT SUMMARY: Mitchneck (D) contended that his actions in withholding payment of money may have been actionable civilly, but were not criminal in nature.

🏛 RULE OF LAW
Fraudulent conversion is committed through the fraudulent withholding of property from one who has a possessory interest therein.

FACTS: Mitchneck (D) owned a coal mine and agreed with a store owner to deduct from his employee's wages amounts used to purchase goods and then turn the amounts over to the storekeeper. Mitchneck (D) withheld the amounts but failed to turn the money over, and he was charged with and convicted of fraudulent conversion. He appealed, contending that his actions only constituted a civil rather than criminal breach.

ISSUE: Is fraudulent conversion committed through the intentionally wrongful withholding of property from one who has a possessory interest therein?

HOLDING AND DECISION: (Keller, J.) Yes. Fraudulent conversion is committed through the intentionally wrongful withholding of property from one who has a possessory interest therein. The employees in this case were owed a debt, yet they had no possessory interest in the money. Thus, the money did not belong to the employees and their assignment to the store transferred only the right to collect the debt. Thus no criminal conduct occurred. Reversed.

▌ ANALYSIS

This case illustrates the difference between civil liability and criminal guilt. The creditor cannot invoke the power of the state to collect a private debt. To allow such would invite the return of the debtor's prison.

■═■

Quicknotes

POSSESSORY INTEREST The right to possess particular real property to the exclusion of others.

■═■

The Case of The Carrier Who Broke Bulk Anon v. The Sheriff of London

Bailee (D) v. Government (P)

Star Chamber (1473). YB. Pasch.13 Edw.IV, f.9, pl. 5 (1473), 64 Selden Soc. 30 (1945).

NATURE OF CASE: Trial for felony theft.

FACT SUMMARY: A bailee (D) broke open the package with which he was entrusted with and converted the goods inside.

🏛 RULE OF LAW
Bailees who break open their entrusted packages and convert the contents are not guilty of felony theft.

FACTS: A man (D) agreed to carry bales of woad (a type of dye) and other things to Southampton for another man. The bailee (D) then opened the bales, took the goods, and converted them to his own use. The issue at trial was whether this constituted felony theft. The defense argued that bailees with legal possession cannot feloniously steal those goods. The prosecution argued that by breaking open the bales, the man committed a felony.

ISSUE: Are bailees who break open their entrusted packages and convert the contents guilty of felony theft?

HOLDING AND DECISION: (Bryan, [C.J.C.P.]) No. Bailees who break open their entrusted packages and convert the contents are not guilty of felony theft. The bailee (D) was given possession of the package and therefore cannot be guilty of anything except in an action of detinue.

(Chokke, J.C.P.) Possession of the goods within the bulk package is not given to a bailee. The bailee cannot be guilty of felony theft for converting the bulk package in his own possession; the package contents were not entrusted into his care. Accordingly, when a bailee breaks open a bulk package, the bailee commits felony theft of the contents. The bailee (D) in the present case is guilty.

(The Chancellor) All judges hold that bailees who break open their entrusted packages and convert the contents are not guilty of felony theft.

DISSENT: (Nedeham, J.K.B.) A bailee can feloniously convert the package contents just as a man may feloniously convert his own possessions. Possession does not excuse the felony. A man cannot convert themug in which a tavern owner serves him a drink although the drink itself is the man's possession.

▌ ANALYSIS

This case, decided in 1473, was a major decision in the development of theft and larceny. It was the first decision to consider a bailee's to liability for larceny. The distinction between possession and custody of goods remains the foundation of modern statutory theft offenses.

Quicknotes

BAILEE Person holding property in trust for another party.

FELONY A criminal offense of greater seriousness than a misdemeanor; felonies are generally defined pursuant to statute as any crime that is punishable by death or by a term of imprisonment exceeding one year.

LARCENY The illegal taking of another's property with the intent to deprive the owner thereof.

Rex v. Chisser

Government (P) v. Customer (D)

K.B. (1678). T.Raym 275, 83 Eng. Rep. 142.

NATURE OF CASE: Appeal from jury verdict of guilty in felony larceny trial.

FACT SUMMARY: Chisser (D), after asking a sales clerk to see two items, ran out of the shop without paying for the merchandise.

🏛 RULE OF LAW
Leaving a store with merchandise a sales clerk has offered for inspection shows an intent to steal and is a felony.

FACTS: Abraham Chisser (D) went into the shop of Anne Charteris and asked to see two crevats. She handed him the crevats to look at and told him the price. He offered her a lower price and immediately ran out of the shop with the crevats.

ISSUE: Is leaving a store with merchandise a sales clerk has offered for inspection a felony?

HOLDING AND DECISION: [Judge not stated in textbook excerpt.] Yes. Leaving a store with merchandise a sales clerk has offered for inspection shows an intent to steal and is a felony. There was no completed contract between the parties in this case, and the goods were still in Charteris's possession even though she had handed them to Chisser (D) to inspect. Chisser's (D) running away with the goods in the presence of Charteris reveals the same intent to steal as if he had taken the goods while no one was in the shop. Chisser (D) committed a felony.

▶ ANALYSIS

The common law elements of larceny were: (1) a trespassory taking and carrying away of property, (2) from the possession of another, (3) with the intent to permanently deprive the owner of the property. Because of the "trespassory taking" requirement, determining when possession passed from the owner of the property to the thief was a critical issue. This case was among the first to expand the interpretation of the "trespassory taking" requirement from its literal meaning.

■═■

Quicknotes

FELONY A criminal offense of greater seriousness than a misdemeanor; felonies are generally defined pursuant to statute as any crime that is punishable by death or by a term of imprisonment exceeding one year.

LARCENY The illegal taking of another's property with the intent to deprive the owner thereof.

■═■

The King v. Pear

Government (P) v. Horse thief (D)

Ct. for Crown Cases Reserved, 1 Leach 211, 168 Eng. Rep. 208 (1779).

NATURE OF CASE: Appeal of larceny conviction.

FACT SUMMARY: Pear (D) hired a horse for a trip, but immediately sold it without going on the trip.

🏛 RULE OF LAW
Trespass for larceny may be accomplished by fraud where the taking involved is done by a trick to gain possession of property, and with the intent to steal.

FACTS: Pear (D) rented a horse from Samuel Finch, stating his intention to make a journey to another town and return that night. He never returned, but, rather, sold the horse that same day. Pear (D) was indicted for larceny (horse stealing). At trial, the jury found that Pear (D) had intended to sell the horse from the beginning. Upon conviction, he appealed, contending that his acts did not constitute the crime of larceny.

ISSUE: Is the crime of larceny committed when possession of property is altered by some fraud (trick) and not by physical trespass?

HOLDING AND DECISION: (Ashhurst, J.) Yes. Trespass for larceny may be accomplished by fraud where the taking involved is done by a trick to gain possession of property and with the intent to steal. The taking by fraud does not alter the nature of the victim's possession of the property at the time of the crime. Even though the victim's act of parting with the property is deliberate, the fact that he was induced to do so by fraud negates his intent to transfer possession. As such, the taking from him of his property is trespassory in that it is done against his actual will. Here, Pear (D) intended, at the time of renting the horse, to sell it. Finch did not give it to him for that purpose. As such, the taking of the horse with the intent to sell it was a trespass against the property of Finch. The conviction must stand.

▶ ANALYSIS

This case points out the generally accepted relationship between the larceny requirement of a "trespass in the taking" and the use of fraud to effect such a trespass. The trespass, of course, is to an interest in the property of another (possession or ownership). The crime was larceny in the case above because there was a trespass to the owner's "ownership" interest in the taking (legally) of his "possessory" interest in the property. If the taking had been of the full ownership interest (title), the crime would not have been larceny since there would have been no trespass to any property interest of the owner. Note, finally, that the word "stealing" when used in the name of a crime generally denotes the crime of larceny. Thus, horse stealing is larceny of a horse. "Intent to steal," however, for larceny, generally denotes the "intent to permanently deprive."

■=■

Quicknotes

FRAUD A false representation of facts with the intent that another will rely on the misrepresentation to his detriment.

LARCENY The illegal taking of another's property with the intent to deprive the owner thereof.

TRESPASS Unlawful interference with, or damage to, the real or personal property of another.

■=■

People v. Sattlekau

State (P) v. Solicitor (D)

Sup. Ct. N.Y., App. Div., 120 App. Div. 42, 104 N.Y.S. 805 (1907).

NATURE OF CASE: Appeal from conviction of grand larceny by false pretenses.

FACT SUMMARY: Sattlekau (D) induced a woman to give him $1,000 for a phony hotel investment after placing a personal ad in the newspaper for the possibility of marriage.

🏛 RULE OF LAW
The elements of larceny by false pretenses are a deliberate intention to defraud, the representation of false pretenses, and the reliance of the victim upon such pretenses.

FACTS: Sattlekau (D) placed a personal ad in the newspaper soliciting women for a housekeeping position in his hotel as well as the possibility of marriage. He signed the ad "Bachelor." Rosa Kaiser responded and they corresponded by mail before arranging to meet for an interview. Over the course of their correspondence, Sattlekau (D) told Kaiser that his name was Ernest Paul, that he was unmarried, that he owned a hotel, and that he was in need of $1,000 for the purposes of purchasing another hotel, which would become their home. Kaiser gave Sattlekau (D) the money and shortly thereafter received a letter stating that there had been a fire at the hotel and that she would need to wait for him for a while. Sattlekau (D) was arrested after setting up an "interview" with another woman, and a jury convicted him of larceny by false pretenses. Sattlekau (D) appealed, alleging that the indictment was defective and the elements of the charge had not been proven.

ISSUE: Are the elements of larceny by false pretenses a deliberate intention to defraud, the representation of false pretenses, and the reliance of the victim upon such pretenses?

HOLDING AND DECISION: (Clarke, J.) Yes. The elements of larceny by false pretenses are a deliberate intention to defraud, the representation of false pretenses, and the reliance of the victim upon such pretenses. Kaiser's testimony at trial, along with Sattlekau's (D) own admissions on several issues, fully supports the conviction. Sattlekau (D) made several key misrepresentations, i.e., that he was not married, that he was the proprietor of a hotel, and that the hotel he named and used in his ads and letterhead was located in Pennsylvania. Kaiser, in parting with her money, relied upon Sattlekau's (D) false representations. The deliberate intent to defraud, the falsity of the pretenses made, and the reliance by Kaiser were fully established at trial and alleged in the indictment. Affirmed.

▶ ANALYSIS

This case was prosecuted under 18 U.S.C. § 1341, the mail fraud statute. The statute's broad scope has been used to prosecute numerous cases involving schemes to defraud sent or delivered through the U.S. Postal Service. In addition, there is a parallel wire fraud statute, 18 U.S.C. § 1343, which covers schemes to defraud transmitted via wire, radio, or television.

Quicknotes

FALSE PRETENSES The unlawful obtaining of money or property from another with an intent to defraud and with the utilization of false representations.

Durland v. United States

Bond fund operator (D) v. Federal government (P)

161 U.S. 306 (1896).

NATURE OF CASE: Appeal from conviction of federal mail fraud.

FACT SUMMARY: Durland (D) was charged with running a dishonest bond fund for which he solicited participation through mailed brochures promising return rates of 50% in only six months.

🏛 **RULE OF LAW**
The fact that a scheme to defraud was not effective in that it did not induce reliance by any victim does not preclude prosecution for federal mail fraud.

FACTS: Durland (D) mailed brochures from the Provident Bond and Investment Company with which he would trick individuals into "investing" a small amount of money each month, promising very large returns. He claimed the rates went up the longer the money was left in the fund and that they would reach as high as 50 percent in six months. At trial, it was found that Durland (D) was running a scheme to defraud and that he had no intention of the "bonds" ever maturing. Durland (D) was convicted under the U.S. mail fraud statute, 18 U.S.C. § 1341. On appeal, Durland (D) argued that the statute does not apply to him because at common law the definition of false pretenses applied only to the representation of existing facts, not to a mere promise regarding the future.

ISSUE: Does the fact that a scheme to defraud did not induce reliance by any victim preclude prosecution for federal mail fraud?

HOLDING AND DECISION: (Brewer, J.) No. The fact that a scheme to defraud was not effective in that it did not induce reliance by any victim does not preclude prosecution for federal mail fraud. The scope of the mail fraud statute is very broad, and a scheme can be promoted through representations or promises of future rewards. Just because no one was issued the phony bonds does not mean that Durland (D) can escape charges. The record clearly reflected that Durland (D) had no intention of making an honest effort at investing the money he received. Therefore, his intent to defraud was sufficient to justify punishment. Affirmed.

▌ *ANALYSIS*

Following *Durland*, other courts have held that although actual injury need not be proven, the government does have to show that the defendant intended harm or injury. In *United States v. Regent Office Supply, Inc.*, 421 F.2d 1174 (2d Cir. 1970), a salesman who falsely stated that he had been referred by a customer's friends was found not guilty because the representations had no bearing on the quality of the merchandise he was selling. Even though the salesman's misrepresentations may have played a part in inducing his customers to make purchases, the court found no actual injury because the goods were what he said they were.

■■■

Quicknotes

FALSE PRETENSES The unlawful obtaining of money or property from another with an intent to defraud and with the utilization of false representations.

■■■

People v. Dioguardi

State (P) v. Extortionist (D)

N.Y. Ct. App., 8 N.Y. 2d 260, 203 N.Y.S.2d 870 (1960).

NATURE OF CASE: Appeal from reversal of several extortion convictions.

FACT SUMMARY: Dioguardi (D) was convicted of extortion for taking money to ensure against labor disputes.

🏛 RULE OF LAW
Extortion is committed by obtaining property by a wrongful use of fear, induced by a threat to do an unlawful injury.

FACTS: Dioguardi (D), through a front man, guaranteed a peaceful resolution to Kerin's labor problems if he was retained as a labor consultant. Kerin paid the retainer for some time before going to the district attorney. Dioguardi (D) was convicted of extortion, yet his conviction was overturned on appeal. The State of New York (P) appealed the reversal.

ISSUE: Is extortion committed by obtaining property by a wrongful use of fear, induced by a threat to do an unlawful injury?

HOLDING AND DECISION: (Froessel, J.) Yes. Extortion is committed by obtaining property by a wrongful use of fear, induced by a threat to do an unlawful injury. Kerin was fearful that the labor problems would drive him out of business. Dioguardi (D) used this fear by wrongfully threatening continued problems unless payment was made. Thus the elements of the crime were established. Reversed.

▶ *ANALYSIS*

The court indicated that the defendant need not have created the events instilling the fear. Further, fear of economic injury is sufficient to meet the second element. It was sufficient that the defendant controlled the situation to an extent that he could end the problem causing the fear.

■═■

Quicknotes

EXTORTION The unlawful taking of property of another by threats of force.

■═■

McCormick v. United States

Legislator (D) Federal government (P)

500 U.S. 257 (1991).

NATURE OF CASE: Appeal from conviction of extortion under color of official right.

FACT SUMMARY: McCormick (D), a member of the West Virginia House of Delegates, was charged with extortion when he supported a bill to grant foreign doctors medical licenses after he had received cash gifts from an organization of the doctors.

🏛 RULE OF LAW
In order to convict an elected official under the Hobbs Act, it is necessary to prove that payments were made in return for an explicit promise by the official to perform or not to perform an official act.

FACTS: McCormick (D) was a member of the West Virginia House of Delegates and represented a district that had long suffered from a shortage of medical doctors. For several years, the State had allowed doctors who had graduated from foreign medical schools to practice under temporary permits while they studied for the State's licensing exam, and McCormick (D) had supported this program. In 1984, when there was a move to end the program, several of the foreign doctors formed an organization to represent their interests and hired Vandergrift as their lobbyist. Vandergrift met with McCormick (D) and they discussed the possibility of introducing a bill that would grant the doctors permanent medical licenses by virtue of their years of experience. During his reelection campaign later that year, McCormick (D) contacted Vandergrift and informed him that his campaign was very expensive and that he had not heard anything from the doctors. Shortly thereafter, on four occasions, Vandergrift delivered envelopes containing cash payments from the doctors to McCormick (D). McCormick (D) never listed the contributions on his income tax returns, and the doctors' records did not list them as campaign contributions but referred to them only by initials and symbols. In 1985, McCormick (D) sponsored the legislation previously discussed with Vandergrift, and the bill was ultimately enacted into law. Two weeks after the bill's enactment, McCormick (D) received another cash payment. McCormick (D) was indicted on five counts of violating the Hobbs Act by extorting payments under color of official right. McCormick (D) was convicted at trial under the Hobbs Act on one count, receiving the first payment, but a mistrial was declared on the other counts. The court of appeals affirmed the conviction and the United States Supreme Court granted certiorari.

ISSUE: In order to convict an elected official under the Hobbs Act, is it necessary to prove that payments were made in return for an explicit promise by the official to perform or not to perform an official act?

HOLDING AND DECISION: (White, J.) Yes. In order to convict an elected official under the Hobbs Act, 18 U.S.C. § 1951, it is necessary to prove that payments were made in return for an explicit promise by the official to perform or not to perform an official act. The nature of politics requires that campaigns be run and financed. While there are ethical considerations at issue, to hold that legislators commit the federal crime of extortion when they act for the benefit of constituents, or support legislation furthering the interests of their constituents, would be an improper interpretation of what Congress had in mind in drafting the Hobbs Act. Although there may be situations in which an elected official could be held to have violated the Hobbs Act, proof of a quid pro quo would be required. The court of appeals erred in holding that a quid pro quo was not necessary. Reversed and remanded.

▶ ANALYSIS

The Court was careful to distinguish the regular solicitation of campaign contributions from the crime of extortion. The Court understood that to have accepted the Government's (P) claim that a quid pro quo was not required would have meant that every politician who accepted a contribution from a lobbyist whose cause they support commits extortion. While skeptics may argue that they do, the Court seems to have reached the only possible conclusion short of a complete revision of the campaign and lobby system.

■=■

Quicknotes

QUID PRO QUO What for what; in the contract context, used synonymously with consideration to refer to the mutual promises between two parties rendering a contract enforceable.

■=■

Lear v. State

Robber (D) v. State (P)

Ariz. Sup. Ct. 39 Ariz. 313, 6 P.2d 426 (1931).

NATURE OF CASE: Appeal from a robbery conviction.

FACT SUMMARY: When Lear (D) was convicted of robbery for grabbing a bag of silver from the victim, Lear (D) argued that the elements of the crime of robbery were not present since he used no force or fear.

🏛 RULE OF LAW
A taking must be accomplished by force or fear to constitute robbery.

FACTS: Lear (D) entered the shop of George Gross. Gross had placed a bag of silver on the sales counter. While Gross was untying the bag, Lear grabbed the bag from Gross's hands and ran out the back door. Lear (D) said no word at the time, exhibited no arms, and used no force other than to grab the bag. Lear (D) was tried and convicted of robbery and appealed, arguing that the facts did not sustain a robbery conviction since there was no evidence that the taking of the bag was by force or fear.

ISSUE: Must a taking be accomplished by force or fear to constitute robbery?

HOLDING AND DECISION: (Ross, J.) Yes. A taking must be accomplished by force or fear to constitute robbery. The crimes of robbery and larceny are not the same. The former is classified as a crime against the person and the latter as a crime against property. In robbery there is, in addition to the felonious taking, a violent invasion of the person. If the victim is not made to surrender the possession of the personal property by means of force or fear, the key element of robbery is not present. In the instant case, the element of force or fear is absent. Lear (D) made no threat or demonstration. He simply grabbed the bag of silver from the hands of George Gross and ran away with it. There was no pulling or scrambling for possession of the bag. This was not the type of force necessary to constitute robbery because it was not of such a nature as to show it was intended to overpower the party robbed and prevent his resisting. "Snatching, as here, which is sufficient asportation in simple larceny, may or may not carry with it the added violence of robbery . . . ." (Bishop on Criminal Law, Ninth Edition, Vol. 2, page 864, section 1167.) In this case, no violence or fear was manifested, hence the evidence was insufficient to sustain the conviction for robbery. Reversed.

▶ ANALYSIS

The force or intimidation of a robbery usually must occur during the course of the commission of the theft. Common law courts often interpreted this rule narrowly to require that the harmful or threatening behavior occur during the actual "taking" and, further, that the taking be successfully completed. In contrast, Model Penal Code § 222.1 has interpreted this requirement broadly to include force or intimidation occurring during an attempted theft or during flight from a completed or attempted crime. The Model Penal Code takes the position that the primary concern is with the physical danger or threat of danger to the citizen and not the property aspects of the crime.

Quicknotes

FORCE The exercise of power over a person or thing.

ROBBERY The unlawful taking of property from the person of another through the use of force or fear.

State v. Colvin

State (P) v. Burglar (D)

Minn. Sup. Ct., 645 N.W.2d 449 (2002).

NATURE OF CASE: Appeal from a burglary conviction.

FACT SUMMARY: When Peter Colvin (D) was convicted of burglary for violating the no-entry provision of a protective order, he argued that his mere entry was insufficient to establish the independent crime of burglary.

🏛 RULE OF LAW
Violation of the no-entry provision of a protective order is not sufficient to establish the independent crime element of burglary.

FACTS: Michelle obtained an emergency statutory order for protection (OFP) against her ex-husband, Peter Colvin (D), containing a provision that Colvin (D) was not permitted to enter Michelle's residence. When Colvin (D) violated the order by entering her residence, he was charged with, and convicted of, violation of the OFP and first-degree burglary. The intermediate appellate court affirmed, and Colvin (D) appealed, arguing that his wrongful entry with the intent to violate the OFP was insufficient to establish the crime of burglary absent the commission of, or intent to commit, any crime other than the OFP violation.

ISSUE: Is violation of the no-entry provision of a protective order sufficient to establish the independent crime element of burglary?

HOLDING AND DECISION: (Lancaster, J.) No. Violation of the no-entry provision of a protective order is not sufficient to establish the independent crime element of burglary. Trespass cannot serve as the crime committed or intended to be committed to establish burglary. To allow an intent to commit a trespass to satisfy the requirement of intent to commit a crime would mean that a mere trespasser who had no intent other than to enter or remain in a building without the consent of the owner could be convicted of burglary. Like trespass, the violation of a no-entry provision of an order for protection is excluded from the crimes that can be the bases for the independent crime of burglary. Both offenses are designed to protect the interests that are invaded by the unauthorized entry that the burglar makes. Thus both trespass and violation of the no-entry provision of an OFP satisfy the legal entry element of burglary. Further, both offenses are complete upon entry. However, the same entry is insufficient to satisfy both the illegal entry element of the burglary statute and the independent-crime requirement. Under the statute, for a burglary conviction to stand, the State must prove that a defendant intended to commit some independent crime other than mere trespass. Reversed.

DISSENT: (Anderson, J.) If the state has misused its charging authority given the facts in this case, that action should be addressed directly rather than through a strained interpretation of the district court's straightforward ruling.

▶ ANALYSIS

In *Colvin*, the Court noted that if the legislature wanted to sanction violation of an OFP based solely on entering a home similarly to first-degree burglary—with a presumptive sentence of 48 months for a first-time offender—it could do so by amending the appropriate statute.

■═■

Quicknotes

BURGLARY Unlawful entry of a building at night with the intent to commit a felony therein.

PROTECTIVE ORDER Court order protecting a party against potential abusive treatment through use of the legal process.

TRESPASS Unlawful interference with, or damage to, the real or personal property of another.

■═■

Perjury, False Statements, and Obstruction of Justice

Quick Reference Rules of Law

Bronston v. United States

Convicted perjurer (D) v. Federal government (P)

409 U.S. 352 (1973).

NATURE OF CASE: Petition for certiorari on federal question arising out of perjury conviction.

FACT SUMMARY: Samuel Bronston (D), sole owner of Samuel Bronston Productions, Inc., arranged for his corporation to enter bankruptcy proceedings. During the bankruptcy hearing, he testified in response to a question about his personal bank accounts. The testimony was literally true but implied a falsity. Bronston (D) was convicted of perjury and he petitioned for a writ of certiorari.

🏛 RULE OF LAW
A witness may not be convicted of perjury for an answer, under oath, that is literally true but not responsive to the question asked and arguably misleading by negative implication.

FACTS: Samuel Bronston (D) was the sole owner of Samuel Bronston Productions, Inc., which produces motion pictures in European countries. Bronston (D) opened and directed bank accounts in multiple European banks on behalf of the corporation. In 1962, for example, the corporation transacted with 37 bank accounts in 5 countries. The corporation petitioned for Chapter 11 bankruptcy protection. At the hearing, Bronston (D) gave the following testimony to questions asked by a creditor's attorney:

Q. Do you have any bank accounts in Swiss banks, Mr. Bronston?
A. No, sir.
Q. Have you ever?
A. The company had an account there for about six months, in Zurich.

Bronston (D) had a personal bank account in Geneva, Switzerland, for about five years. Prosecutors charged Bronston (D) with perjury under 18 U.S.C. § 1621 because his second answer, while literally truthful (i.e., the company did have an account in Zurich for about six months), implied that he did not ever personally have any Swiss bank accounts. The jury convicted Bronston (D) after being instructed in part that conviction was appropriate if the answer was not literally false but constituted a false statement in context. Bronston (D) appealed and the court of appeals affirmed his conviction. The United States Supreme Court accepted the case on a writ of certiorari to address the application of § 1621 to a nonresponsive and arguably misleading answer.

ISSUE: May a witness be convicted of perjury for an answer, under oath, that is literally true but not responsive to the question asked and arguably misleading by negative implication?

HOLDING AND DECISION: (Burger, C.J.) No. A witness may not be convicted of perjury for an answer, under oath, that is literally true but not responsive to the question asked and arguably misleading by negative implication. Bronston (D) asserted at trial and in his appeal that he could not be convicted of perjury because his answer was admittedly truthful. The trial court and the court of appeals held that perjury occurs when the truthful statement is intentionally given in place of a responsive answer as a means to lie by negative implication. Section 1621 cannot apply, however, to Bronston's (D) answer. The statute defines perjury as a willful statement not believed to be true. Bronston's statement was believed by him to be, and was in fact, true. It was the examining lawyer's responsibility to note the evasiveness of Bronston's (D) answer and clarify whether Bronston (D) had personal Swiss bank accounts. It is not the place of the jury to determine whether Bronston (D) intended to mislead or deceive; the jury can only consider the actual answer given and whether the witness believed it to be true. Section 1621 must be read in its historical context as well. The French imposed capital punishment on perjurers because no witnesses for the accused were called and it was thus imperative that the truth be spoken on the stand by the accusers. The English tradition called for pillorying as the significantly lesser punishment for perjury because witnesses for both sides appeared and filled out the details of a case. This statute is in the Anglo-American tradition because the courts have other safeguards in place against false testimony. Congress did not intend § 1621 to cover false statements by negative implication. The witness must be made aware that his or her answer was misleading or non-responsive and given an opportunity to correct the error. The remedy is a new question, not a perjury conviction. Reversed.

▶ *ANALYSIS*

This case switches the responsibility for the "evasive" answer from the witness to the questioner. One result of the case was the belief that the witness could now lie with impunity if the answer was carefully crafted, but the focused attorney should always catch a non-responsive answer and ask a follow-up question designed to get an affirmative response. A famous case that involved the so-called *Bronston* defense was the President Bill Clinton impeachment case in which President Clinton invoked

Continued on next page.

the defense to the perjury charges because his answers may have been evasive but were technically true.

■■■

Quicknotes

CERTIORARI A discretionary writ issued by a superior court to an inferior court in order to review the lower court's decisions; the Supreme Court's writ ordering such review.

PERJURY The making of false statements under oath.

■■■

United States v. Moore

Federal government (P) v. False form-signer (D)

612 F.3d 698 (D.C. Cir. 2010).

NATURE OF CASE: Appeal from conviction for a false statement based on insufficiency of the evidence as to "materiality."

FACT SUMMARY: Moore (D) was convicted of making a materially false statement because he signed a false name on a United States Postal Service delivery form. While Moore (D) admitted he willfully signed a false name, he argued that no rational jury could have found the false name was "material" to warrant a conviction.

RULE OF LAW
A false statement is sufficiently material if it has a natural tendency to influence, or is capable of influencing, either a discrete decision or any other function of the agency to which it was addressed.

FACTS: As part of an investigation, inspectors from the United States Postal Service intercepted a package containing drugs addressed to a female at an address. A "controlled delivery" was made by an undercover postal inspector to the address. When no one answered, the inspector prepared to fill out a Postal Service form notifying the addressee that a parcel was waiting and could be obtained by picking it up or by arranging for another delivery. Moore (D) arrived before the form could be completed and accepted delivery of the package by signing a false name. Moore (D) admitted at trial that he signed the delivery form using a false name, but argued it was not a materially false statement. Moore (D) was convicted of making a materially false statement in violation of 18 U.S.C. § 1001(a)(2).

ISSUE: Is a false statement sufficiently material if it has a natural tendency to influence, or is capable of influencing, either a discrete decision or any other function of the agency to which it was addressed?

HOLDING AND DECISION: (Ginsburg, J.) Yes. A false statement is sufficiently material to have a natural tendency to influence, or is capable of influencing, either a discrete decision or any other function of the agency to which it was addressed. To prove Moore (D) made a statement in violation the criminal code, the Government (P) must show he (1) "knowingly and willfully" (2) "[made] any materially false, fictitious, or fraudulent statement or representation" (3) in a "matter within the jurisdiction of the executive . . . branch of the Government of the United States." In determining whether a false statement is material, the issue is whether the statement has a tendency to influence a discrete decision of the body to which it was addressed. The evidence showed the name

that Moore (D) signed was immaterial to the undercover postal inspector's decision to deliver the package to him. While the statement need not actually influence an agency in order to be material; it need only have "a natural tendency to influence, or [be] capable of influencing" an agency function or decision. Moore's (D's) false statement was capable of affecting the Postal Service's general function of tracking packages and identifying the recipients of packages entrusted to it. Moore's (D's) use of a false name also could have impeded the ability of the Postal Service to investigate the trafficking of narcotics through the mails. Affirmed.

ANALYSIS

The "materiality" element to support a conviction for making a false statement requires only a showing of a tendency to influence a discrete decision of the body to which it was addressed. Here, the effect on the undercover postal inspector was immaterial, as Moore's signing a false name on a delivery form would disrupt the general function of the Postal Service to tracking packages and identifying the recipients. Ironically, the court explained the false name given by Moore (D) was "material" because it could have prevented the Postal Service from identifying and locating him in pursuit of its investigation.

Brogan v. United Sates

Union officer (D) v. Federal government (P)

522 U.S. 398 (1998).

NATURE OF CASE: Writ of certiorari to address federal question.

FACT SUMMARY: James Brogan (D), a union officer, accepted payments from a company whose employees he represented. Federal agents visited his home and asked him questions about the payments. Brogan (D) answered "no" when asked if he accepted payments from the particular corporation while he was a union officer.

> 🏛 **RULE OF LAW**
> There is no exception to criminal liability for a false statement to a federal agency that consists of a mere denial of wrongdoing, the "exculpatory no."

FACTS: James Brogan (D) was a union officer in 1987 and 1988. JRD Management Corporation (JRD) was a real estate company whose employees the union represented. JRD gave cash payments to Brogan (D). The Internal Revenue Service and Department of Labor began investigating JRD. During the investigation, federal agents visited Brogan's (D) home and asked him several questions. Brogan (D) answered "no" when asked if he accepted payments from JRD while he was a union officer. Prosecutors charged Brogan (D) with, *inter alia*, making a false statement to federal agents in violation of 18 U.S.C. § 1001. The jury convicted Brogan (D) and the court of appeals affirmed his conviction. The United States Supreme Court granted certiorari on the federal question of whether the "exculpatory no" was an exception to the criminal offense in 18 U.S.C. § 1001.

ISSUE: Is there an exception to criminal liability for a false statement to a federal agency that consists of a mere denial of wrongdoing, the "exculpatory no"?

HOLDING AND DECISION: (Scalia, J.) No. There is no exception to criminal liability for a false statement to a federal agency that consists of a mere denial of wrongdoing, the "exculpatory no." Section 1001 covers "any" false statement and Brogan (D) concedes he is guilty of the literal reading of the statute. Brogan (D) asserts, however, that the Court should adopt the more expansive reading adopted by several circuits that permit the "exculpatory no" exception. The major premise is that § 1001 only criminalizes statements that pervert governmental functions. The minor premise is that simple denials of guilt to federal investigators do not pervert governmental functions. Therefore, Brogan (D) argues, the "exculpatory no" is an exception. These arguments fail completely. A federal investigation is a governmental function that

depends on the truthfulness of its subjects, so the major premise fails. The minor premise is inaccurate because it arises out of the assumption that prosecutors will over-zealously use § 1001 against persons who say "no" instead of remaining silent as a means of "piling on" offenses. Congress created this separate criminal offense with serious consequences. It is not the Court's place to second-guess that decision. The plain language of the statute supports Brogan's (D) conviction. Affirmed..

DISSENT: (Stevens, J.) This Court has previously found statutory language to be broader than that intended by Congress. Further, the Court should respect the uniform understanding of the bench and bar that the exception applies.

▌ *ANALYSIS*

The "exculpatory no" doctrine was judicially created to limit the rather broad scope of § 1001. The Supreme Court flatly rejected the creation and focused on the plain language of the statute. Prosecutors, however, are advised not to pursue prosecutions for "exculpatory no" violations. *See* United States Attorneys Manual, at www.usdoj.gov. The practical result of the *Brogan* decision remains unseen.

■=■

Quicknotes

CERTIORARI A discretionary writ issued by a superior court to an inferior court in order to review the lower court's decisions; the Supreme Court's writ ordering such review.

■=■

United States v. Aguilar

Federal government (P) v. Indicted judge (D)

515 U.S. 593 (1995).

NATURE OF CASE: Appeal from conviction for obstruction of justice.

FACT SUMMARY: Judge Aguilar (D) became involved with a case set before Judge Weigel and later lied to federal investigators about his involvement. He was prosecuted for obstruction of justice.

🏛 RULE OF LAW
The crime of obstruction of justice does not apply to defendants who make false statements to investigators working independently of the court's or grand jury's authority.

FACTS: Michael Tham, a union official, sought post-conviction relief before Judge Weigel. Tham asked Edward Solomon and Abraham Chalupowitz (Chapman) to help him with his relief because both men knew Judge Aguilar (D) who heard cases in the same courthouse as Judge Weigel. Weigel testified Aguilar simply asked him to place the matter on his docket and did not attempt to influence the outcome. The FBI was separately investigating Tham on another matter and sought a wiretap from Judge Peckham, who also sat in the same courthouse as Judges Weigel and Aguilar (D). The FBI informed Peckham about meetings between Judge Aguilar (D) and Chapman. Peckham told Judge Aguilar (D) to avoid Chapman because his name showed up on a wiretap authorization. Judge Aguilar (D) told Chapman about the wiretap. The Grand Jury opened a new investigation into the attempt to influence Judge Weigel. During that investigation, Judge Aguilar (D) lied about his knowledge of the wiretap and his involvement in the Tham investigation. Judge Aguilar (D) was convicted of obstruction of justice for lying to the FBI. The jury could not reach a unanimous verdict on the obstruction charge for influencing Judge Weigel. Judge Aguilar (D) appealed his conviction on the ground that his false statements did not "corruptly influence" the investigators and the grand jury had not authorized the investigation. The circuit court reversed the conviction. The Government (P) appealed.

ISSUE: Does the crime of obstruction of justice apply to defendants who make false statements to investigators working independently of the court's or grand jury's authority?

HOLDING AND DECISION: (Rehnquist, C.J.) No. The crime of obstruction of justice does not apply to defendants who make false statements to investigators working independently of the court's or grand jury's authority. Judge Aguilar (D) was charged with violating the Omnibus Clause of 18 U.S.C. § 1503, which prohibits corruptly endeavoring to obstruct justice. This is a broad statute limited by caselaw involving persons who knew or had notice that the specific court was administering justice. The proceeding alleged to have been obstructed must also not be an ancillary one, such as an investigation independent of the court's or grand jury's authority. This is the "nexus" requirement of § 1503. Finally, the obstruction does not need to be successful but only an "endeavor" needs to be made. Judge Aguilar (D) did make false statements to an investigator. Nothing was shown, however, that the investigator would have testified before a grand jury, so the nexus requirement was not met. The majority's interpretation of "endeavor" permits punishment of the defendant who intends to obstruct and tries to obstruct but is foiled. Affirmed.

CONCURRENCE IN PART AND DISSENT IN PART: (Scalia, J.) The majority's interpretation of the word "endeavor" in the statute requires "natural and probable consequence" to substitute for "intent." This is an impossible interpretation. Endeavoring then occurs only when unnatural and improbable success results. The majority now limits the reach of this statute.

▶ ANALYSIS

Judge Aguilar was the first federal judge prosecuted under the federal racketeering statute. His testimony was pitted against the testimony of other federal judges who served with him; none of them testified he had committed a crime. In 1996, Judge Aguilar resigned his judgeship in exchange for the Department of Justice dropping the remaining felony charge against him. The charge was related to his sharing the information about the wiretap in violation of 18 U.S.C. § 2232(c).

■━■

Quicknotes

RACKETEERING A conspiracy organized for the commission or attempted commission of extortion or coercion.

■━■

United States v. Cueto

Federal government (P) v. Convicted obstructer (D)

151 F.3d 620 (7th Cir. 1998).

NATURE OF CASE: Appeal from conviction for obstruction of justice.

FACT SUMMARY: Amiel Cueto (D) filed multiple cases, motions, and proceedings involving his client, Thomas Venezia, and an investigator, Bond Robinson. Investigation uncovered Cueto (D) did so to protect his financial interest in Venezia's illegal gambling operation. Cueto (D) was convicted of obstruction of justice for his delay tactics and interference with judicial administration.

RULE OF LAW

Zealous advocacy for a litigation client becomes criminal obstruction of justice when the intent is to corrupt the administration of justice.

FACTS: Thomas Venezia owned B & H Vending/Ace Music Corporation, a vending and amusement business, which operated an illegal video poker operation in area taverns and in the Veterans of Foreign Wars (VFW) hall. Venezia hired attorney Amiel Cueto (D) to defend him and the tavern owners. The Illinois Liquor Control Commission (ILCC) opened an investigation into illegal gambling in southern Illinois taverns. ILCC Agent Bonds Robinson became an undercover investigator working with the FBI for the case. Robinson suggested to Venezia that he should offer a bribe to discourage the investigation. Venezia asked Cueto (D) for advice and Cueto (D) referred him to his law partner, Tom Daley. Daley reported Robinson to the ILCC for allegedly soliciting a bribe. Venezia and Robinson met and Robinson taped the conversation. The ILCC then raided the VFW and seized B & H gambling machines. Venezia consulted Cueto (D) about the raids. Cueto (D) and Venezia wrote a letter to the state's attorney detailing Robinson's "corruption" and then filed a lawsuit against Robinson for his "corrupt" practices. Cueto (D) got a court order for Robinson to appear at a hearing on one of the raided taverns and served him there with notice of an injunction hearing in fifteen minutes in the lawsuit against him. Robinson's request for an attorney was denied, he was not allowed to put on a defense, and he was forced to answer questions about the covert investigation. The state court entered a preliminary injunction against Robinson enjoining him from interfering with Venezia's business. Despite the injunction, Robinson visited another tavern and discovered more B & H gambling machines. The tavern owner confessed to participation in illegal gambling activities. Cueto (D) then wrote another letter accusing Robinson of violating the injunction and threatened to file a suit against ILCC and a suit against Robinson.

Robinson moved to remove the show cause order to federal court; the court determined Robinson was working undercover for the FBI, which provided federal jurisdiction. The district court removed the case, dissolved the injunction against Robinson, and dismissed the complaint. Cueto (D) appealed and this court affirmed. The U.S. Supreme Court denied certiorari. The investigation revealed Cueto (D) and Venezia developed secret partnerships involving B & H. Cueto (D) continued to advise Venezia even when he was not the attorney of record and threatened further prosecution of Robinson. Cueto (D) filed multiple motions to hinder a grand jury investigation into B & H activities and Venezia. Venezia was convicted of several counts of racketeering and a jury convicted Cueto (D) of obstruction of justice under the Omnibus Clause of 18 U.S.C. § 1503. Cueto (D) appealed.

ISSUE: Does zealous advocacy for a litigation client become criminal obstruction of justice when the intent is to corrupt the administration of justice?

HOLDING AND DECISION: (Bauer, J.) Yes. Zealous advocacy for a litigation client becomes criminal obstruction of justice when the intent is to corrupt the administration of justice. Cueto (D) first argues the Omnibus Clause is vague because much of legal work is intended to influence the justice system. It is not the means the attorney employs to influence, but the intent to corruptly influence. Cueto (D) was acting to protect his financial interests in the illegal gambling operations, not performing those acts attorneys typically perform in litigation. His first defense fails. Cueto's (D) next defense also fails. The government must prove: (1) a pending judicial proceeding; (2) defendant knew of the proceeding; (3) defendant obstructed or endeavored to obstruct the due administration of justice; and (4) defendant acted corruptly. The defendant does not need to be successful in the attempt to obstruct. Cueto (D) filed repeated motions and appeals to delay and obstruct the cases involving Robinson. These delay tactics were done to protect Cueto's (D) financial interests. Further, Cueto's (D) attempts to get the state's attorney to prosecute Robinson was also obstruction of justice because the conduct had the requisite nexus to the judicial proceedings involving Robinson and Venezia. Affirmed.

ANALYSIS

Cueto (D) was sentenced to 87 months in prison. Criminal defense attorneys split into those supporting the

Continued on next page.

conviction and those condemning the conviction on the basis it would result in criminal defense attorneys failing to zealously advocate for their clients. Consider whether the court could have limited the holding to attorneys who are involved in illicit businesses with the clients or used unlawful means to defend the client. The current holding requires courts to determine the attorney's "intent" rather than take an objective look at the attorney's actions. Had the court limited the holding as suggested, criminal defense attorneys could zealously advocate without fear of crossing some indefinite line so long as the attorneys were not involved in a client's illicit business or employing illegal defense techniques.

■══■

Quicknotes

SHOW CAUSE Generally referred to as an order to show cause or a show cause order. The order is directed to the opposing party to appear and show cause why a certain order should not be enforced or confirmed, or give reason why a court should take or not take a proposed action.

■══■

Arthur Andersen LLP v. United States

Convicted auditor (D) v. Federal government (P)

544 U.S. 696 (2005).

NATURE OF CASE: Appeal from convictions for corrupt persuasion and document destruction.

FACT SUMMARY: Arthur Andersen LLP (D) was the accounting firm for Enron Corporation at the time Enron was under investigation by the Securities and Exchange Commission (SEC) for its accounting practices. Arthur Andersen (D) repeatedly instructed its employees to follow its document retention policy, which resulted in significant document destruction during the investigation. Arthur Andersen (D) was convicted of corruptly persuading its employees to withhold the documents from the Government (P).

RULE OF LAW

The requisite mens rea for the offense of corrupt persuasion is the defendant's consciousness of the wrongdoing.

FACTS: Enron Corporation, an energy conglomerate, engaged in aggressive accounting practices. Enron hired Arthur Andersen LLP (D) to audit its publicly filed statements as well as review its internal accounting practices. When Enron's financial troubles became public, Arthur Andersen (D) formed an Enron crisis-response team with in-house counsel, Nancy Temple. In-house counsel was aware an SEC investigation into Enron's practices was "highly probable." Enron provided a general training course during which it reminded its employees of the document retention policy and urged employee compliance. Temple requested Arthur Andersen's (D) crisis response team be reminded of the Enron document retention policy. On October 19, Enron forwarded its SEC notice of investigation to Arthur Andersen (D). Temple emailed the Arthur Andersen team and attached the document retention policy to the email on that same day. The next day, October 20, Temple reminded the team again during a conference call to abide by Enron's document retention policy. Her supervisor held two additional meetings to remind the team to comply with the document retention policy. A substantial number of paper and electronic documents were destroyed following these reminders. The SEC opened its formal investigation on October 30 and requested Enron accounting documents. The document destruction continued until November 8 when the SEC subpoenaed documents. Arthur Andersen (D) was indicted for violating 18 U.S.C. §§ 1512(b)(2)(A) and (B), which criminalize knowing corrupt persuasion of persons with intent to cause that person to withhold documents from a government investigation. A jury convicted Arthur Andersen (D) and the Fifth Circuit affirmed. The

United States Supreme Court accepted Arthur Andersen's (D) writ of certiorari to address the mens rea requirement of § 1512(b).

ISSUE: Is the requisite mens rea for the offense of corrupt persuasion the defendant's consciousness of the wrongdoing?

HOLDING AND DECISION: (Rehnquist, C.J.) Yes. The requisite mens rea for the offense of corrupt persuasion is the defendant's consciousness of the wrongdoing. § 1512(b) addresses witness tampering in obstruction of justice crimes. The Court historically acts with restraint in assessing the reach of a criminal statute. Here, the underlying act of "persuasion" seems innocent enough. Further, persuading a client to withhold documents is also not necessarily a corrupt practice, for example when the documents are protected by attorney-client privilege. Many companies have document retention policies created with the intent to protect documents from production to the Government (P). The words "knowingly" and "corruptly" in the statute require conscious awareness of the wrongdoing committed. The jury instructions in this case failed to address completely the mens rea element. In fact, the jury instructions stated the jury had to find Arthur Andersen (D) guilty even if the evidence showed Arthur Andersen (D) believed it was acting honestly and lawfully. The statute requires knowledge of the wrongdoing, not a belief of lawful behavior. The instructions also failed to require demonstration of a nexus between the document destruction and knowledge that those documents might be material to a proceeding. Here, Arthur Andersen (D) merely reminded its employees working with Enron documents to follow Enron's document retention policy. Reversed and remanded.

▶ ANALYSIS

Prior to the Enron debacle, Arthur Andersen LLP was one of the largest accounting and consulting firms in the world. After its conviction in 2002 for obstruction of justice for the massive document destruction, it was prohibited from auditing publicly traded companies. Arthur Andersen LLP soon lost the vast majority of its auditing clients and was forced to fire thousands of employees. The unanimous Supreme Court ruling reversing its criminal conviction did little to repair its destroyed reputation and Arthur Andersen LLP is now little more than a shell company with few assets. The spectacular failure of Enron Corporation and Arthur Andersen LLP did prompt Congress to enact the

Continued on next page.

Sarbanes-Oxley anticorruption legislation, which in part criminalizes the corrupt destruction of a document with the intent to impede an official proceeding.

■══■

Quicknotes

CERTIORARI A discretionary writ issued by a superior court to an inferior court in order to review the lower court's decisions; the Supreme Court's writ ordering such review.

MENS REA Criminal intent.

■══■

Glossary

Common Latin Words and Phrases Encountered in the Law

A FORTIORI: Because one fact exists or has been proven, therefore a second fact that is related to the first fact must also exist.

A PRIORI: From the cause to the effect. A term of logic used to denote that when one generally accepted truth is shown to be a cause, another particular effect must necessarily follow.

AB INITIO: From the beginning; a condition which has existed throughout, as in a marriage which was void ab initio.

ACTUS REUS: The wrongful act; in criminal law, such action sufficient to trigger criminal liability.

AD VALOREM: According to value; an ad valorem tax is imposed upon an item located within the taxing jurisdiction calculated by the value of such item.

AMICUS CURIAE: Friend of the court. Its most common usage takes the form of an amicus curiae brief, filed by a person who is not a party to an action but is nonetheless allowed to offer an argument supporting his legal interests.

ARGUENDO: In arguing. A statement, possibly hypothetical, made for the purpose of argument, is one made arguendo.

BILL QUIA TIMET: A bill to quiet title (establish ownership) to real property.

BONA FIDE: True, honest, or genuine. May refer to a person's legal position based on good faith or lacking notice of fraud (such as a bona fide purchaser for value) or to the authenticity of a particular document (such as a bona fide last will and testament).

CAUSA MORTIS: With approaching death in mind. A gift causa mortis is a gift given by a party who feels certain that death is imminent.

CAVEAT EMPTOR: Let the buyer beware. This maxim is reflected in the rule of law that a buyer purchases at his own risk because it is his responsibility to examine, judge, test, and otherwise inspect what he is buying.

CERTIORARI: A writ of review. Petitions for review of a case by the United States Supreme Court are most often done by means of a writ of certiorari.

CONTRA: On the other hand. Opposite. Contrary to.

CORAM NOBIS: Before us; writs of error directed to the court that originally rendered the judgment.

CORAM VOBIS: Before you; writs of error directed by an appellate court to a lower court to correct a factual error.

CORPUS DELICTI: The body of the crime; the requisite elements of a crime amounting to objective proof that a crime has been committed.

CUM TESTAMENTO ANNEXO, ADMINISTRATOR (ADMINISTRATOR C.T.A.): With will annexed; an administrator c.t.a. settles an estate pursuant to a will in which he is not appointed.

DE BONIS NON, ADMINISTRATOR (ADMINISTRATOR D.B.N.): Of goods not administered; an administrator d.b.n. settles a partially settled estate.

DE FACTO: In fact; in reality; actually. Existing in fact but not officially approved or engendered.

DE JURE: By right; lawful. Describes a condition that is legitimate "as a matter of law," in contrast to the term "de facto," which connotes something existing in fact but not legally sanctioned or authorized. For example, de facto segregation refers to segregation brought about by housing patterns, etc., whereas de jure segregation refers to segregation created by law.

DE MINIMIS: Of minimal importance; insignificant; a trifle; not worth bothering about.

DE NOVO: Anew; a second time; afresh. A trial de novo is a new trial held at the appellate level as if the case originated there and the trial at a lower level had not taken place.

DICTA: Generally used as an abbreviated form of obiter dicta, a term describing those portions of a judicial opinion incidental or not necessary to resolution of the specific question before the court. Such nonessential statements and remarks are not considered to be binding precedent.

DUCES TECUM: Refers to a particular type of writ or subpoena requesting a party or organization to produce certain documents in their possession.

EN BANC: Full bench. Where a court sits with all justices present rather than the usual quorum.

EX PARTE: For one side or one party only. An ex parte proceeding is one undertaken for the benefit of only one party, without notice to, or an appearance by, an adverse party.

EX POST FACTO: After the fact. An ex post facto law is a law that retroactively changes the consequences of a prior act.

EX REL.: Abbreviated form of the term "ex relatione," meaning upon relation or information. When the state brings an action in which it has no interest against an individual at the instigation of one who has a private interest in the matter.

FORUM NON CONVENIENS: Inconvenient forum. Although a court may have jurisdiction over the case, the action should be tried in a more conveniently located court, one to which parties and witnesses may more easily travel, for example.

GUARDIAN AD LITEM: A guardian of an infant as to litigation, appointed to represent the infant and pursue his/her rights.

HABEAS CORPUS: You have the body. The modern writ of habeas corpus is a writ directing that a person (body) being detained (such as a prisoner) be brought before the court so that the legality of his detention can be judicially ascertained.

IN CAMERA: In private, in chambers. When a hearing is held before a judge in his chambers or when all spectators are excluded from the courtroom.

IN FORMA PAUPERIS: In the manner of a pauper. A party who proceeds in forma pauperis because of his poverty is one who is allowed to bring suit without liability for costs.

INFRA: Below, under. A word referring the reader to a later part of a book. (The opposite of supra.)

IN LOCO PARENTIS: In the place of a parent.

IN PARI DELICTO: Equally wrong; a court of equity will not grant requested relief to an applicant who is in pari delicto, or as much at fault in the transactions giving rise to the controversy as is the opponent of the applicant.

IN PARI MATERIA: On like subject matter or upon the same matter. Statutes relating to the same person or things are said to be in pari materia. It is a general rule of statutory construction that such statutes should be construed together, i.e., looked at as if they together constituted one law.

IN PERSONAM: Against the person. Jurisdiction over the person of an individual.

IN RE: In the matter of. Used to designate a proceeding involving an estate or other property.

IN REM: A term that signifies an action against the res, or thing. An action in rem is basically one that is taken directly against property, as distinguished from an action in personam, i.e., against the person.

INTER ALIA: Among other things. Used to show that the whole of a statement, pleading, list, statute, etc., has not been set forth in its entirety.

INTER PARTES: Between the parties. May refer to contracts, conveyances or other transactions having legal significance.

INTER VIVOS: Between the living. An inter vivos gift is a gift made by a living grantor, as distinguished from bequests contained in a will, which pass upon the death of the testator.

IPSO FACTO: By the mere fact itself.

JUS: Law or the entire body of law.

LEX LOCI: The law of the place; the notion that the rights of parties to a legal proceeding are governed by the law of the place where those rights arose.

MALUM IN SE: Evil or wrong in and of itself; inherently wrong. This term describes an act that is wrong by its very nature, as opposed to one which would not be wrong but for the fact that there is a specific legal prohibition against it (malum prohibitum).

MALUM PROHIBITUM: Wrong because prohibited, but not inherently evil. Used to describe something that is wrong because it is expressly forbidden by law but that is not in and of itself evil, e.g., speeding.

MANDAMUS: We command. A writ directing an official to take a certain action.

MENS REA: A guilty mind; a criminal intent. A term used to signify the mental state that accompanies a crime or other prohibited act. Some crimes require only a general mens rea (general intent to do the prohibited act), but others, like assault with intent to murder, require the existence of a specific mens rea.

MODUS OPERANDI: Method of operating; generally refers to the manner or style of a criminal in committing crimes, admissible in appropriate cases as evidence of the identity of a defendant.

NEXUS: A connection to.

NISI PRIUS: A court of first impression. A nisi prius court is one where issues of fact are tried before a judge or jury.

N.O.V. (NON OBSTANTE VEREDICTO): Notwithstanding the verdict. A judgment n.o.v. is a judgment given in favor of one party despite the fact that a verdict was returned in favor of the other party, the justification being that the verdict either had no reasonable support in fact or was contrary to law.

NUNC PRO TUNC: Now for then. This phrase refers to actions that may be taken and will then have full retroactive effect.

PENDENTE LITE: Pending the suit; pending litigation under way.

PER CAPITA: By head; beneficiaries of an estate, if they take in equal shares, take per capita.

PER CURIAM: By the court; signifies an opinion ostensibly written "by the whole court" and with no identified author.

PER SE: By itself, in itself; inherently.

PER STIRPES: By representation. Used primarily in the law of wills to describe the method of distribution where a person, generally because of death, is unable to take that which is left to him by the will of another, and therefore his heirs divide such property between them rather than take under the will individually.

PRIMA FACIE: On its face, at first sight. A prima facie case is one that is sufficient on its face, meaning that the evidence supporting it is adequate to establish the case until contradicted or overcome by other evidence.

PRO TANTO: For so much; as far as it goes. Often used in eminent domain cases when a property owner receives partial payment for his land without prejudice to his right to bring suit for the full amount he claims his land to be worth.

QUANTUM MERUIT: As much as he deserves. Refers to recovery based on the doctrine of unjust enrichment in those cases in which a party has rendered valuable services or furnished materials that were accepted and enjoyed by another under circumstances that would reasonably notify the recipient that the rendering party expected to be paid. In essence, the law implies a contract to pay the reasonable value of the services or materials furnished.

QUASI: Almost like; as if; nearly. This term is essentially used to signify that one subject or thing is almost analogous to another but that material differences between them do exist. For example, a quasi-criminal proceeding is one that is not strictly criminal but shares enough of the same characteristics to require some of the same safeguards (e.g., procedural due process must be followed in a parole hearing).

QUID PRO QUO: Something for something. In contract law, the consideration, something of value, passed between the parties to render the contract binding.

RES GESTAE: Things done; in evidence law, this principle justifies the admission of a statement that would otherwise be hearsay when it is made so closely to the event in question as to be said to be a part of it, or with such spontaneity as not to have the possibility of falsehood.

RES IPSA LOQUITUR: The thing speaks for itself. This doctrine gives rise to a rebuttable presumption of negligence when the instrumentality causing the injury was within the exclusive control of the defendant, and the injury was one that does not normally occur unless a person has been negligent.

RES JUDICATA: A matter adjudged. Doctrine which provides that once a court of competent jurisdiction has rendered a final judgment or decree on the merits, that judgment or decree is conclusive upon the parties to the case and prevents them from engaging in any other litigation on the points and issues determined therein.

RESPONDEAT SUPERIOR: Let the master reply. This doctrine holds the master liable for the wrongful acts of his servant (or the principal for his agent) in those cases in which the servant (or agent) was acting within the scope of his authority at the time of the injury.

STARE DECISIS: To stand by or adhere to that which has been decided. The common law doctrine of stare decisis attempts to give security and certainty to the law by following the policy that once a principle of law as applicable to a certain set of facts has been set forth in a decision, it forms a precedent which will subsequently be followed, even though a different decision might be made were it the first time the question had arisen. Of course, stare decisis is not an inviolable principle and is departed from in instances where there is good cause (e.g., considerations of public policy led the Supreme Court to disregard prior decisions sanctioning segregation).

SUPRA: Above. A word referring a reader to an earlier part of a book.

ULTRA VIRES: Beyond the power. This phrase is most commonly used to refer to actions taken by a corporation that are beyond the power or legal authority of the corporation.

Addendum of French Derivatives

IN PAIS: Not pursuant to legal proceedings.

CHATTEL: Tangible personal property.

CY PRES: Doctrine permitting courts to apply trust funds to purposes not expressed in the trust but necessary to carry out the settlor's intent.

PER AUTRE VIE: For another's life; during another's life. In property law, an estate may be granted that will terminate upon the death of someone other than the grantee.

PROFIT A PRENDRE: A license to remove minerals or other produce from land.

VOIR DIRE: Process of questioning jurors as to their predispositions about the case or parties to a proceeding in order to identify those jurors displaying bias or prejudice.

Casenote® Legal Briefs